Every Contact Leaves a Trace

Liz Floutier

The lily is our flower. My wedding gift to my husband was a pressed and mounted stem from the very first bouquet he ever bought me and he has gifted me with many more since.

We both love them for their beauty and their fragrance, but it is also true that they are dangerous flowers. On contact, lily pollen will leave an indelible stain and the slightest brush against it will mark whatever it touches forever. A fair illustration of my life, as over the years I've brushed against things I shouldn't, intentionally or otherwise and found myself deeply, even brutally marked by those experiences. It is one reason for the title of this book.

Unlike lily pollen though, which is impossible to remove, my own indelible stains have been washed away by the blood of Jesus, the only thing that has the power to do so, freeing me to breathe deep and enjoy the beautiful fragrance that is Christ in me.

Forward

I first met Liz in the early nineties with Prue Bedwell when she came to us for prayer counselling at St Andrew's, prompted to do so by recurring and frightening nightmares. We were struck by her desire to be free from her past and her willingness to engage fully in the process, as she shared her life story with us.

As we met weekly over many months, we watched as God did open heart surgery on her as only He can. Facing the actual pain of abuse and betrayal was terrible, but once it was done she was able to start forgiving, with the full knowledge and understanding of the havoc which the traumas had wrought in her heart.

If you want to be assured that God is still in the business of rescuing, healing and turning a person's life upside down, then read this book. Liz's story is a wonderful example of God's love and mercy. She tells her story with openness and honesty and it's a real page-turner. It will encourage you to believe God for more.

Mary Pytches, Author and Speaker

Introduction

The time is now……..

So, there was an invitation from the Lord to begin a journey into what started as the unknown.

It went something like this, 'If you will set aside an hour a day, to sit with your iPad open and your fingers poised, I will give you the words'. Interested but unsure, and as the bearer of what has seemed perpetual disappointment at projects started and not finished, I inquired further before committing myself.

'What form is this 'writing' to take….teaching, devotional, memoir, testimony, fiction, what?' no answer. Just the invitation and a challenge to trust and discover in the process.

Two months in, there were daily, well almost daily, jottings, that amounted to all of the above. Minus the fiction. There has been enough fiction in my life.

I was continually surprised at the flow. That each day as I sat, almost without thinking and unbidden, my fingers would begin tapping the keypad and the words would flow out. And each day, without planning or contrivance there was a short but finished piece that resolved. Beginning, middle and end.

It is a long time since I was at school but the statutory requirement for the beginning, middle and end of a piece of written work is indelibly stamped on my brain. There began a stirring in my spirit, that maybe, just maybe, there was something happening here.

During one of my frequent walks with my Heavenly Father, I realised that for some days I had recently spent much of this walking time, recalling various parts of my own story. Not the usual 'big deal' testimonies that get shared often in the course of my ministry work, but less remembered things. This realisation prompted me to inquire of Him again for direction and this time I clearly heard an answer.

'Write your own story'.

This suggestion has been made to me before many times by my husband, who will laugh when he reads this. My response has always been the same, 'Why? Who on earth will want to read MY story.' He has always graciously backed off and I have less graciously resisted the little tug that always happens in my spirit, dismissing the thought as fanciful.

But God……..

Resistance this time would be disobedience, so here I am. Fingers poised, about to write my own story.

I dedicate it to Mike who has always encouraged me, even in the face of my own persistent discouragement to do so.

I write it to the glory of God, my wonderful Heavenly Dad, Jesus my closest friend and Holy Spirit my true counsel and help.

I offer it to you, whoever you may be, in faith, that somehow through reading it, you will be both blessed and encouraged.

Part One

Chapter 1

The first time I was entrusted with my Father's box brownie camera, I was four or five. We were crossing the Mersey on the New Brighton ferry. I clicked before I even looked through the viewfinder but still managed a reasonable shot, of the candy-striped safety rail and an expanse of grey sea. Of course the snap was black and white, so everything appeared grey. But I remember the Mersey and it was.

The occasion was a day trip to New Brighton and as near as I would get to going abroad for a few years to come. We had travelled from Nottingham to Liverpool on the bus, to spend a few days with my paternal grandparents. They had made their home in Knotty Ash from their native Ireland when Grandad left the Merchant Navy, him a Protestant from Belfast, her a staunch and devout Catholic from Cork.

To marry my Grandma he'd had to 'convert', renouncing the very little faith he had, to pursue the 'true' one, which he didn't believe in at all. But needs must when you're in love and determined.

She was Elizabeth Anne and I honestly don't think I ever knew his name. Other than Grandad Moore. This is not as shocking as it seemed when I first realised it. In my hearing, my parents referred to each other as Mum and Dad, and neighbours were never on first name terms unless they became really close friends. The few that did became Aunty .... to me, but the husbands always remained Mr. for some reason. It was of an age I suppose.

Grandad spent the rest of his working life as a docker, walking the five or so miles to the port each day in the hope of being 'put on' and getting paid, and then walking home again. It was a hard life, but so was he, and he laboured faithfully to provide for his wife and ever growing family.

1

There were nine children, eight boys and one girl, my Dad was second to youngest. He shared scant memories with me of his own childhood but I doubt it was huge fun. There was love though if only expressed through the shoes on his feet and the daily food that was put on the table.

My own memories are patchy too. I recall two or three holidays spent there, one of them the only time we went away together as a family ourselves. There is a photograph of me as a very small girl, standing on a stepladder in the back yard with my brother in the 'on guard' position, an epee in his hand. I think it is doubtful my Grandad ever fenced, he'd been on the circuit as a bare-knuckle boxer in Ireland, it doesn't really follow. Maybe it was a souvenir from Merchant Navy days. Whatever, I vaguely recall a happy day and know that in later years that photo always made me smile.

I have several abiding memories from the times I spent in Liverpool and looking back, I always recall them as good days.

This was an age when children were routinely asked to run errands (go on a message, in the local vernacular) for whichever adult they were responsible to. One day Grandma had asked me to fetch something for her from the shop on the high road. She gave me a small list and a ten-shilling note with strict instructions to go straight there and back, talk to no one on the way and make sure that I brought back all of the change.

Rather than resenting the time the chore would take, I loved being considered grown up enough to be trusted with it, and with ten-bob note in hand, I skipped off down the street full of purpose and looking forward to the praise that I knew would come when I'd completed it.

Rounding the corner from the narrow terraced street onto the high road, still skipping along, I was startled by a woman coming straight towards me. Dressed in belted mac and headscarf typical of the day, she stopped me in my tracks and looked at me sternly. Then she took the note from my hand, folded it into a very small square and placed it back into my palm, closing my fingers into a fist to hold it.

I don't recall her exact words though I can still make that broad scouse accent ring in my ears, but I do recall that she was kind in her firmness. It probably ran along the lines of, 'you don't want to be walking along with a brownie flapping about like that, someone'll have it off of you!'

The shopping completed and the change safely in my pocket, I ran back home to Grandma and she was pleased. I didn't tell her about my encounter and so received the smile and the pat on the back that I craved, rather than the finger-wagging I would otherwise have got.

It was the first incident I remember to suggest to me that people are not always good and don't always mean well. It was a seminal lesson and it went deep. Fifty-five years or so later, here I am recalling it again.

Auntie Josie lived around the corner from my Grandparents and as their third child, was significantly older than my Dad. Her own daughter, my cousin Jean, was significantly older than me and I adored her.

Well into her teens she was all mini-skirts, eyeliner and earrings, and to me, visiting her was a joy. My Mum preferred the natural look, she possessed no makeup whatsoever and for her, ears were strictly for hearing, not adorning. Getting to mess around with Jean's old make-up and parade around in her earrings genuinely thrilled me. She kindly filled a Scottie dog biscuit tin with her cast-offs and presented it to me as a parting gift. Mum hated it, but I treasured it for years and never lost the thrill.

Unusually in that place at that time, Jean and Jim were the proud owners of a car and could both drive. We weren't and neither of my parents possessed a license, so this elevated my Aunt and Uncle to stardom status in my five-year-old eyes.

I have no recollection of the make or model, it was small and basic but it was freedom, and afforded us rides along the seashore at Ainsdale Sands and the odd trip to Blackpool. All of this was so outside of my experience at that point that it was as exciting as going to the moon, which happened in reality a few years later to four American astronauts. They may have broken through the boundary of possibility but I bet no-one bought them a lolly off the pier. Huge it was, dark red with yellow cats eyes and black whiskers........

There also actually was a Scottish terrier called Angus and although I didn't recognise it at the time, a passionate love of animals that has stayed with me was birthed during those visits.

There was a lovely family who lived in the house next door and I became good friends with their daughter Marian. She was to be confirmed into the Catholic Church during one of our stays and much to my Grandma's pleasure and my own parents' disapproval, I was invited to share the occasion with them.

They let me accept of course, it would have been churlish not to, but they were concerned that just as mucking around with make-up and trashy earrings might tempt me to tartiness, attending a ceremony where little girls dressed in white became the bride of Christ, might give me a predisposition to joining a cult in later life.

The ceremony was meaningless to me but I loved it. The solemnity and the ritual and most of all the beautiful 'bridal' dresses and the satin shoes. Grandma who was also invited, gave me a square of black lace as a head covering, which I was disappointed to have to return when it was all over.

Marian's own head was adorned by long golden hair which had been lovingly styled into a beautiful 'up do' for the occasion. My own, extremely dark and always kept cut boyishly short, felt ridiculous to me by comparison, and the first seeds of rebellion against the strictures of my childhood were probably sown at that time. They were to be well watered over the next few years.

There are no other specific incidents of note that I remember, but I do retain a very strong sense of 'belonging' in that place. Neither of my grandparents was effusive in their affection, towards me or indeed one another, but there was a profound bond between them that was

4

inescapable. This pervaded the atmosphere in their tiny home and more than compensated for its own shortcomings. It was a freezing house, proper ice on the sash windows in the winter and no hot water till the fire was stoked and well burning.

It was probably for this reason that every day began with a hearty breakfast, that would warm and sustain them both through the mornings' hard work, his at the shipyard, hers at the washboard and mangle. And it was the same breakfast every day, porridge. A thick, glutinous mass of oatmeal made with milk and water and seasoned with salt, rather than sweetened with sugar. The only concession to a small child was a puddle of extra, very cold milk, poured at the table, to at least reduce the temperature to below danger level. I hated it and to this day, that hatred remains in almost phobic proportions.

No other food from that time sticks in my memory, except that there was bread and jam for tea, and it was there that I was introduced to Roses Lime Marmalade which I still love, so overall it's evens on the culinary front.

The house was a two-up, two-down pre-war terrace and there was still a tin bath hanging in a space off the kitchen. It boasted two toilets though and this afforded some sort of status, even if one was sited in the back porch and the other at the end of the back yard. It scarred me with a deep dislike of having to put shoes on to go the loo and goes some way to explaining the abiding aversion to camping that I developed later.

Though the spare bedroom was tiny, the bed seemed huge. It was piled high with eiderdowns and blankets and once snuggled in, it was like being cocooned in a feathery nest. There were a couple of pictures on the walls and a small dressing table, home to a brush and comb set and a pink glass atomiser bottle that never had anything in it, and which completed the decoration.

The pictures captivated me and I've never forgotten them, they were Art Deco style foil art. Pretty ladies on black backgrounds and so different from the cheap Vermeer style reproductions of drab Dutch women hefting heavy brown vases or cleaning out grates, that hung on our walls at home.

My Grandma gave me those pictures and a few other trinkets to treasure the last time I stayed with them. A couple of ropes of paste flapper beads that glinted in the light, the dressing table set and the pink glass atomiser. She also gave me the first bible I ever owned. An old Catholic illustrated edition with scary pictures depicting biblical stories.

She left me these things and so very much more. At the time, and for way too many years, I was oblivious, but I know in my spirit now and without doubt, that she filled a heavenly bowl with her prayers for me. I hope she knows I know it. I will be forever thankful.

Of Dad's siblings, seven were still alive at this time and except for the youngest who married a southern girl and moved to Hertfordshire, they all made their homes in Liverpool. In those days closeness looked like letters rather than visits and apart from sister Josie who was practically around the corner, and Ron in St Albans who was closest in age to Dad, we never visited the others. So I grew up knowing that I was part of a large family but not knowing most of my relatives.

We were close to Ron and Eileen though. If my Dad stretched expectations by training to be a teacher straight after the war, and then settling in my Mums hometown of Nottingham once they married, Uncle Ron broke the mould completely. Ten years younger than my Dad, he benefitted from improved opportunities in education and went to university in the south where he met Eileen. She was lovely and a devout catholic and so won the heart of my Grandma too. They settled in St Albans, where Ron became a lecturer in a red-brick and learned to fly a helicopter, which for some reason was always a problem for my Mother. He spent a lot of years trying to lose the Liverpool in him and cultivate a southern accent, and the perceived duplicity was hard for her. She had to go through it all again down the line with me, but more of that later.

I loved Uncle Ron and Auntie Eileen and on the death of my Grandparents when I was six and seven, migrated my holiday sojourns to St Albans to stay with them and my two younger cousins. Before visiting them at their house, I was always excited and happy when they came to ours. They arrived first in their little Messerschmitt 'bubble car' and later when the children were born, in a Zephyr Zodiac. I have a sweet snap of my brother and me at the wheel of the bubble car, which is precious, but it was the big Zephyr I remember more fondly. They came to collect me in it for my first stay with them, and barrelling down the newly opened section of the M1 between Nottingham and Luton was simply wild in my young eyes, stretching out on the bench seats and eating up the miles on this huge road.

Ron and Eileen were sweetness itself but I was completely overawed when we arrived at their house in the leafy suburbs. We lived on what was at the time, the biggest council estate in Europe, and although these were the days when most tenants took pride in their homes, the uniformity and the crowding and the pebble dash were inescapable. Their house had a wrap-around garden, a drive, a double garage and five bedrooms. It was a mansion, and I knew that mansions were where the 'posh' people lived. It dawned on me that we didn't even speak the same language. I dropped my 'h's and they never did and not only that, they added an 'r' where it didn't belong. Their lounge was the size of the whole of our downstairs and they ate their meals in a dining room. How could we even be related?!

They were both kind and sensitive and gently coaxed me back to confidence, but for a time I was completely intimidated and after seeing them in their own home, I was always vaguely embarrassed when they came to see us in ours. It was the first time I would understand that there were real people, normal people, who were materially better off than we were, and it didn't take me long to decide that I preferred their circumstances to our own.

We did have a grand time together though. Eight years my senior, my own brother was by now involved with his own friends, rendering me almost an only child, so having younger cousins to play with was wonderful. With them were many 'firsts'. My first trip to London, first ride on the tube and first visit to a model village (that I was later to live very close to and visit with my own stepchildren). There was also my first experience of Chinese food, which was exotic beyond words and a gift from Eileen of my first handbag, which she bought for me so that I wouldn't feel underdressed when I went with her to Mass at the Catholic Church. Which was another first, and nothing like the confirmation ceremony I'd attended in Liverpool. I remember being embarrassed that I didn't know by heart the responses and couldn't take communion. St Albans was an intimidating place indeed. But at no time was I made to feel like the poor relation or be anything other than loved and welcomed.

They emigrated as a family to New Zealand about five years later, as Ron had been selected for a professorship at Auckland University. Letters, cards and phone calls were exchanged over the years and we did get to meet again when I was in my twenties and Ron was on sabbatical at Ashridge College in Hertfordshire. It was timely, he died not long after and way too soon. Although we saw little of each other in later years, it was an enduring relationship and the memories I do have are sweet. I am thankful for that and for them. They opened my eyes in ways I wasn't to appreciate until I was much older.

Chapter 2

Back in Nottingham, I navigated pretty uneventfully through my infant school years.

Determined on my first day that I was a 'big' girl, I resisted every attempt on the part of my Dad to accompany me on the short walk to school. He was adamant, so I acquiesced eventually and was safely delivered with the rest of the new intake. There was retribution at the end of the day though, as I dug in my heels and insisted that I walk home by myself. He left me at the gates and I made my own way once he was out of sight. It has baffled me since, that as a five-year-old, I could exert that much influence and to an extent, it still does.

Miss Fry, my teacher throughout my infant years, was a diamond and I really loved her. I was bright and a bit of a teachers' pet, so that when my first public shaming came from her it was devastating.

The school day always culminated with a storytime, where the children gathered at the teacher's feet and listened. On this particular day, we had been a rowdy lot and were slow to settle and her patience with us was spent. Distracted when she issued a warning that the next pupil to talk would get a spanking, it was me who spoke, and she had no choice but to make good on her threat. She called me to the front of the class and administered three short sharp slaps to my thigh. I was mortified. Tears stinging the back of my eyes I returned to my place feeling as though my whole world had just collapsed. Surely she knew that I wasn't deliberately disobedient, I was a good girl, helpful and responsible.

It was my first taste of what I saw as betrayal and I was desperately hurt. I also knew that there would be a letter to my parents and that compounded my shame. Dad taught in a secondary school and the importance of a spotless school record was drummed into me early as mandatory. It was with a heavy heart I trudged home that day. My lack of recollection about what happened when I got there, suggests to me that it amounted to nothing; it was the first of many subsequent life lessons to prove that anticipated dread is often worse than reality.

Of course what I was unable to grasp at all at the time, was that for Miss Fry this was also an unpleasant experience. Whether it taught her anything about the gravity of making threats I don't know, but she never failed to treat me kindly and well from that point onwards and no reference to it was ever made afterwards. As far as I was able, I forgot about it but it left a scar that sadly festered for years.

With year 3 of infant school came responsibility, as a number of us older children were selected to take a new pupil under our little wings at the start of the new school year. My charge was Rosie Brown, a tiny, absurdly pretty little girl from an upmarket part of the estate. And yes, there was such a thing back then, newer houses constructed from red brick, with upstairs toilets.

We became instantly firm friends and I fell completely in love with everything about her. She was a bona fide 'only child' and loved as such by her ever doting parents, who, probably recognising my loneliness, extended serious hospitality to me. Every Sunday was spent with them for a couple of years, me pitching up at their house sometimes before they were even out of bed. They never turned me away, simply laid another place for their special Sunday cooked breakfast, full English with red sauce in a plastic tomato bottle on the table.

In the afternoons we would often go for a 'ride out' in the car, a dark green mini, which was a whole new experience for me, taking in the scenery of the quaint outlying villages and enjoying sipping a bottle of cherryade through a straw in a pub garden.

They took me into the bosom of their family, including me in visits to both sets of their parents and various aunts and uncles. I vividly remember visiting Rosie's paternal grandparents on a few Sunday evenings and being taken by them to evensong at the church they attended. These visits doubled my religious experience to date. It was an old Anglican Church, huge, cold and low and very far removed from the strict ritual and solemnity of the Catholic Churches I'd been taken to in Liverpool and St Albans.

Although the building was bitterly cold, the fellowship was warm, and it was clear even to my young self that here were people who really cared for each other. Until that point church had simply been ceremony, here it was relationship and even better, cake.

Again, my own parents weren't best pleased with what they saw as a new threat, but on balance they deemed the Catholics scarier than the Anglicans, so they never forbade me going.

The church was in The Meadows district, which was at that time one of the poorest areas of the city. About twenty years later it underwent complete slum clearance but back then, in the midst of all the poverty, was community, and community was what took place in that church.

If my broadening religious horizon was difficult for my parents, what must have been even harder for them to bear, was me coming home from these Sunday visits full to bursting with what we'd done together. Having no family car meant we rarely ventured that far from home other than on special occasions, and we never passed the time together sitting in a pub garden. On top of that, I was always very vocal about all the new 'stuff' that Rosie had. And she did have everything.

It wasn't so much that she was spoiled, or particularly overindulged, simply that her parents had the means and they adored her, so if she wanted it, they bought it for her. She was generous in her sharing but I often went home acutely aware that my own toy box was empty by comparison. And although I don't really remember it, I know myself well, and can easily imagine that I was less than kind to my parents in expressing my 'lack'.

Even worse was to come in my perception of my parents' shortcomings. To this point our holidays constituted either a visit to Grandparents in Liverpool, or a visit to my Aunt and Uncle in St Albans and the odd day out on a coach trip. All perfectly enjoyable and perfectly acceptable until at the end of the school year when Rosie announced they were going to Spain for theirs. Abroad. On an aeroplane. The package holiday had been launched and they were among the first to discover its joys.

The delights of Liverpool, St Albans and Alton Towers (which back then was public gardens with a pagoda and a boating lake) could not compete. I was devastated and no amount of cajoling would make me understand that truly, I wasn't missing out on something wonderful.

I sulked when the postcard arrived, showing a long white sandy beach against a deep blue sky and even bluer sea. I sulked even more when they returned home with Mediterranean suntans and flamenco fans. They kindly gifted me a souvenir suedette donkey wearing a sombrero and carrying twin flower-baskets across its back and a flamenco fan, but they were no consolation. We were poorer and it was my parents' fault and it wasn't fair.

And then came the dancing. Creative stuff at school was difficult for Rosie, she had an aversion to getting dirty and so hated the traditional artistic things like painting and clay modelling. But she did find her creative expression early through dance, and she had real flair on the floor. She went for lessons each week in Modern and Latin American, held at our local community centre by the glamorous 'Miss Ann', and after pleading with my parents, who had already kitted me out for ballet which I didn't pursue, I was generously allowed to enrol too.

Our paths didn't really cross there as I joined as an absolute beginner and she was already a junior intermediate, but I did enjoy it and to my folks' amazement stuck with it to Junior Gold level.

I was always highly commended in the exams but I never possessed the same feel or flair Rosie had, passing hers always with distinction. I think I derived as much enjoyment from practising on the landing at home and driving my brother to distraction with the accompanying pop tracks, as I did from any exam achievement. I still know how to Cha, Cha, Cha though, over fifty years later.

Our friendship cooled as we grew and were placed in different classes, and then our results in the 11+ exams sent us in different directions and we lost touch, but not completely. Much later in my early twenties and long since left home, I would drop round to see Rosie and her parents when visiting my own. They gave me the same warm welcome and always invited me to stay for tea. The plastic sauce bottle in the shape of a tomato was still on the table.

There was no deprivation in my childhood, our finances were limited but sufficient. My Dad received a grade 1 teachers salary, promotion eluding him for years as he only had a basic qualification, gained through a fast track system after the war, and Mum mostly worked in textile factories earning little, so although we were deemed culturally middle class, we survived on a working-class income.

This in fact suited them well. Disaffected by the war years and by hard and poor circumstances growing up, they had both independently embraced left-wing ideology and met for the first time at a Young Communist League summer camp in Chesterfield. When they married they became active members of the real thing and the social gatherings of my childhood were party meetings, where they sat around drinking Camp coffee and defaming the bourgeoisie.

So there was always a political angle and that had no small impact on what I was allowed and not allowed on the toy front. Realistic, naked, Tiny Tears was seen as playful and educational and allowed. Barbie on the other hand, was a tarty, shallow, materialistic airhead, who obviously got up to no good with her hunky boyfriend Ken every time they went for a ride in that vulgar American sports car.

I was allowed a Penny Bright doll, and in fairness, I loved her, but she was horribly tame once I'd been introduced to her rivals by Rosie.

Eventually I negotiated for Sindy, who at least had dark hair which somehow qualified her for intelligence, and over quite a few years managed to acquire various accessories for her. My parents nearly baulked at the grand dining table set, with its eight-piece cutlery settings, but they generously gave in eventually. It meant nothing to me really, and I was well into my teens and in the arms of a public school educated boyfriend, before I learned anything at all about table etiquette.

But the doll I really wanted eluded me. Tressy, she was the one. Tressy had extending hair, that could be pulled through her skull and then styled in any manner of ways. I yearned for a Tressy doll, not because of any brooding ambition to dress hair, but simply because she had it, and I didn't. Well, not much of it.

For some reason that I have never understood, my Mother was determined that my hair was kept severely, boyishly short throughout my childhood. To my knowledge I never had a nit infestation so there was no clinical need for this, long hair was just not allowed. It occurred to me in later years, that perhaps my Mother had wanted another boy, and keeping my hair short was a way of keeping the dream alive. I will never know the real reason, it was one of the many questions I never asked her, but it did provoke rebellion in me. As soon as I was of an age to refuse to go to the hairdresser, I did exactly that, and by the time I was twelve my hair was long and lush. She never brushed it, dried or styled it and she said it looked like rats tails. It was a serious dislike.

There were many things about my Mum that I was never to know. She lost her own mother as a teenager, and her elder sister became a substitute. Sadly she also died a couple of years later, leaving Mum and a much younger sister Athelea, who she then had to mother herself. Maybe long hair had been a bone of contention between them.

Mum had no schooling beyond fourteen and I think had been lonely. Assuming responsibility for the household so young, alienated her from her girlfriends, and her father was strict and unwelcoming anyway. I remember one or two visits from him and one from my Aunty Athelea, but there was some family disagreement that escalated to war and became estrangement, so neither was ever part of my life.

My Mother read of her Father's death in the obituary column of the Nottingham Evening Post many years later. I think my Dad accompanied her to the funeral where they saw her sister, but sadly there was no future rapprochement.

It was hard for families not living in close proximity to stay close in those days. Communication was in the main by mail. A phone call involved the saving of threepenny bits and later sixpences, a walk to the box and a queue, and so were saved only for the sweetest relationships or emergencies. A death meant a telegram.

My Father learned of the death of both of his parents via telegram, a short sentence, nothing more, and this probably goes some way to explaining his own terse communication of significant events to me in later years. I don't know whether we were unusually distant as a family, it was just our normal, and it was only later, as I began to meet those of friends, that I wondered whether perhaps during this time, I was missing out on something important.

Never encouraged to bring friends to our home, I visited them in theirs and with the ease that only children possess, assimilated myself into the families of several. Rosie's was one but there were a few others, before and after hers. Prior to starting school at age five, the friend pool was the immediate neighbourhood and friends were not hard to make. These were the days of unlocked doors and borrowing cups of sugar and everyone knowing everyone else, even if they weren't on first name terms. We played in the street and across the street. French skipping and hopscotch and catch.

The family next door had five children, which Mum thought was a grossly unfair imposition on their Mother, who she always referred to as 'poor Mrs Brown'. There were four boys and a girl and we played together but were never close. I remember once heading off with them 'Famous Five' style to have an adventure near the river. There was nothing unusual back then in kids being dispatched off for the day, with instructions to not get into any trouble and 'be back in time for tea', and we were trusted to do just that.

It was springtime and spawning season and we decided it would be fun to bring home tadpoles and watch them grow. Loaded up with a couple of old plastic bowls that had been lying around in the Brown's back garden, we headed to the pasture grounds by the banks of the Trent. It was a bumper day and when we duly returned in time for tea, we were weighed down with our haul. Naturally, I wanted to keep my share with me and needed to find a container. There was nothing immediately obvious at home so I used my initiative and grabbed three saucepans from the kitchen so we could divide the catch. Later, unable to find the saucepans so that she could prepare the evening meal, which was always called tea, I was asked by my Mum whether I knew anything about their disappearance. Caring far more about tadpoles than tea, I could see no problem and proudly took her out to the garden to show her how I had put her pans to vital use.

Her response was a horrified gasp followed by an exasperated 'Oh Elizabeth!' and a tirade about her best pans being full of frogspawn and completely ruined. I can quite see her point now, but absolutely couldn't then and was indignant and confused at her anger. In my eyes, it was a worthy and educational project which I had imagined they would applaud, and I thought her reaction completely unjust. Dad, always a diffuser of disputes, located an old container from the coal shed and the gloopy spawn was decanted into that. But Mum was adamant about the pans, and despite his assurance that a thorough scouring would be adequate to restore them to hygiene, they had to be replaced.

I'm not sure what we had for tea that day but I did discover why, although always referred to as Liz or Lizzy, I had in fact been named Elizabeth. From that point on, 'Elizabeth' meant I was in trouble.

There was a memorable occasion sometime later, when I had volunteered to take care of the class gerbils at home over the Easter holiday and was given permission to do so. Thinking I was, and wanting to be highly responsible, I took it on myself to clean out their cage one day whilst Mum was at work. She came home halfway through my endeavour to find me in a heap of sawdust on the living room carpet. This elicited another 'Oh Elizabeth' compounded by a wail of 'this is too much!' I dare say it was, but at the time really didn't understand how my good intentions could be so misunderstood!

The house opposite was home to an ex-army couple with three young daughters and a bulldog. I became good friends with the middle daughter, Jaqueline, affectionately called pie-eye by her Father, who I hope wasn't prophetic.

But my first real friend was Stephen Fletcher, an only child who lived around the corner. The connection was made through our respective back gardens which shared a boundary, the houses set diagonally opposite each other. Stephen and his mother came round one day to retrieve a mis-thrown ball and an invitation to tea followed. I will never know whether my own mother wanted another son, but Mrs Fletcher certainly longed for a daughter and I was more than happy to oblige. Mrs Fletcher became my special adult friend and it seemed to me that, unlike my own Mum, she was never ruffled by anything, attentive to every childish need and happy to be so.

They were the first 'quiet' family I ever met, apart from my own, but I had no understanding whatsoever that the quietness simply reflected a strict disciplinarian of a father, who controlled every aspect of every day, except for the time when he was out working. He was more scary than wilfully cruel. It sadly transpired later that his behaviour was rooted in mental illness, but at the time his wife and his son lived cowering in his shadow.

To stay so calm in such an atmosphere came from a deep inner serenity on her part, and the measure of comfort she derived from creativity. Mrs Fletcher loved crafts and flowers and most of all sewing. She could really sew. For one Christmas she made me a complete nurses outfit, tunic, apron, cuffs, hat and cape which she'd surreptitiously measured me for during play visits with Stephen. But her 'piece de resistance' was a bridal outfit for my much-maligned Penny doll, which was a surprise to them but served as a real favour to my Mum and Dad. It elevated boring Penny to preferred status and stopped me whingeing about my dolly deficit. It must have taken her hours to complete. Hand-stitched in an embroidered cream satin, with tiny pearly buttons all the way down the back. It was beautiful and I wish I'd kept it, a labour of love without a doubt and very, very special to me. It is still clear in my mind's eye all these years later.

Every Christmas Mrs Fletcher would come to our door to deliver a card and a gift for me. It was the only time that she would come into the house, as visiting was frowned on by her austere husband. She'd accept a small glass of Harvey's Bristol Cream sherry for a seasonal toast, and confided to my parents that it was the only alcohol she ever took, as 'Arthur didn't approve'.

Mr Fletcher was indeed the smartest man I had ever met. He worked as an accountant at Griffin and Spalding a large, independent department store in the city, and left every morning dressed in a dark woollen overcoat and trilby hat, and carrying a black umbrella. He polished his shoes every evening on returning home and had Stephen do the same with his own. He placed huge value on tidiness and no matter what playful chaos took place in the daytime, the evidence of it was completely removed before his homecoming.

I recall one particular occasion when I'd been at their house to play and was invited to stay for tea. This wasn't unusual, in fact it happened often but it was normally just the three of us, sitting at the kitchen table with boiled eggs and soldiers. This time Mr Fletcher was at home. We were to eat at the dining end of the living room, at the big mahogany table. Writing this I can still feel the anxiety that rose up in me at the prospect, for fear of making a mistake of any kind.

In fact, I was so nervous that instead of asking to be excused when needing to use the bathroom, I simply sat there and wet myself on the dining chair. I was then left with the dilemma of how to leave the table at the end of the meal, which kept me in that state of high anxiety throughout the rest of it. I dare say that a little stain was forever obvious after that but thankfully nothing was mentioned. Maybe Mrs Fletcher's housewifely genius was able to remove it after all.

Mr Fletcher was a man of some rank in the Salvation Army, and in spite of his severity was not completely devoid of tenderness. He drew a pencil sketch of me during the course of one visit, which he had me sit still for. I would much have preferred to be playing fuzzy felt farm with Stephen, but the sketch came out well, and my parents kept it, so it was a blessing to them.

Mrs Fletcher was truly a saint. She never complained or bemoaned her lot, even when mental illness was diagnosed in her husband. She had a deep and well-grounded faith, probably rooted in the Salvationist tradition and honoured all of her responsibilities. His condition worsened over the years and rendered him completely agoraphobic. She spent herself looking after him and Stephen stayed and looked after her. Lives wasted some would argue, but they were lives lived in love.

The childhood friendship ended with the onset of adolescence, and our move away from the estate, but Christmas card exchanges continued right up until the time of my parent's deaths, and long after Mr Fletcher's.

Mrs Fletcher was a lovely woman. She touched my heart deeply as a child and I learned from her, something of the nature of a quiet and gentle spirit. She is fondly in my memory.

There was one other close friend from that neighbourhood during those early years, unusually made through a motherly connection. Nottingham at that time was a centre for the rag trade, and everyone knew someone who worked at a garment factory. Trained as a lockstitcher in her teens, and interrupted only by a short stint as a Clippie on the buses during the war, my Mother met Mrs Betts at the factory where they both worked. Making knickers. She became the closest Mum had to a girlfriend, and I became good friends with her daughter June.

Auntie Sheila, as she was known to me, also took in piece work at home, which she did at an old Singer treadle sewing machine in their front room. It was like a great hairy pet, I remember the whole house always covered in cotton threads, that found their way everywhere and stuck to everything. Although a tiny little bird of a thing, Auntie Sheila was a no-nonsense, salt of the earth woman. A soft heart in a tough exterior developed over years of hard knocks and disappointment.

June was a year or so older than me and I enjoyed looking up to her as only little girls can. She too took dancing lessons and eased my disappointment at not excelling like my younger friend Rosie, by being even more pedestrian than I was.

She also loved swimming and we often went together to the old Victoria Baths in the city. It was there that we got into our first scrape. We'd make the trip on Saturday mornings and week by week we noticed that there was a man who was always there when we were.

He began to chat to us and seemed friendly enough, so much so that we started to look forward to seeing him. Aged eight and nine, it didn't occur to us that the attentions of a man in his thirties was odd. Of course, we'd both been well-schooled in the perils of stopping to talk to strangers, but we felt that the security of the baths gave us just that, security. He started to bring us sweets and that endeared us to him even more. And then came the invitation back to his flat for tea. We thought we were all friends by this time and saw no harm, but when Auntie Sheila overheard us talking about the planned visit the following week, she went spare. Naturally.

She stormed off to get my Mother, so they could decide what was to be done. June and I sat amid the cotton threads, at first somewhat perplexed at the fuss, and then in terror when the Mother's decided the police must be called. They duly arrived, two uniformed constables whose presence was enormous in the small house. We got a lecture about telling the truth, and another one about 'stranger danger'. A stern warning about the consequences of being so reckless followed and then a stern tongue lashing from the Mother's. They were relieved of course, that they'd saved us from an awful fate, but also embarrassed at the presence of the police and all the gossip that a panda car parked outside the house would cause.

Our statements made, the police visited the man, who got a stiffer lecture than we did and a warning to desist. I remember feeling responsible for getting him into trouble and desperately sorry. But there was no way to make amends, we were banned from the baths forever.

It was another life lesson in things not always being as they seem. Like the dear woman in Liverpool, who'd stepped in to save me from a potential opportunist thief, Auntie Sheila had taken action to save us from something potentially much worse. It was a harder one to accept. The man had seemed nice and in my innocent eyes was probably harmless and simply foolish. For the first time I found myself bearing someone else's responsibility. It was to become a trait that would plague me for years.

June and I recovered and focused our attentions elsewhere. Saturday morning swimming was replaced by Saturday morning Pictures, hosted by the Congregationalist Church at the community centre where they met. A cynic might say that this was an endeavour to boost Sunday school numbers, but there was never anything other than an hour and a half of cartoons, a beaker of thin orange squash and a tuck shop. However it did increase Sunday school attendance by two for a short time at least, as we decided we would give it a go. Honestly, I don't remember anything of the meetings themselves but I know that we were given a blue-covered membership card, that got stamped with a red star every time we turned up. It hooked me for a few weeks but the novelty wore off quickly and we stopped going.

Unlike the Catholics and the Anglicans, my parents clearly perceived no threat at all from the Congregationalists, and didn't bat an eyelid throughout this short season. Maybe having me out of their hair on Saturday and Sunday mornings far outweighed the risk of any possible damage, I'll never know, but I enjoyed the freedom and lack of criticism and felt that I must be growing up to be trusted so.

The next venture though was more of a test for them. Their left-wing politics and egalitarian principles, determined for me early, that I would never be a Brownie or a Girl Scout. At age 5 I was enrolled into the Woodcraft Folk, which describes itself today as an 'educational movement for children and young people'. In the early sixties, it still clawed strongly to its roots, closely tied to the Co-Operative Society, to Labour and to pacifism, and much of the 'education' was skewed to the left. It was mixed-sex and there wasn't a hint of state or religion, and it was a huge part of my childhood.

June though was a member of the Girls Brigade, their offer being 'Girls' lives transformed: God's world enriched', and she was my friend and I wanted to go with her. It must have been the ultimate in anarchy to my parents and I can now, well appreciate their angst. However, more deeply ingrained in them even than their politics, was their belief that children should be allowed to discover truth for themselves, so despite many disapproving tuts, they didn't stop me going. They needn't have worried. The 'Barbie' in me quickly worked out that I wouldn't be seen dead in the uniform and I hated the marching drills, so my attendance was short-lived. To protect my friendship with June, I'd offer help at the odd jumble sale but that was the extent of my involvement, and seen for what it was, it posed no problem to my parents.

Poor June was soon to become persona non grata with them though. Prompted by some reason that I forget, she started going to the Catholic Church on a Sunday and again, I wanted to go with her. Mum and Dad were appalled but again, didn't stand in my way. Fortunately for them, it was another short season, as Woodcraft weekend camps often took me away and on balance I enjoyed them more.

The 'June problem' was to be solved for them completely a couple of years later by the 11+ exam. She was a year ahead of me and was directed by her result to the secondary modern school. Mine took me to the grammar the following year when we also moved house, and our paths divided forever. A gradual drifting apart became an abrupt ending but there was never any quantifiable rift, our friendship simply reached its natural conclusion. Auntie Sheila taught me something of the 'milk of human kindness' and her down to earth, no guile, take me as you find me philosophy left its mark. I am grateful.

Chapter 3

An event took place in the middle of this time, that was to leave its mark in more ways than one. At an afternoon rehearsal for the Christmas carol concert at school, I began to experience acute pain in my stomach.

I'd had mild stomach aches for a couple of years by then, but as physical examination revealed nothing untoward, they had reasonably been diagnosed as psychosomatic, which in turn had given rise to many bedtime readings of Aesop's Fables and particularly 'The Boy Who Cried Wolf'. The unfairness of this went to my heart, I knew what I was feeling but sensing the hopelessness of trying to prove it, I determined to grit my teeth and carry on. That afternoon though the pain was too severe. I was directed to sit quietly by myself in one of the classrooms whilst my parents were alerted to come and take me home. It was the day I was to pray my first independent prayer. I remember not being able to sit still, it was too painful, so bent double I strode around the room crying out to God that I didn't want to die. I was too young. I was seven.

Reliant on public transport, neither of my parents was able to get home quickly, so Auntie Sheila was alerted and came to my rescue. One of the teachers drove us back to her house and she made a space in all the sewing chaos for me to sit and wait.

Mum arrived after about half an hour, and together they stood over me and agreed I looked 'grey', a description that came up often in the re-telling of this story as time went on. When Dad arrived back from school at his usual time of 5:30, he too agreed with the greyness and asked me if there was anything I wanted.

The problem was pain rather than sickness but feeling miserable, I'd refused to eat my tea. However, for a few days I'd had my eye on a box of Terry's Weekend chocolates that had been bought for Christmas, and aware even then that I had special 'daughter powers' with my Dad, I asked for and was given them. So surprised at this request being granted, (things bought for Christmas were absolutely only for Christmas) and aware of my increasing pain, I concluded that I must be in serious trouble. Clearly, I was right to pray my earlier prayer.

However for my parents, for whom there was no deity, the nearest thing to God was the Doctor and concerned about incurring his wrath for something that might simply pass, he wasn't called. This decision was made easier for them by my own protestations that it was just tummy ache, only a bit worse, which itself was fuelled by the fact it was practically Christmas and I didn't want to die in hospital!

The next morning I couldn't stand up, Dad rolled me out of bed, carried me downstairs and settled me on the settee. I remember a little whispering going on in the kitchen, and then he went off with his sixpence to the phone box to arrange for the doctor to visit on his rounds. By the time he arrived, I was pretty much out of it. He made a perfunctory examination, had stern words with my parents and then left to call an ambulance. No one close possessed a telephone.

For all my enjoying playing at hospitals in my bespoke nurses outfit gifted to me the previous year, I was not happy at the prospect of being admitted to one. Nor excited by the flashing blue light or ambulance siren. But admitted I was, to the Children's Hospital in the city. I remember lying on a trolley being prodded and poked and undergoing what seemed like a million tests. I remember being alone, scared and not comforted.

Eventually, I woke up in a bed in a long ward. Nurses bustled around and seeing me awake, gave me attention. I was groggy, sick and felt oddly tight around the middle but I was no longer in terrible pain. Eventually, my parents came to visit and explained that my appendix had seen fit to burst and I was lucky to be alive. The next two weeks were surreal. I was fascinated by my torso which was painted red and turquoise with iodine, and by the wound which was cleaned and dressed daily. It was a big scar on a small body which I thought would give me good currency to impress my friends later. As would the removed sutures which I was given to take home as a souvenir.

Christmas in hospital in the mid-sixties was pretty grim. The nurses were kind but the rules were strict and there was a prevailing sense of patients being a nuisance that permeated my very soul. On Christmas Day, Doctor Claus was pulled through the ward in a wheelchair by a team of nurses wearing antler headbands, handing out RVS presents to each child from a yellow hospital waste sack. But visiting times were still kept at one hour in the afternoon and visitors limited to two per patient. It took me far longer to recover from the experience than it did the surgery. But when I returned to school after the Christmas break I capitalised on it, writing the obligatory 'what I did in my holidays' essay. No one took me seriously at first, which was hurtful, but this time I wasn't phased by their doubts, after all, I had the scar, which I was proud to display to prove the truth of my tale.

This whole episode was in a way, a precursor to another which was to occur a few years down the line, where not being believed had a far more damaging and long-lasting effect. The things that shape us begin early.........

Was my childlike prayer for help heard? Now I can say with confidence an unequivocal 'yes', back then I doubt I gave it a second thought once I was back home......I still had a box of chocolates to finish.

As ever, summer follows winter and that summer we were to have our first 'proper' seaside holiday. My brother Karl, now a young teen, was due to go off camping for two weeks and we booked to go to Cornwall whilst he was away. On the train. Overnight. It was an adventure. I can remember we had to change trains at Newton Abbot at about 4:00 a.m. and had to wait for what seemed like hours on a cold and deserted platform, but when we finally boarded the train that would take us to the end of the line our spirits lifted.

It remains a beautiful journey through Devon and into Cornwall. The line hugs the coast and the views are amazing. We rolled into Penzance at around 7:00 a.m. way too early to check into our accommodation, and found a cafe that would serve us breakfast. It was so exciting. We never, ever, ate out. I even remember that I asked for egg and chips and got them, Mums objection that 'you can't have chips for breakfast!' gently overridden by the friendly waitress.

We stayed in a family room at a small guest house near the seafront, run by Mrs Adams who was lovely. She resembled Miss Cramm who was my first year Junior form teacher and a favourite, so I was happy. She gave us a good daily breakfast and an evening meal which we were called to by the banging of a gong that sat in the hallway.

I was quite enthralled with it all at the start, but less so the next day when our daily walk took us past the big hotels on the promenade. Of course, it was our budget that determined where we stayed, but when I asked why we were in a Guest House was told only that 'hotels are not for the likes of us', followed by 'anyway a Guest House is way more upmarket than a B&B'. The contradiction escaped me at the time but it was typical of my Mum, a mass of contradictions.

Having no car, our days were mainly spent taking coach trips. Mounts Bay Coaches still operates today and it was with them we visited The Lizard and Kynance Cove, St Ives, Sennen Cove and Lands End, Porthcurno and Mousehole. Even back then we queued in miles of traffic on little lanes but it was so new and exciting we didn't mind. Everywhere was lovely, capturing my heart way more deeply than I realised at the time, but it was Mousehole that impacted me most. A tiny fishing village with only a few gift shops, a pub and a chippy. Idyllic little fisherman's cottages that in the sunshine belied

27

the hardness of the lives of the families who lived there and made their living from the sea. It is not so very different today although many of those cottages are now chic holiday lets.

The Mousehole Mice were famous and Mum bought me two. They were sweet, hand-sewn, felt creations, presented in their own gold gift box with a transparent plastic lid. A lady mouse and her baby, anthropomorphised and dressed in pretty clothes. I still have them, still in near perfect condition fifty-five years on.

At the end of our fortnight, we bought chocolates for our coach driver and a pot plant for Mrs Adams to express our thanks. Mum in particular was very taken with the unusual flora and was determined that we should be the first on our estate to grow an exotic tree in the garden. Unable to transport a palm sapling on the train with three large suitcases and a child, they opted for a monkey puzzle tree which they bought as a very small cutting with a root ball. Even I, who at that time had no real interest in plants, loved the furry bark of the monkey tree, which grew surprisingly well in our Midlands garden.

We uprooted it and took it with us when we moved house a few years later, but it was more than monkey tree roots that were planted in me that summer. Something of Cornwall had deeply touched my heart and a seed of longing to be there was planted, that was to slowly germinate over time.

We were never to holiday as a complete family, Karl always taking himself off on some expedition or other, and by the time I hit teenage, I was to do the same. Our expeditions were different but in a way we were kindred spirits and the bond between us close.

There were three more childhood holidays for me with my parents, in Devon, North West Wales and another in Cornwall. There were 'incidents' in each but none was desperately memorable. Mum and I spent most of our time on a collision course, fuelled I'm sure by my 'Daddy's girl' status, which no doubt I exploited horribly and which irritated her no end. I can empathise now, and reflecting on those times only gives rise to fond feelings. If as they say, family holidays are second only to moving house in heightening stress levels, we didn't do so badly.

Karl, eight years my senior had been a member of the Woodcraft Folk since infant school, and always wanting to follow in his footsteps, I longed to join. For Mum and Dad, it was the solution to what they saw as the potential church problem and I was enrolled as an 'Elfin' as soon as I hit primary school age. We met weekly in a local school hall and then occasionally joined together with other groups from across the city for hikes and camps.

There was some really valuable education, focused mainly on outdoor pursuits, and we learned the names of flora and fauna and the country code, to which I have ever been obedient. We wore a green 'Folk Shirt' as a uniform, emblazoned with the Woodcraft logo, a rising sun fronted by two tall pine trees, which we sewed on ourselves, as we did with the other badges we attained over time, knots and first aid and cooking and the like.

Our first responsibility was to choose our 'Folk Name' which was the name we would be addressed by throughout and had to be embroidered on the shirt. 'Clover' was quite endearing age five but later I thought it made me sound like an ambivalent cart horse, so I changed it to 'Swift', which was far cooler but much less apt! Karl had chosen 'Kestrel' from the outset and that became uber cool in 1969 when the film Kes, adapted from Barry Hines book, A Kestrel for a Knave, was released to critical acclaim.

The Woodcraft rituals were rooted in paganism as opposed to religion, and these names were meant to ground us in nature and the things of Mother Earth. It wasn't overt though and was sincerely meant even if perhaps somewhat misguided. Each age group had a name, Elfin, Pioneer, Venturer and then Senior Venturer at eighteen, after which if you stayed, you became a leader. Each group had a creed which we learned by heart and recited in a circle at each meeting. Circles were a big thing. As were hiking and camping and most weekends there was one or the other happening somewhere. Tents were always pitched in circles around a central totem pole, which wasn't worshipped as such but was gathered around to recite the creeds.

Until I began this project I'd not considered that there was anything remotely sinister in all the ritual. Most were well-meaning, poetic even in parts, but having read afresh the various liturgies I'm now not so sure. The Folk Marshall's closing address at the end of any gathering or camp read:

'Go ye your ways, and may the Spirit of Woodcraft help you in all your works,

Be ye loyal to our cause and faithful to your fellow citizens.

Be strong! Live kindly! Love the Sun and follow The Trail!

I have spoken'

Whether they still use those same words I don't know, but I would be concerned now at anyone reciting them without understanding the spiritual power of a sworn oath.

Teaching children to become self-reliant and independent, was part of the Woodcraft philosophy and to this end, I was sent off to my first weekend 'camp' almost immediately. It was the first time I had been 'sent' anywhere and whilst I'm sure that my parents asked me if I wanted to go, and equally sure that I said yes, it was a miserable time. It was a gathering held in Scunthorpe, in winter, and we weren't actually under canvas which was a blessing, rather we were each placed individually into a host home for two nights, and then gathered together for activities during the daytime. This took place before my hospital encounter and became the worst experience of my little life to date.

The family I stayed with were perfectly nice, but I was six and they were complete strangers. I hated it and was desperately homesick but received short shrift from my group leader and felt very inadequate and small. So much so, that when quizzed on returning home on Sunday night, I insisted that I'd had the best time and couldn't wait to go again and on a proper camp. Oh boy.

Delighted at my enthusiasm, I was encouraged to participate in as many weekends as our meagre purse would allow. And so began my rather less than illustrious camping career.

My early memories are basically of being miserable, and mud. Elfins always stayed in twelve-man 'stormhaven' tents, made from heavy green canvas, which stayed waterproof until someone touched the side. Someone always touched the side. Groundsheets in those days were not sewn in and simply held down at the corners with pegs, so there was an unpluggable gap that always let in water, mud, insects etc.

There was camaraderie and after 'lights out' feasts and giggles, but there were also fallouts and bullying and fights. Of course there was supervision, but in the interest of child development we were largely expected to resolve our own disputes. It didn't always end well, children aged 6 - 10 can be horribly cruel to each other.

From the get-go I had a very strong sense that if I didn't enjoy these events I would be deemed a failure and not wanting to be so labelled, even back then, I manufactured a brave front that was far from the truth. In so doing, I doomed myself to frequent camping trips throughout my primary school years, each one without exception a gruelling test of endurance.

There were some things I really did love and enjoy though, and they more than evened out the balance in the long run. Much emphasis was put on creativity, especially music and dance. The Woodcraft songbook was packed with old folk songs and new protest songs. At every meeting there was someone with a guitar who could strum sufficiently well to accompany us singing the 'Bold Grenadier' followed by 'We Shall Overcome,' the irony is not lost on me still. The Red Flag was in there somewhere. We folk danced and sang our way through the rest of the sixties and one way or another life in the Woodcraft was a circle. Except on May Day's when it was a march, with banners blazing out for world peace and the 'Family of Man' (a song itself) to unite.

The two major impacts of that time were the founding of my first enduring friendship and a month spent on an International Camp in Finland.

31

Elaine was eighteen months my senior and we met when I was six. She had every quality that I didn't, she was confident, sporty and forthright, a born leader and one I was happy to follow. Our closest years were early teenage and together we got into scrapes aplenty. For a couple of those years I spent more time at her house than I did at my own, and sadly my Mother took against her as a 'bad influence', which was totally unfounded. I never had her sportiness or confidence but was hugely strong-minded and stubborn as an ox, and any leading astray was shared equally between us.

We are still in contact to this day and although we don't talk often and geographically are separated by thousands of miles, each would be there for the other, without question. It is good to know.

The camp in Finland was pivotal for several reasons. It was the first camp that I really enjoyed most of, for a start. Finland is a beautiful country and when you've spent your life mostly on a council estate in a midlands city or a slum in Liverpool, even at age eleven you can recognise the value of clean air. It was helped by beautiful weather and the midnight sun. By larking around in lakeside saunas and then diving into the freezing water. By the first experience of trying to be understood in a foreign language and successfully buying stamps to mail postcards. And then, sadly, by a storm.

We were a delegation of about thirty, of different ages from eleven to twenty, accompanied by a couple of leaders who had experience in travelling in such groups. We journeyed from Nottingham to London by coach, where we met up with the Southern contingent to travel by boat and train through Germany and onto Scandinavia. Friendships were forged on the journey as we sang and danced our way across Europe, entertaining (hopefully) other travellers at the stations we passed through along the way.

By the time we arrived at the campsite in Lahti, we were a well-bonded group and happy to share tent space, boys with boys, girls with girls.

The site was hugely well organised into different villages, with various 'venues' dotted around the perimeter. One was a large covered stage by the lake, a three-sided affair complete with full electrics and a sound system. Our group was involved in presenting an evening of dance and song there at about our third week in, and it happened to be on the night the weather broke. Protected by the roof, we were undeterred and even in the rain, many turned up to watch. At some point in the programme, the structure took the full force of a lightning strike and the electrics completely blew with a horrific bang.

Twenty screaming children were comforted by as many concerned leaders who hurried onto the platform in its wake. Except there were no longer twenty, there were nineteen. Angela from Muswell Hill had been playing her guitar leaning against the back 'wall' of the stage. The wiring ran along the joists and she took the full force. There was nothing to be done, although every effort was made to revive her.

Her parents were informed and flew out a couple of days later to collect her and we were counselled and gently consoled by our leaders, who were amazing. It was decided that we would see the camp out, and respectful tribute was paid during the remainder. But it was deeply affecting for us all and sadly is the overriding memory that remains. It was my first experience of the fragility of life and the harsh reality of death. It has never left me.

It was a sombre group that disembarked the train at Nottingham Midland Station where the parents who had arrived to meet us were gently briefed of events by our leaders. It was of course the first they had heard, and it must have been hard for them to know how to respond.

My own heart, although hurting, didn't really break until I got home, when somewhat subdued, my Dad had to tell me that while I was away my pet mouse Jinx had died and they'd given away my white rabbit, Christmas, as I didn't seem that interested in him anymore. I was sad about the mouse but distraught about the rabbit, whose re-homing, though possibly justified, felt like betrayal to me.

My world shifted on its axis that summer and with the onset of the autumn term in September would be forever changed. Grammar School beckoned.

Chapter 4

If life could reasonably be described as a rope, tied fast to something secure, then it would be fair to say that mine frayed, unravelled and lost its anchorage in my teens.

There were several cords, each distinctly separated from the others. It went something like this.........

As their own had been so elementary, a huge value was placed on the benefits of a good education by my parents. So much so in fact, that when Karl was selected to sit for and awarded a scholarship place at Nottingham High Boys, they sacrificed their strong political objections to public schools completely. This was partly fuelled by the alternative for him being the boys' comprehensive on the estate, which even back then had a reputation for being notoriously rough, giving rise to understandable concerns about how he'd manage.

Never his academic equal, no such opportunity was offered to me, which actually was to my great relief. I didn't like the grey uniform or the idea of having to bus into the city every day, and was more than happy to be offered a place at Clifton Hall Girls' Grammar. The school was literally around the corner and the uniform was purple and gold, better by far on both counts. Mum was less relieved and whilst she was pleased that I had passed the eleven plus, I think she always felt somewhat cheated that we weren't both in the elite. I tempered my own feelings of being a disappointment to her, by reasoning that at least I had passed the exam and wasn't condemning her to the lifetime of shame that my being sent to the secondary modern would have caused her. But my grammar school career was to prove almost spectacularly unsuccessful and failed to bring either of us much joy in the five years that it lasted. It didn't bring shame exactly, but it dashed completely her hopes of me attaining the dizzy heights of academe and following Karl to Cambridge.

The nervousness that assails some children at starting their secondary education, evaded me. I was simply excited to move up and desperate to stop being a child. But sadly being one of the new babies in a selective school went nowhere near to scratching that particular itch. By the time I was twelve, all of my friends outside of school were considerably older and I liked to think myself their equal, being back at the nursery end of things was a complete affront.

I hated it from the start. I considered myself more mature and more experienced than most of my classmates and must have been insufferable to them. I was soon knocked off my superior perch though. Throughout junior school, I had pretty effortlessly topped the class and wrongly imagined that the same lack of effort would continue to see me through. It soon became clear that in this new environment, I was in fact decidedly average and even behind in some subjects. Rather than rising to the challenge to improve, I adopted a more laissez-faire approach, convincing myself that the first couple of years weren't that important and I would be able to cram for the exams. I had little parental pressure, Karl had enjoyed his studies and never needed coaxing, they imagined I would be the same. By the time they realised this wasn't the case, the damage was done and much to their disappointment I scraped through each year only by the skin of my teeth.

There were no practical substitutions to compensate for not excelling academically at Clifton Hall, although music and sport were highly lauded, as both gave opportunities to represent the school. I was gifted in neither, although I did enjoy being a member of the choir for a time. We travelled and won competitions with renditions of The Goliath Jazz and The Jonah Man Jazz, under the direction of the wonderful Miss Cator, but sadly she left at the end of my second year and I lost the heart for it.

Scraping through became my modus operandi for survival and although I was reasonably well thought of by my teachers, my end of term reports always bore the same statement in practically every subject, 'with more application, could do better'. I was made so aware that I was not fulfilling my potential, that I became determined not to. At least I could succeed in that. Rebellion was again in the air.

Never a loud rebel, my stance was to simply refuse to conform. Skirt too short, sleeves rolled up that sort of thing. Always asking 'why' and never content with a, 'because that's the way it is' answer. I carried a sullenness about me that wasn't endearing, and I had few friends. However I was known for my ability to distract a teacher away from a boring lesson, onto a subject that would amuse the class, and was feted on some level for that. Invariably, I would get pushed forward as class spokesperson if ever there was a contentious issue to be overcome.

The only thing of note that I did for the school, was to enter a county-wide public speaking competition in my third year. I wrote and put forward a well-reasoned argument against the Rio Tinto Zinc Copper Mining Company, and came first in the set-piece. I lost it in the impromptu section though, when I could find nothing of note at all to say about the random subject I was given. I've erased it from memory, it was so embarrassing, but think it was something to do with vegetables. My Dad who had come to watch me speak was so disappointed, at the time I presumed in me, which compounded my shame. I discovered much later his feeling was empathy for me rather than judgement against me. But sadly I was to make the same mistake many times over the years before I made this discovery.

Our third-year form teacher was Mr Rogers, a small, sarcastic, bespectacled man who taught French and Russian. He used to throw the board rubber and call us 'miserable creatures' when we failed to understand, and for some inexplicable reason, I had a strange respect for him. He was also my French teacher and I had been unable to complete the viva exam in my third year due to sickness. Returning to school a few days later, and wanting to get it out of the way, I knocked on the staff room door at lunchtime and asked if I could speak to him. To his credit he came, but his response to me was like a slap in the face. He was appalled at my arrogance in thinking that I could determine when to re-sit, and I have never forgotten his words. 'Who do you think you are?! How conceited can you get?!' followed by a torrent of angry rhetoric that cut me to the quick. Lip quivering, and tears stinging my eyes I fled the staff room and out to the foyer, where I bumped into Miss Tait, the deputy-head. The floodgates opened and I sobbed like my heart would break. Perturbed, she kept asking, 'Elizabeth whatever is the matter, what has happened?'. I think I got his name out but nothing else, I refused to be comforted and was dispatched to the sick room to calm down.

In reality for me, this incident was the tip of a huge iceberg that was set to keep shattering over the next twenty years, but I had no concept of that at the time. Mr Rogers was an authority figure who questioned my motives and completely misunderstood me and unlike the others, who weren't part of my school life, I liked and respected him and it hurt. It really, really hurt.

At the close of my second year, life began to get very stormy outside of school and from that point my focus was always elsewhere. To my mind, school was a mandatory obligation that got in the way, and I lived for the day I could leave it behind.

In my final year I attended as little as possible, somehow managing to convince my teachers that I was completing the necessary work to get me through the forthcoming O' Level exams. Against everyone's advice, I was determined not to continue to the sixth form and nothing was going to sway me. In any case, the school was closing at the end of the academic year in a countywide shake-up of the system, meaning further studies would have had to be undertaken elsewhere and this diffused the pressure somewhat.

So, having not been there much for months, I finally left Clifton Hall on the day I took my last O'level exam. I said no goodbyes and carried no friendships forward. It was a very final leave-taking and even now, looking back, I cannot imagine how it could have been any other way.

Chapter 5

My birthday falls at the beginning of the academic year in September, which made me twelve when I started at the grammar and the oldest in my class, in fact almost a year older than one of my classmates. At the very beginning it was of little consequence, we were all simply trying to find our feet in a new environment. It wasn't long though before the cracks started to show. My 'best friend' at this time was Elaine, also in the school but two years ahead. She looked out for me in a motherly sort of way but we saw little of each other during the day for the first year or so I was there.

We were becoming ever closer socially though. Together, we were helping to lead a group of Woodcraft Elfins that met every Tuesday evening at a school in the Meadows, still a much-deprived area of the city. We both loved it and took our responsibilities very seriously. The leader, Joe was a lecturer at the Teacher Training College also in Clifton but lived with his wife and family in the classier suburb of Keyworth, a few miles out. We would meet him at the college and he'd take us back home where his wife would give us tea, before travelling into the city to do the group. The whole thing was an education for me, I ate my first pizza at their house and had my first taste of garlic. We drank 'real' coffee from a percolator and had discussions about the best way forward with our little 'elfins'. Ridiculous really, I was twelve, I could see the poverty most of them were living in and I felt 'something' like compassion, but the best way forward? Was that playing British Bulldog or learning to dance Strip the Willow? I was clueless.

My biggest responsibility was as treasurer, which amounted to no more than collecting and keeping the subs and a record of them. Each child contributed a couple of pence a week, which went towards the cost of hiring the school hall and providing refreshments. It was a tiny amount and not unreasonable but no child was ever excluded because of an inability to pay. What should have been a very simple exercise, turned into a bit of a nightmare for me. Handling money was not a life skill that I had been taught, so when I found myself short, I took to 'borrowing' from the subs tin, without ever really giving a thought as to how I would repay it. Of course there came a day of reckoning, when an account was required and I recognised that I was in some trouble. Too proud to make my confession to Joe or even to Elaine, I went to my Dad and turned on the little girl charm. It worked, and although it came with a lecture, he bailed me out and recouped his outlay by reducing my pocket money until the debt was cleared.

It was a soft lesson, and taught me nothing that I needed to learn and much that I didn't. I learned that by sweet talk and cheap promises, I was able to achieve my own ends and with that knowledge, watered the seed of the manipulator that was inherently present in me. Being held to account would have been a far better, if harder option, for my Dad, who at that point was reluctant to admit any flaw in me. Skill in handling money eluded me for many, many years but I grew well in the art of manipulation.

We helped with this group for about a year and then stepped down. We remained Woodcraft members but other pursuits were beckoning, more enticing than playing games.

We started to spend time with the older 'Pioneers' and most of our friends were around seventeen and eighteen. Not so huge a gap for Elaine, but I was still only thirteen, so pretty huge for me.

My parents' goal had always been to encourage us to be as independent as possible as early as possible. With Karl it worked out well, he was equally happy with his books and his outdoor pursuits and if not studying, was to be found climbing a mountain or descending into a pothole somewhere in Derbyshire or Wales.

He managed to never get injured and it was all very wholesome. Even when he decided that he wanted to learn to play the guitar, it was safe, his preference being for traditional and contemporary folk music, rather than any of the emerging 'pop' so unbearable to them.

It was not to play out so easily with me. I grasped the basic concepts of right and wrong (although as the subs issue showed, was more than happy to compromise for my own gain) but was in the main undisciplined. Neither settled nor happy at school, I was desperate always to be out and about and glued myself to Elaine like a limpet. Although eighteen months apart in age, we were well matched and pretty much inseparable. She was a natural leader and I was happy to follow in her wake, simply thankful to not be condemned to hanging around with girls my own age. Most afternoons I went to her house after school and remained there through the evening. It was a busy house. She had three older sisters, two living at home at the time, and there were many frequent visitors. Life just seemed to happen there and if you were in the house you were considered a valued part of it and included.

For my parents, my Mum particularly, this constituted both desertion and betrayal and she laid the responsibility for it firmly at Elaine's door. She felt that I was being lead astray, which was grossly unfair to Elaine who was made to feel so obviously unwelcome at our house that she stopped coming. This only served to exacerbate things and lead me to spend even more time at hers.

There were ridiculous contradictions in my parents' attitude played out during this time. I went with Elaine, to my first all-night party at thirteen, a flat-warming and gathering of Woodcraft friends. It was deemed acceptable by them as the host was the son of a couple they respected and therefore judged to be above reproach. The fact that he was in his late teens, as was everyone else apart from us, and that it was 1972 escaped them completely. There was everything there that you would expect, apart, thankfully from trouble, and the following morning wasn't a pretty sight. Karl, who was friends with the older lads and on vacation from university, had turned up at some point.

At first, I was cross thinking he'd cramp my style, but later grateful as his presence kept me out of the clutches of one of the boys. However old I felt, I knew I wasn't old enough or ready for that.

But I did so enjoy being one of the crowd, and with Elaine as my peer was accepted easily, no one questioning my age. It helped that I looked much older than my years. At eleven, I had looked eleven, but at thirteen, with newly plucked eyebrows, a smattering of Mary Quant and long dark hair, I could easily be mistaken for eighteen and often was. I can honestly say that I have never been challenged about my age in any setting, although it would be the most welcome ego boost if someone were to do it now!

We enjoyed some happy times with the older Woodcraft folk. Less was expected of us in terms of participating in organised activities, and we mostly would hang out together as a group, singing and chatting and putting the world to rights, in the way that only those with little experience of it can. There were ceilidhs, and socials, and hikes, and marches and great camaraderie. I recall all of it with nothing but fondness. It is true, I have never learned to love camping but I am glad to have done it, and done it with those folk at that time. They are cherished memories.

In many ways, thirteen was a seminal year for me. Having older friends meant that I largely missed out on the usual rites of passage that come with early adolescence and I found myself catapulted forward and often out of my depth.

In addition to the Woodcraft Folk, the Co-Operative Society sponsored several other worthy institutions in the city, including the Arts Theatre. The Society had purchased the former Particular Baptist Church in 1946 and converted it into a small but fully functioning theatre, run by its members and overseen by a full-time manager. It was an amazing venture, its aim to produce good quality amateur drama and musical theatre for the pure joy of it, and in so doing, train future generations of actors and backstage professionals.

More than a few notable names cut their teeth on that dusty stage and for a while, I hoped that I might be one of them.

My first time at the Youth Group was eye-opening. Run by a wonderful and highly committed couple who both worked as full time, school-based, drama teachers, it attracted a really mixed bag of kids aged thirteen to sixteen. Most were, or seemed to be, confident and extrovert and more than comfortable in what seemed to me initially, a wholly bizarre environment. There were breathing exercises, and attitude exercises, trust-building exercises and being still exercises. I was so exercised by it all that I nearly ran before the end of that first session, but something like fascination pulled me back.

For all my apparent poise, at heart, I was both timid and shy and desperately ill at ease. Astute observers of their students, Robin and Sue seemed to recognise both my need and my desire to fit in and be part of something, and were patient and kind in trying to coax me out of my shell.

The Youth Group staged a week-long production annually and that year it was to be The Crucible by Arthur Miller, a meaty play about the Salem witch trials. I wasn't hopeful for a part, so was surprised when at the casting they invited me to take the role of Betty Parris. I'd read the script of course and as she only seemed to have three lines thought I could probably handle it.

The main requirement was to lie still on a bed throughout the whole of Act 1, and then sit up quickly and scream the house down for a couple of minutes at the end. Given the signal to do so, at the first read-through rehearsal, I opened my mouth and nothing came out. The second time wasn't much better, I managed a sound but it was more like a frightened mouse squeaking than a child possessed, which is what it was supposed to be. My shameful embarrassment was compounded when I overheard a couple of the other, older girls (who later became friends but were then not) confirming to each other that I was terrible and likely to wreck the whole thing.

I remember after this, at the next read through, Sue sitting on one side of me and Robin on the other, and when my cue came both whispering in my ears simultaneously, 'close your eyes and just scream!' Amazing both them and myself, I managed to do exactly that for minutes on end, and each scream seemed to evict a little more of my timidity. By the time we came to do the show I could scream for England, or at least New England, which is all that was required. I had also learned to lie absolutely still on my side for nearly forty-five minutes, which brought me some acclaim. So still in fact, that the audience thought I was a dummy, and when I sat up and opened my lungs it caused gasps aplenty. I was going to be a serious actress for sure.

With this little success came recognition and acceptance within the group, and instead of being simply tolerated by the more seasoned members, I was embraced. I loved it. From that point, I immersed myself in every aspect of theatre life and got myself involved wherever I could.

Greenroom life was vibrant. It was a social space where everyone gathered after meetings and rehearsals; casts, stage crew, wardrobe department, anyone and everyone, and was where the serious, senior members entertained us all with their own theatrics. I was completely enthralled with all of it and spent many evenings starry-eyed, just listening and drinking what remains to this day, to be the most disgusting coffee I have ever tasted.

There were opportunities to get involved in every production in some way, and I took whatever I could get. From painting flats for a set, to prompting, to box office, coffee bar and usherette. Everything to me was playing a role and I took each as an opportunity, resenting nothing.

The Youth Group production the second year was Ann Veronica by H.G. Wells and the casting was determined by group read-throughs of the script. After the acclaim for Betty Parris, I was this time hopeful for a slightly bigger part, but had no great expectations.

Having a natural talent for imitating other accents, I was at home reading in the plummy voice required for the characters of Morningside Crescent, and I loved reading out loud and could do it well. But no one was more surprised than me when they offered me the eponymous leading role. It wasn't actually the best role but it was huge. Ann Veronica appears in practically every scene of the play and has hundreds of lines. I was thrilled and increasingly insufferable at home as I grappled to learn it all. But home had become a truly difficult place to be by this time, so I was careless of my moods and behaviour.

For reasons that will become apparent, it was the very act of becoming someone else for a while that captivated me, allowing me a form of escape that nothing else did. But as with most things, it came at a price. My long-standing friendship with Elaine began to suffer, as I immersed myself deeper into theatre life at the expense of everything else. We didn't fall out exactly but there was a cooling in our relationship and we saw less of one another. She felt I had changed and was becoming 'affected', hanging out with the more arty set, and in fairness, she was probably right although I couldn't see it at the time. In turn I felt somewhat abandoned by her, it was all rather uncomfortable for a while. But overall it was a good, focused time and it kept me from completely losing my footing which would have been almost inevitable otherwise.

By the time production week arrived, I was a ball of adrenalin and as high as a kite. First night nerves were hideous but once over them, it went pretty much like a dream. The notices in the Evening Post were excellent and the letters to the theatre magazine 'Cyclorama' even better. Cyclorama was actually a double-sided sheet, run off on a Roneo machine and posted out, but the letters were penned by highly esteemed members of the theatre and that was far more important to me than the format or how it was printed. At a point in my life where I felt otherwise totally without value, here it was expressed in print. I was valued and rated, and at last I could see that I might have a purpose. It was worth the cost to me at that time.

I remember leaving the theatre at the end of the third night and being stopped by a woman as I walked to the bus station, 'that was so lovely dear' she said, 'well done'. I floated the rest of the way, I had been recognised!

There was a good role the following year in the Roses of Eyam, another weighty piece about the plague, and a lead role after that as Rose Trelawny in Pinero's Trelawny of the Wells, which was reasonable but not so well received as the others. There were a couple of opportunities in the senior productions too, small parts in Hobson's Choice and Jane Eyre and a chorus part in the annual panto which was a hoot. I loved these, especially as they were the real deal in my young eyes, catapulting me out of the Youth Group and making the seniors my peers.

One night there was a revue staged by the members for the members, on the rehearsal room stage. As a Youth Group, several of us were given individual set pieces to perform. Mine was an excerpt from a play by Ladislas Fodor called The Vigil, a retelling of the Easter story in a modern US courtroom setting. Somewhat incongruous, sandwiched between a reading of Jabberwocky and Eliza Doolittle's 'Wouldn't it be Loverly' from My Fair Lady, but powerful nonetheless. I played Mary Magdalene describing her first encounter with the risen Christ and her deliverance by His hand. It affected me deeply, although at the time I had no idea why.

There was also a flip side to all the wholesome dramatics, which began in the Green Room and was cultivated shamelessly by me. I'd had no real 'boyfriend' experience up to this point but was not uncomfortable in male company, having got to know plenty of lads in the Woodcraft over the years, so when I began to receive attention in the Green Room, I was neither unduly disturbed nor immune to the silver-tongued charm.

The attention came from one guy in particular, a known lothario and so beguiling that I turned to jelly whenever he spoke to me. He nicknamed me JB and in my innocence I had absolutely no idea what it meant, but was not unhappy even when he explained that I was jailbait. His attention made me feel special and I lapped it up. The idea that I could present a temptation to him gave me a huge ego boost and still emerging from a shell of shyness, helped me no end. He was thirty-four and married of course. A product of the swinging sixties and free love, with a 'very understanding wife' (his words), who made it his business to bed every woman he found attractive. He belonged to both the theatre and the Operatic Society and played a big field. To me, he was simply a star and when he turned his attention my way I was immediately hooked. That he was twenty plus years my senior didn't occur to me in the slightest, that he was 'famous' and drove a Triumph Stag probably did.

In as far as I was capable at thirteen, I fell totally in love with him, way beyond any crush. I lied to him about my age, increasing it by a couple of years so as not to seem childish, and he offered to drive me home one night after a green room session. We left to a few knowing nods and winks and he chatted amiably throughout the journey. I was flattered and not remotely disturbed when he drove past my road and down a quiet lane, saying that he 'wanted to say goodnight to me properly'. Nothing serious ever happened really, just a lot of fumbling and some talk, but it went on for many months and there became an understanding that at some point, he would be 'my first'.

As I recall all this, there is a part of me that thinks I should be appalled. And it is true, I should be and would be if I was hearing it from someone else. But this is my story, and I am not. He was only ever kind and he made me feel good about myself and in June of 1973, he was there when my world imploded and helped to put me back together.

I was heartbroken, when he announced he had secured a new job in Southampton and would be leaving. Amazingly, I found myself there a few years later and we met a couple of times. In fact, we kept in touch until I was in my early twenties and although many others had by that point, he never bedded me. What had begun as arguably the most wrong relationship I've ever had, ended up as the most chaste. I loved him, he was a true friend.

My parents were of course completely unaware of all this. Not so much as kept in the dark by me, but preferring to trust that the Theatre was a safe place for my development, keeping me out of trouble and wholesomely occupied and not taking any further interest. Whilst they would have preferred me to be pursuing something that would lead me into a secure career, they had reasoned that my thespian ambitions were probably the least-worst of many possibilities and were happy to leave their concern there. They were never that supportive but neither were they dissuasive.

The theatre remained a big part of my life right up to the point of leaving home for the final time when I was sixteen. My commitment lessened though when I embarked on my first serious relationship and plummeted at the end.

As a youth group, we were entered into a competition to be held at The Royal Albert Hall in London, the prize being recognition and the possibility of being spotted by talent scouts. The individuals invited to be part of this troupe were asked to give an absolute and firm commitment to the project, no back-outs. I was one of them, I said yes and then weeks before the competition, I backed out.

Simplistically speaking this constituted a terrible letdown by me and it was, but I was broken and reeling and had been offered a way out and I took it. I will never forget making the phone call to Robin and Sue to say I was leaving; she could have rightly responded angrily and with justifiable accusation but she didn't. She didn't even say she was disappointed in me, but simply that she had always been 'a great believer in doing what seemed right at the time' and then she released me with her blessing.

It was one of the kindest things anyone had ever done for me. At the time when I needed it the most and no one else was prepared to, she absolved me of responsibility. The irony was that in this instance I was responsible and she released me anyway. I am ever indebted to them both. To my knowledge they were not Christians but they always treated me fairly and in this final act, however unbeknown to either of us at the time, showed me a reflection of God's love.

Whether by leaving, I did the right thing, I will never know.

Chapter 6

My life took a curveball one night in June 1973 that would cause ripples to fan out for the next twenty-odd years. Leaving the Green Room one mid-week evening, I ran to Broadmarsh Station to catch the last bus home, and missed it. It wasn't a disaster in itself, I was able to take a different route that meant that I had a longer walk once dropped off but I'd done it many times before and wasn't worried.

The walk took me on a cycle track alongside the main A453 and at 10:45 at night it was still busy with traffic. Not for one second was I aware of anything untoward, but about 200 yards along the track, I felt a hand go round my neck and something sharp pressed against my back. Instinctively I bit down hard, but the grip tightened and I heard a man's voice which was carried on sour breath, 'I don't want to hurt you, you just do as I say and you'll be alright'.

Terror is a surreal experience, it comes like a red mist and with a curious numbness. I remember feeling faint and my legs threatening to buckle as he dragged me through the hedge of nettles and marched me across a field. There was a housing development under construction just above the banks of the Trent and I remember clearly thinking that I would end up in the river, and in that moment being concerned for my parents.

In the shell of a house, on a concrete floor, I surrendered the virginity that I thought had already been reserved by someone else. Or rather this man took it. After my initial bite and a bit of kicking, it was clear he was far stronger than me and my resistance from then on was simply to plead. Driven by something that can only have been evil, he was immune, and not deterred by my screaming at him that I was only thirteen. It was brutal and painful and thoroughly demeaning, but mercifully it was not long.

Afterwards, rather than stabbing me and leaving me dead for the building contractors to find, or throwing me into the waters of the Trent, which for some reason is what I convinced myself he would do, he pulled me to my feet, took me by the hand and lead me back across the field and through the hedge. Once on the cycle track again, he pushed me in the direction I'd been walking and told me to go, with a warning that if I looked back he would find me and kill me.

Still scared enough to believe he would make good his threat, I ran towards home and only slowed when I was sure that I was out of his sight. With the initial rush of adrenalin at being safe subsiding, my thoughts turned to what I would say to my parents when I got there.

As I'd expected they would be, they had already gone to bed when I arrived. This was not unusual, creatures of habit to the last, they turned in for the night at 10:30 on weeknights and I had long since had my own key for such an eventuality. (Actually, I'd had my own key since I first started school at five, often arriving home half an hour or so before Mum got back from work). Once through the front door though, all my reasoning left me and I was simply a thirteen-year-old girl desperately in need of comfort. I raced up the stairs to their room and barged in. What happened after that was a catalogue of errors, and at first certainly, they were mostly my own.

As was their habit, they were sitting up in bed reading. In pyjamas and winceyette nightie, Mum hairnetted and both devoid of their teeth, now soaking neatly in plastic containers on their bedside tables, they looked small and diminished somehow. And alarmed, having heard me so out of character dashing up the stairs and bursting into their room. Although desperately wanting to, I knew as soon as I opened their door, that I couldn't tell them everything. Mum especially would never cope (the unkind thoughts about her manipulating the whole thing to be about her, didn't come till later) and anyway what purpose would it serve for them to know all the details in the long run. However, it was clear to them that something was seriously wrong, so I told them that a man had grabbed me from behind and threatened me as I walked up the cycle path, but that I was ok and they weren't to worry. Giving this misinformation was my first mistake and no matter how sound or naive my motives, was to cost me dearly.

Vainly, I had hoped that they might make a bit of a fuss of me and leave it there, but quite rightly, their concern was that this man was out there and having tried once, might now attack someone else and there be dire consequences. Ironically we had not long had our first telephone installed and the Police were duly summoned.

Dressing gowned and with teeth back in place, they divulged what I had told them to the two officers who attended. In their turn, they asked me to confirm, which I did, and then suggested it might be worth me accompanying them on a drive around the area to see if my assailant was still lurking somewhere. I agreed to this, but when they assumed that my Dad would also come, I said no and asked for Karl instead, who was home from Cambridge for the long vac. This must no doubt have been deeply hurtful to Dad and caused anguish to Mum, who would have spiralled into worry about 'what the Police must think' and the state of our family relationships.

Nonetheless they made no objection, and Karl and I were bundled into the thankfully, unmarked, police car. The search yielded nothing and after half an hour or so we were back home. Accompanying us into the house, the officers explained to my parents that they would need to bring me to the local station in the morning to make a statement, but for now they needed to take away everything I had been wearing. They also said it would be best if I was to be examined by the police doctor that night.

They gave me a bag for my clothes, and reduced to a state of terror not dissimilar to that I'd experienced earlier, I went to my room to change. I'd been wearing a maxi skirt and smock top, both favourites, and a pair of Indian sandals and I duly bagged them. I also put in my tiny bra but when it came to my knickers, I just couldn't. They were bloodied and disgusting, and I was ashamed and embarrassed and scared, and so substituted a clean pair from my underwear drawer. They accepted the bag without examining its contents and turned to leave, expecting me to go with them to see the doctor.

At that point I simply said no. I knew an examination would reveal the greater extent of the assault and I had already denied this to Mum and Dad, it was impossible that I should go. The officers sat me down and explained the power of evidence gathered early but I dug in my heels and refused to be persuaded, and eventually they left. Unbeknown to me I had just made mistakes two and three, each as serious as the first.

I have no idea what went through my parents' minds when I said I needed to bathe. It was by now after midnight and taking a bath was not a spontaneous thing in our house. Through the whole time I knew my Dad, he took a bath once a week on a Saturday afternoon, finishing exactly in time to watch 'Final Score' on the tv and tally his Pools coupon. But whatever they were thinking, they were kind enough to ask no further questions and let me get on with it. A sleepless night followed. I knew I was in trouble, but at that point had no idea of how much, and innocently imagined that I could explain it all privately to the Police when I went to give my statement the next day.

We were asked to report at 10:00 a.m. and Dad felt it impossible for him to take time away from the classroom, so it was Mum who walked with me the short distance to the local station. It was a tiny place, comprising a reception area and a couple of meeting rooms. We were seated in one of these by a kindly WPS, who gently explained the procedure. She asked me to tell her, in detail, exactly what had taken place. I repeated what I had offered the previous evening, knowing that with Mum sitting beside me, there was no way I could divulge everything.

However gently prompted by the officer's questions, I was persuaded to reveal slightly more.

'Did he threaten to hurt you?'

'Yes'

'Did he, at any point threaten to rape you?'

'Yes'

'Did he touch you intimately'

'Yes'

All and more met by sharp intakes of breath from Mum. I was asked to sit in the reception area while she was questioned herself and can only imagine the line that would have taken.

'Tell me Mrs Moore, is it usual that your thirteen-year-old daughter would be coming home from the city late at night by herself?'

I doubt it was very pretty or kind, and suspect that to be put in this position by me, caused indignation to rise in Mum. Of course, I had no understanding of that at the time and when I was summoned back in, my expectation was simply that they would try and trace my attacker and if they couldn't do so, all this would go away.

The next few minutes in that room, are indelibly imprinted on my memory, although thankfully, through the goodness of God and His healing, those memories no longer have any power to hurt me. Mum sat upright in her chair, with a face that looked like thunder and defeat in equal measure.

The WPS looked me in the eye and said, 'well Elizabeth, thank you for telling me about the events of last night, I want you to know that I believe you. Your statement will now be referred to CID in the city, who will want to speak to you themselves. You will also have to see the Police doctor for an examination sometime today'.

She had lost me at, 'I believe you'. How could that even be in question? I had told the truth, admittedly not all of it, but there was hugely good reason for that and anyway it didn't invalidate anything that I did say. I began to experience that cold clammy discomfort that accompanies fear and the recognition that all is not well.

It was a very quiet walk, from the station to home and we sat pretty much in silence waiting for Dad to get back from school. They had words privately when he did, and I just sat, waiting.

A CID officer arrived at about 5:00pm to take us into Nottingham Central Police Station. All three of us went, not really knowing what to expect or how we would deal with it. What happened over the next two and a half days still constitutes the worst time of my life to this point. It was 1973. The Rape Suite did not yet exist. The thought that a girl assaulted by a man would relate better to 'the gentle touch' of a female officer when questioned, had not yet entered anyone's mind. And Police Surgeon's, well whoever was on duty, was on duty, no special training or experience required.

We were taken to an upper floor room and introduced to a detective inspector and his sergeant, both huge men, both taking their positions on the other side of a huge desk. They were not deliberately unpleasant but they were very matter-of-fact. The introductions over, the DI explained that before we did anything else I had to undergo a medical examination, and questioned why I had been so resistant to this the previous night, when it would have been more helpful. He was clearly unimpressed when I said that I simply couldn't face it and responded with something like, 'well you're going to have to face it now'.

Dad remained with them, and Mum and I were escorted to the bowels of the station, where the on-duty doctor had his 'consulting room'. A suite it certainly was not. It was a tiny, shabby room with a desk, two hard chairs and an examination couch. He was clearly, a disinterested man, assured of his power and position and not in the least concerned about ours. He told Mum to sit and me to undress and lie on the couch. There was no privacy screen or even a curtain and Mum's embarrassment was so acute, that despite my precarious position, I felt it.

As the incident the previous night had been my first experience of physical intimacy, this was my first experience of an internal medical examination. They were as brutal as each other. With my Mother looking on and trying not to, the Doctor said pretty much the same words as my attacker had, if less aggressively, and once I was suitably positioned, began his work.

Gloved hand inside me, he looked at me and then Mum and said, 'someone's been in here before haven't they?' Unaffected by my cry of denial, he elaborated, 'and not a boy either, a mature man'. It was absolutely untrue. Prior to the attack the only fumblings down there had been mine, and nothing more than the usual explorations of an emerging young woman.

Mum was distraught. As I have said, she was a fount of contradictions and for all the communist anti-establishment rhetoric, had a respect for the professional classes that bordered on idolatry. If the doctor said it, it must be true. Confusion and shame descended on me with tsunami force, and as we were returned to the CID office, with Mum mumbling, 'where did we go wrong?' to me, her fallen daughter, I simply went numb with the shock of it all.

Dad was still there, and someone brought us tea as we waited for the detectives to return. No-one spoke. We sat apart from one another almost like strangers.

On their return, the detectives resumed their positions behind the massive desk, any previous trace of friendliness completely absent. Addressing only me, the DI laid out their summations. The forensic report was in, and the clothes I had surrendered, although dirty with soil, plant debris and concrete dust, revealed no evidence of violence or sexual assault. They made no mention that the underwear was completely clean and clearly freshly laundered. However, the Police Surgeon's report showed that I was indeed sexually active and there was evidence that intercourse had taken place. No mention was made of the nettle-rash that covered most of my legs, nor the bruising around my neck.

He went on to say that in the light of this information their conclusion was that I had told them nothing but a pack of lies and that I should go home now, and return in the morning ready to make a new and true statement, detailing exactly what had taken place.

Neither Dad nor Mum made any response, like me numb with shock but without the sense of injustice that was growing in me by the minute. We were so clearly summarily dismissed, there was absolutely no point in trying to respond even had I been able to.

Dad thanked them and assured them that we would be there in the morning and we were returned home in a Panda car, drawing attention to ourselves as we turned into our small estate.

It was the stuff of nightmares.

Once home, with front door closed, there were no outbursts. They smoked and drank whisky to calm their frayed nerves, and Mum continued to mumble about how could they have gone so wrong. Dad said absolutely nothing. In spite of the shock, I was indignant, I had told them the truth, I insisted, this was so unfair, the doctor was a beast, his findings simply wrong. And after that, I asked Dad a fated question.......

'I am telling the truth Dad, you do believe me don't you?'
He sighed and responded, 'Well, the doctor and the police seem to think otherwise, so.....'
He didn't go so far as to say he believed I was lying but the implication was clear, I turned and went to my room and something in me died. It broke us. He was not unkind to me, but I was no longer his little girl and he was no longer my rock.

In their parenting of me there had been little discipline, but they did ground me in the moral principles and one of them was to always tell the truth. Feeling abandoned by them in that moment, I reasoned that I would simply keep telling the truth until I was believed, because the truth had to win out in the end. And when the detectives accepted it, then so would they. It was to prove a vain hope. But it got me through the night and filled me with resolve the next morning, as I waited to go again to Nottingham Central Police Station.

Dad accompanied me this time, silent throughout the journey. He was asked to wait separately as I was lead again to the CID office, where the huge DI still sat behind his huge desk. Did this man ever go home? He took me through the statement I had made the day before. He said he didn't believe a word of it and that I was now to tell him the truth of what happened. I told him, simply repeating my statement of the previous day.

We ping-ponged through the morning. Someone brought a sandwich and a drink. We didn't leave the room. The doctor's report was the problem, outweighing everything else, and I knew then that I would have to give every detail, despite still wanting to somehow protect my Mother from the worst.

So I told him, accounted for every minute of the whole sordid thing, tears streaming but with the biggest voice I could muster. He sat there, shaking his head. His questions actually weren't unreasonable, why would I have given them clean underwear if I had nothing to hide? I explained about Mum's disposition and my need to shield her but he didn't buy a word of it.

'Let me tell you, what really happened last night Elizabeth........'
His scenario was that I had arranged a clandestine meeting with a boy/man, after the theatre. We had gone somewhere for sex and I had lost track of the time, making me very late home. Worried about the reception I would get from my parents I made up this elaborate story to get myself out of trouble, and all it had served to do was to land me in a whole load more.

It was pitiful in reality and any lawyer would have taken it apart, but there was no lawyer, there was not even parental support. So it went on, all afternoon, him goading and me fighting for the truth, which I sincerely believed, he had to believe in the end.

It was still an impasse at the end of the day when he brought the interview to an end with a warning. He for the life of him couldn't understand what I thought I could possibly hope to gain by holding out, but tomorrow things had to change. I was to report back and if I remained unwilling to make a fresh and truthful statement, I would be formally charged with wasting Police time, which was a serious offence.

Dad was recalled and for the second time, we were summarily dismissed.

All I remember of the rest of that day was the quiet. Back at home Mum and Dad whispered to each other, excluding me and allowing no possibility for discussion. Karl absented himself, understandably unable to handle what was palpable tension.

I went to bed dejected and frightened and comforted myself by reading the whole of H.G. Wells' novel Tono Bungay. I remember absolutely nothing of the story even to this day, but it holds a place of affection in my heart as it got me through the night without terrors.

Well aware that I was in trouble, but still convinced that the truth would win out, the next day we returned yet again to Central Police Station and the CID office. And again I faced the huge Inspector sitting at his huge desk.

He sighed impatiently when I repeated my stance of the previous day and responded that he simply wasn't prepared to listen to any more of my nonsense. He had nothing against me personally and he was sorry that I'd got myself into such trouble, but I had to now take responsibility and face the consequences at home, whatever they may be. He gave me a cup of tea and ten minutes to think about it and then it was up to me. Alone in that office, confused and bewildered, I realised that my only way out of this was to lie. To go completely against one of the founding principles on which I'd been raised, and it made no sense to me whatsoever.

Reasoning that being charged with wasting police time would cause more embarrassment and shame than me recanting my statement and inventing a new story, and also frightened by the prospect of a criminal record at thirteen, I got my imagination to do its work. I was very tired and it was very limited.

When the Inspector returned, I said I was ready to start again and he breathed a sigh of relief. So, there was this guy I'd met before at some party and he'd asked to see me again. I liked him but he was much older and my parents wouldn't have approved, so we arranged to meet on a night I was already out and the rest was as they'd guessed.

'What was his name?'

'Mick Thomas'

'And where does he live?'

'Bulwell, I don't know the address or phone number'

'Where had you arranged to meet?'

'Council House Lions'

A few more perfunctory but personal questions followed to which I gave equally perfunctory answers. The truth was I had met a guy called Mick Thomas at a party and he did live in Bulwell, but I had never seen him again and had made no arrangement to. All dates met at the stone Lions outside the Council House, so I figured that was easily believable.

Somehow it was enough, I signed it as a true and complete statement and they called Dad back in.

With him present, the Inspector said to me, 'I have interviewed some hardened criminals in my time Elizabeth, but honestly, I don't think I've ever met anyone quite as stubborn as you, and whilst I can't condone what you've done and the trouble you've caused us, I do respect you for fighting so hard. Maybe you can turn that stubbornness into a quality for good in the future'.

For the final time and not quite so summarily as before, we were dismissed and taken home. At least I hoped it was the final time. Never a liar until that point, it began to dawn on me that I had a lot to learn. Would they be able to trace Mick Thomas? How much time would they give to it? Would they question everyone at the theatre? The party I'd referred to had been held by one of the older members of the Youth Group, would they drag her into it? Guilt set in, the poor guy had done absolutely nothing wrong, what if I had landed him in a whole load of trouble?

Oh my, fear started to seep into my system like poison and it was much worse than any of what had gone before.

At home, Mum and Dad weren't unkind but they gave me a stern talking to and they agreed for me, that I would never again make mention of this sorry episode. I would go back to school as if returning from a short sickness and that would be that, we would carry on as before. Taking refuge from all the injustice, I went to my room feeling like dirty dishwater being emptied down the plughole.

A couple of other unthinkable possibilities hit me that night, sleepless again and full of contempt for everyone and everything. 'What if's' that until that point mercifully hadn't occurred to me. What if I was pregnant? What if I had contracted some filthy STD? How on earth would I manage either of those situations, or worse still both of them? The thoughts came to compound the fear that was already gnawing away at me and by morning I was a wreck. Walking to school every car that passed sent a shockwave through me, was it the Police coming to haul me back in having disproved my story?

Once at school, I was summoned to the Headmistress' office where I was given a lecture about the importance of telling the truth and a letter to take home to my parents. There were whispers going around the corridors and it was soon made known to me that the Police had been in and that I was the subject of their enquiries. Unable to find it within me to become the celebrity of the piece, I simply ignored it all. Dodging questions, hiding in the toilets between lessons. It died down after a few days and I was seen as simply the quirky girl who refused to mix.

The letter to my parents from Miss Squires, I did sneak a look at. It was opened, read and kept in the desk letter rack in the living room, like a souvenir, odd considering we weren't supposed to ever make mention again. It was short and to the point and began,

'Dear Mr and Mrs Moore,

I was sorry to hear about the recent trouble with Elizabeth and in any case, the Police came to see me on Thursday……..'

Years later and long since left school, I found that letter still in the desk and I took it. I don't know if they knew, it was, in true form, never mentioned. I kept it for years, taking it out at intervals and brooding on it and the nature of betrayal, usually when something else had gone horribly wrong and I needed to feed my own angst.

A few weeks passed and it became mercifully obvious that I wasn't pregnant, I didn't think either that I had contracted any disease, there were no symptoms. I was relieved to say the least, thinking that maybe my luck was changing and I'd dodged a couple of bullets, but even so I remained frightened of my own shadow.

One day coming home from school, there was a panda car parked in the spaces near our house and I imagined it was all over. I went through the front door convinced that my fate was sealed. When Mum saw my face she asked what on earth was wrong with me and I realised, just in time not to give myself away, that there was no police presence in the house. It transpired that there had been a bike or something stolen from a house down the road and they were attending to that.

After a couple of weeks Mum and Dad began to ask why I hadn't been going out, had I become fed up with the theatre, was something wrong? The abandoned little girl in me wailed but I said nothing. The truth was I was absolutely terrified of walking back from the bus stop at night, but of course they couldn't see that.

Eventually, screwing up my courage and stealing my nerves against the possibility of being the subject of gossip, I did go back. Thankfully no one was cruel and I was welcomed, and for the first time since the incident I slowly began to find myself again. Fortunately I was able to beg myself lifts home at the end of most evenings and when he was there, the man who knew me as JB always offered.

Stopping in a lay-by the first time, he put his arms around me and let me talk. It all came out, no tears, but still he rightly gauged the pain and held me, telling me gently that 'lightning didn't strike twice'. Well I had seen it strike once at a lakeside in Finland, and now this had happened, so it was hard to believe, but I took the comfort anyway, it was in short enough supply.

A little more comfort was to come, though from the most unlikely of sources. Clifton Hall was essentially a very traditional school. Each day began with Assembly, with everyone gathered in the hall, it was not optional. Headmistress and Deputy Headmistress, in their gowns, seated on the stage, teachers on either side of the hall, the sixth form on chairs at the back and the lower school, cross-legged on the floor in year order, first years at the front.

To begin, a piece of classical music was played on a record player operated by the music teacher, situated by the grand piano to the left of the stage, and after the notices, we stood to sing hymns to her piano accompaniment. There would then be a short message, usually given by the Head and usually taken from a worthy article in the Readers Digest.

On this particular day, the article referenced the famous 'love' scriptures from Paul's first letter to the Corinthians chapter 13. The words spoke to my heart although I was only half-listening, and I was moved to tears. It seemed to me that lately love had been none of the things Paul said it should be, and I found solace in the hope that perhaps there was a chance that at some point, things could be different.

Assembly over, we went to our lessons with me determined to look out that scripture later. The school day took its course and when I got home I was disappointed to realise that I had forgotten to do so. Then I remembered the old Catholic Bible that my Grandma had given me the last time I stayed in Liverpool, so many years before.

I recalled nothing from the morning, other than the passage was from the New Testament and my knowledge of the Bible was limited to the very little I had learned in early childhood. This amounted to nothing really but I knew that I had to find that scripture. So I sat in my tiny bedroom and went through every New Testament page until I did, or something like it in antiquated language. As I had in the morning, I found solace again in the evening through Paul's words, and even a glimmer of hope that maybe there was a better way.

I prayed that night for the first time since I was seven and struck down with a bursting appendix, and to be honest it was in a similar vein. God if you're real, I need you. Now. Nothing at all happened but I had expected nothing, so wasn't disappointed. Finding the passage and reading it for myself gave me the impetus I needed. It was the night of a life-changing decision.

Addressing myself in the mirror (something I am still apt to do from time to time) I gave myself a good talking to. 'You have a choice to make Liz and you have to make it now. It is sink or swim time. Stop it all now or survive, it's up to you, what will you do?'

'Survive', I told my reflection.

'And how will you do that?' my reflection answered.

It was not the life-saving decision I could have made, given more understanding, but within its limitations I did at least make the right choice. I had found comfort in Paul's words but by reading no further, not the salvation offered in Jesus.

Instead, I began at that moment to construct a tower around myself that would be completely impenetrable and far too high to scale. It turns out, I was a good builder. And also a good demolisher. I tore down every principle on which my life had been built and replaced each one with what I decided would form my new truth.

Trust absolutely no one, ever. Live for yourself and use whatever means available to achieve what you want. Try not to hurt anyone but recognise that sometimes you may have to. The world now owes you a living, take it. Dangerous principles on which to build a life and an open door for bitterness to enter in and take up residence. And with all its cohorts in tow, it did just that.

It was as if, in that instant of entry, bitterness soured every word of those beautiful verses that only moments before had given me such comfort. Actually, love was not patient. Or kind. It was totally self-seeking and self-serving. It did not delight in truth, truth was an idealistic concept that served no purpose whatsoever. Love never protected, and trust, hope and perseverance counted for nothing. It was all lies.

Partnering with this stark negativity had no apparent immediate effect. In fact, I felt better having made what I saw then as a wholly positive decision, choosing to be a victor and not a victim, irrespective of the cost. When I donned my school uniform the next morning, I stood taller and felt stronger than I had since that fateful night, and ready to face the world. The foundations of the fortress that I was to construct around myself over the coming years were firmly laid and I already felt the protection that the lies I had chosen to believe afforded me.

All told, June 1973 was a sorry month and it set the tone for many years to come.

At the time, I had no idea of the spiritual impact of the decisions that I'd made. I was simply satisfied, that in making them, I had given myself a strategy for moving on and released myself from the constant worry and hurt and pain and confusion that I was feeling. And it sort of worked for a while, like a local anaesthetic for the soul, I was numbed to just about everything.

The only place I came to any life was the theatre. Even in my numbness, I recognised that there was an escapist freedom to be found in assuming the character of a role. Learning to scream as Betty Parris was a great help and exuding the upper-class confidence of the suffragette Ann Veronica, making a stand against her family, went some way to relieving the bitter disappointment that I felt with my own.

Chapter 7

Turning fourteen in September made me eligible to take on a Saturday job, which was attractive on two fronts that actually amounted to the same thing. By now always wanting to be out, bus fare money was always needed and always in short supply, so the small wage was welcome, also the job got me out of the house for the whole of Saturday. It was my first win, win situation!

Elaine was already doing the same at a large branch of John Menzies in the city and put a word in for me. Before long I joined her on the record counter and although unbeknown to me at the time, took a huge and fateful step into the next chapter of my life.

Music had been important to me since childhood, singing Bob Dylan songs on my swing before school in the morning. Much of my soundtrack was handed to me through my brother but I was continually developing my own tastes, usually to Karl's disapproval. Every Saturday provided the opportunity to hear something for the first time and a whole new world began to open up. I hadn't expected working to be so much fun and that fuelled my ambition to be out of school as soon as possible.

Increased trade as Christmas approached opened up overtime opportunities. I took whatever extra shifts I could get and so began a habit of skipping lessons whenever I thought I could get away with it, to go instead to work. It was surprisingly easy and I sailed through the Christmas season undetected and richer than I had ever been.

The extra help was required purely for the season, so it was Saturday's only again for a while afterwards. Conversely, it was probably for this reason that I didn't at that point get caught, so it was all to the good really, although still not having learned anything about budgeting, the bus fare squeeze was soon back on. However, that didn't last for long. The young manager of the store began to show an interest in me, having become aware of my increased presence over the busy period, and one day he phoned to ask me out. I could think of no reason why not to go, so agreed, and a date was set. Some months had passed since 'all the trouble with Elizabeth' so the parental detachment from my comings and goings had resumed and when I said that Jon was picking me up to take me out, not an eyelid was batted. That I saw anyway.

He was almost twice my age, an ex public-school boy and a graduate in political science from Leeds University. He wore square steel framed specs and sported a bushy beard and he talked about dreamy things like poetry and plays and music. He took me to a pub in Long Eaton with plastic banquette seating, and a jukebox that grabbed the record you'd selected, or possibly one you hadn't, from a revolving rack and jammed it on the turntable as you watched. He bought me a half of bitter and lime and we listened to Ricky Valance singing 'Tell Laura I Love Her' on repeat. It was already a golden-oldie but I loved the pathos.

Jon was relaxed and talkative, he asked me about myself and my hopes and dreams and was not deterred by the awkward silences when I was unable to think of anything interesting to say. He was not pushy or forceful, and gave me only a very chaste kiss goodnight when he dropped me back home. He said he'd enjoyed my company, would like to see me again, how about next week? As usual Mum and Dad had gone to bed when I stepped through the front door at 11 o'clock, but this time I had no need or desire to run to them for comfort. I was on cloud nine.

We started to see each other regularly and whilst admittedly I was enthralled by him, he also was sincerely drawn to something in me, apart from the appeal of a 'nubile young thing' which he called me from time to time. But he was in his late twenties and it wasn't too long before he wanted more than conversation.

When I had called myself to account before the mirror the previous June, one of the 'lies' that I demolished was that I was worth waiting for, that my body counted for something. Already violated, it seemed worthless to me, so what did it matter who I gave myself to? There was also the added pressure of the free-love generation and the acceptance that sex was justifiably expected. The difficulty for me was not that I wasn't willing, or that I was worried about pregnancy or my reputation, I cared about neither. It was simply that aside from those chaste kisses I hated being touched. With the exception of my actor friend, who I'd trusted prior to the rape, I flinched if anyone came close.

Jon obviously picked up on this quickly and asked what had happened to me, in his maturity understanding that something had, rather than feeling rejected and giving up. So I told him. He was only the second person I had confided in.

He didn't say as much, he was understanding and patient and kind, but I imagine Jon saw me as a bit of a project for a while. He was a dreamer, and told me once that he could see me as some tragic figure, weighed down by her tears as she went through life. Maybe I do him a disservice; if I was a project, I was one he came to love, and he looked after me and out for me for a long time.

He brought me back to life and with patience and gentleness showed me that sex did not have to be violent or sordid, and could be more than something just to be endured.

I thought then that he treated me with respect and as a woman, even though I was still very much jailbait. Today, I'm not sure quite what I think. I volunteer as a Police Chaplain and I have heard first-hand the rancour of Officers called to deal with child sex cases, especially of those with young daughters of their own. But at fourteen, already robbed cruelly of my innocence, I was not a little girl. And however much my sixty-plus year old self can see and understand the moral arguments, my own truth is that I was not exploited by this man in any way, and in the end it was me who did the leaving, arguably sufficiently healed to pursue my own exploits. I was to find myself wishing more than once, that I had stayed.

We quickly became 'an item' seeing each other as often as possible, and Jon continued my education in things other than the simply carnal. He taught me how to hold a knife and fork properly (who knew?), to pronounce the 't' at the end of words and not to drop the 'h' at the beginning. He couldn't soften my 'u' or persuade me to add an 'r' where the wasn't one, for example in 'bath', but both of those things came by osmosis later on. Way more importantly, he taught me the value of beautiful things and words and affirmation, and helped me to recalibrate and find within myself some desire again to actually enjoy being alive.

These things must have been apparent in me, but Mum and Dad were less enthusiastic about him. 'He's too old for you', was one concern, but it was far outweighed by the fear that in his grip I would let go of my socialist roots and embrace another way. 'He's admitted that he votes Tory, Liz', was a phrase I heard more than once, as if this was the ultimate betrayal. Our relationship by then was so broken, I simply took no notice of these comments, making sure always to get back from a night out after they had gone to bed, so that Jon could come in for coffee without fear of their disapproval. When they did have occasion to meet, he was simply nice to them, so it was impossible for them to do anything other than reciprocate, if in a somewhat subdued manner.

I'm inclined to think now, that his easy confidence frightened them. Although they were supposed to despise everything his background stood for, they were also slightly in awe of it, especially Mum, who always had a hankering for better things. In any case, they never voiced their opposition to his face, and as if a fait accompli, he was tolerated, although never embraced by them.

For his part, Jon had no need for their approval and their standoffishness was no problem to him. So we continued on. Increasingly I would spend the night at his house, telling them for form's sake, that I was staying with a girlfriend from the theatre. They knew I was lying, but it made it more palatable, so they accepted it. I never gave a thought to any concerns they might have about condoning an underage relationship, and they must have had them given our history. I simply barrelled ahead with my life and they couldn't see how to stop me, reasoning I believe, that they would be there to catch me when I fell.

There was one lesson that I would have been far better not learning from Jon, but to my detriment I was a good pupil and learned it well. At university in Leeds, he had developed a penchant for 'real' beer and whilst most activists were still banning the bomb, he joined the Campaign for Real Ale (CAMRA). Most of our dates involved trips to pubs, often with other members of the Nottingham branch, and imbibing vast quantities of the stuff.

To do this well, of course, I had to be eighteen and so invented a whole legend for myself, easily becoming a first-year student at the teacher training college in Clifton. I knew its layout from the days of helping lecturer Joe with the Woodcraft Elfin Group, and this gave me the confidence to lie authoritatively, if somewhat vaguely, about life there. I nearly came unstuck when the CAMRA chairman said his girlfriend went there too, but she hardly ever joined us and on the odd occasion that she did, paid me no mind. It was a big college, it wasn't inconceivable that we should never meet.

And so before I was legally old enough to drink, I had consumed my own body weight in beer and many times over. Most days I woke with a hangover, but as with almost everything, drinking capacity improves with practice and I practised hard. Four or five glasses a night was not unusual by the time I was fifteen, and it was only that I began by drinking half-pints, rather than pints, that I didn't get into serious trouble.

My frame is small, and my weight then hovered around the seven stone mark, I kept it there by eating less than I drank, but how I maintained my health I don't know. It never occurred to me that I was developing a habit that would become a problem. Some of these guys measured their worth by how much they could consume and being able to keep pace with them, even if in half quantities, was almost an accolade. I remember one evening in the pub, a guy who worked as an engineer for what was then the GPO, interrupting his pint to go outside and be sick and then coming back to the bar to finish his drink to a round of applause. There was no obvious pressure to join in but there was a lot of encouragement.

Nottingham at the time had three breweries, each producing real ale, so there was no shortage of hostelries to frequent in the city. One of them was The Newmarket Inn, run by an ex-Police Officer who had been injured in the line of duty and had taken early retirement on health grounds. I didn't know his history until after I'd been accepted as part of the CAMRA group as Jon's girlfriend, so that when I did find out, the police connection didn't rock me too much.

I was rocked a lot harder when I was introduced to another member, who was a stalwart supporter of the cause but not often around as he worked shifts. He turned out to be an active service Police Inspector and for a while, I was terrified of him. He was actually a lovely man and he and his wife Ann became friends to us, often inviting us to their home for meals. They simply believed my lies and accepted us as a couple. What an irony, and one that only went to support my new belief that being truthful profits you nothing.

On top of this, the pub was fifty yards from the stage door of the Arts Theatre, so the perfect venue to meet Jon after a rehearsal and quickly became our 'local'. Synchronicity indeed.

Over the next couple of years, we travelled in coaches all over the country with CAMRA, visiting breweries and attending beer festivals, drinking our way non-stop through the weekends.

There was a three-day festival held at the Corn Exchange in Cambridge whilst Karl was still a student there. It was fun, bunking down on his filthy floor in the attic of a huge old house in the city and being part of the 'student fraternity' for the weekend. It was the nearest I ever got to attending university. Years later I was to have an office in Marlow, right next to what had then been part of Brakspear's brewery, and could remember the guided tour through the brewing process on a visit there. By the time I was legally entitled to drink it, there wasn't much I didn't know about beer. I don't remember too much of it now, lost as it was in the haze of spirit fumes that were to follow later.

Apart from this decidedly, unhelpful influence, Jon was a positive force in my life. He certainly helped me to believe better of myself and raise my very low levels of self-confidence. He used to pick me up occasionally from school, in his old Mark 2 Jaguar, which earned me huge points on the schoolgirl credibility and interest scale. But it was by then water off a duck's back to me, in my head I had already left and the need to impress my peers had long since passed.

For all his encouragement, he showed no interest whatever in the things that had taken up my time prior to meeting him, namely the theatre. He wasn't exactly unsupportive, but he never came to see any production I was in and was the sole reason for my lessening commitment to it as time went on.

This was difficult for me to understand and I was particularly hurt when he didn't come to see me as Ann Veronica, pleading work and other commitments. He more than absolved himself by presenting me with a first edition copy of H.G. Wells original book, which aside from the nurse's outfit, lovingly stitched for me by Mrs Fletcher so many years before, was the most thoughtful gift I had ever been given and remained so for a long time. On reflection, there was probably an unhealthy level of control but I could see nothing other than his goodness and as far as I was capable, which wasn't far, I trusted him.

One thing I was acutely aware of, was that I wanted to retain control of was my body, and on turning 16 when the pill became available without parental consent, I booked an appointment with the Doctor. The same Doctor who had diagnosed my appendicitis years before and the only GP I had ever seen.

From the moment I entered the surgery I was ill at ease. He questioned me deeply about the nature of my relationship with Jon and asked for almost graphic detail. He then told me that he was willing to issue me with a prescription but that it was important for him to assess my health first by performing an internal examination. I felt trapped but desperately wanted the script and so agreed. It was like a replay of the scene with the Police Surgeon, minus the disdain but with lewdness enough to compensate for it. He fiddled around way beyond the need for examination purposes and asked questions like, 'does this feel nice?', 'is it better this way?'. I was absolutely revolted, this man had known me from babyhood, it was an unquestionable abuse of his position. When it was over and with prescription firmly in hand, I bolted from the surgery, shaken to my core and desperately upset. But I did nothing about it and told no one, the fear of not being believed far greater than my pain and indignation. It was another betrayal by someone in authority and served only to add another brick in my wall of self-protection.

In the autumn of 1975 after a huge and what seemed like it might be a terminal blow up with my Mother, I packed a bag and went to stay with Jon in his shared house in the city. From a practical point of view it was a nonsensical move, getting to school meant a bus ride rather than the walk around the corner from home, but from a survival point of view it made huge sense.

My Dad, who by then was at his wit's end with our bickering, let me go without resistance, on the understanding that I would continue to attend school and to study. Almost inevitably though, my attendance dropped and my studying took a massive hit, but my resolve to show everyone that I could meet the challenge of living as an adult and pass next years exams grew wings. I would make this work.

And I almost did. Jon was insistent that I should continue to see my parents, however difficult and he made it part of the deal if I wanted to stay with him, so I did. It wasn't comfortable or easy for any of us but it was sound advice, not least because a change was on the horizon that would separate us for a short while.

There had been some problem for him at work that called his management into question and he was given notice to leave. He quickly found an Area Management position with a rival company but it meant a geographical move west, as the territory was too big to cover from Nottingham. I was heartbroken and distraught and the timing was rubbish, a couple of months before I was to sit O'Level exams.

Mum and Dad saw this as the fall that they had been waiting to catch me from, and welcomed me back home. It was good of them, but they cooled in their attitude when it became obvious that we hadn't split up and were biding our time and making plans for when I was released from school obligations.

I'd been meeting those obligations only very lightly for the whole of that academic year. Skipping as often as possible, and leaving early to go to work. There was a call from my form teacher to my parents, expressing concern at my poor attendance and suggesting to them that emotionally I wasn't very strong. They shared this with me and I was aghast and furious, I really liked this teacher and it felt like yet another betrayal. No one else took much notice as long as I submitted enough work to scrape through and I did. Seemliness was everything.

We arranged that Jon would come for me the day I sat my last exam and I can still hear my mother's voice downstairs, as I collected my packed belongings from my bedroom, saying to my Dad, 'Well, I can't say as I want her to go, but I'm buggered if I'm going to try and stop her'. I doubt it would have made any difference had she tried. We said goodbye without affection and I walked away from all of it and them, determined to be without regret.

And so ended my first chapter, I was never to live in the family home again, or even visit it for a long time. Jon had rented a small cottage on the edge of Minchinhampton Common in Gloucestershire. The cottage itself was sparse but the area was stunningly beautiful.

We had visited a few places during the eighteen months or so we had been together. Jon booking rooms in pubs which we brazenly checked into as Mr & Mrs to no objections, and taking me to places new. We'd explored North Wales and Oxfordshire and the Chiltern's but the quaintness of the Cotswolds was like something from a fairytale. I loved it.

There was a stone cattle trough outside our front window and we would be woken in the morning to the sound of cows coming down from the common to drink. Jon was away occasionally, on overnight trips to the further-flung stores in his area, but I thought nothing of being left alone. CAMRA hardened, I happily wandered up to The Black Horse on the Common, and enjoyed a couple of drinks with the locals in the evenings. It was run by a lone Landlady and she took me under her wing a little. Ridiculous really, I was still shy of seventeen, drinking by myself in a pub full of old men.

A short walk to the local bakery provided a hot and fresh loaf, and bread and homemade marmalade, bought from the lady next door became a staple. To a council kid from Nottingham, it was some sort of Eden.

It was not all idyllic though. Whilst we were there, we had our first serious 'domestic'. I said something apparently out of turn one evening when I was making a meal and Jon simply stopped speaking to me. I questioned, pleaded and cajoled trying to discover what I'd done wrong, but he refused to be drawn. It went on for days and I was at a loss, even trying to manipulate him into speaking by feigning falling and hurting myself upstairs, whilst he was sitting downstairs, but he wouldn't respond. For the first time, I began to question whether I had done the right thing in leaving to be with him.

To compound the awkwardness I also had no money and no transport, it was only a short spell but it was horrid. After two or three weeks of silence, he slowly began to come around but he would never explain what had caused the problem. I assumed that it was my fault and bore the responsibility for it on my shoulders. For all that he had taught me and for all his encouragement, I thought that I was nothing without him and was completely dependent on his goodness and generosity.

Our stay there was short, only a few months. Yet again there was a problem with Jon's management style and he was asked to leave. He shrugged it off and we decamped and went to stay with his Mother in Solihull, whilst he searched the appointments section of The Times for something new.

His Mother was kindness itself, preparing what had been her marital bedroom for us to stay in. She had long since been deserted by Jon's father, a cruel husband, and slept herself in a smaller room. Despite her sweet welcome, I remained terrified of her throughout.

She was beyond 'posh', she spoke like the queen and even when she ate by herself she laid the table with silver and napkins. Having to support herself, Jon and his younger brother once abandoned by her husband, she became a clerk to the court. But even her regaling us with a story about a plummy barrister, who in cross-examination said to the accused, "And did you say to him, 'Where's the f***ing stuff'" in her high pitched upper-class voice, didn't temper my fear of her. What she thought of me I never found out, I imagine that she was somewhat perplexed at her eldest son's choice.

After a couple of months, our next move was south, Jon having secured a management position at the new Carrefour Hypermarket recently opened in Eastleigh. He was given a relocation allowance and we stayed at a small hotel on the outskirts of Southampton. Whilst he worked, I became friendly with the young couple who managed the hotel, and they in turn, introduced us to a crowd who hung out at a local Folk Club, held in a real ale pub just down the road. So we quickly made some friends. Most of them were students at the University, soon to go home for the long vac. Five of them were in a house share and asked if we would be interested in taking a room vacated for the summer. Thinking this would be a more sociable option than the hotel, we agreed and checked out.

The student house was without doubt the most squalid place I had ever been in. A small terrace on a long road of the same, close to the docks. The floors were sticky, the beds old mattresses on dirty carpets and the kitchen host to all manner of crawly things. I convinced myself it was simply a 'student thing' and determined to stick it out, it had after all been my idea, and in any case was only for a few months. So I settled myself, and started to apply for jobs.

It seemed impossible to even secure an interview, even for the lowliest position. Of course, I was not trained for anything but had proof of seven O'levels at reasonable grades, surely that must count for something. In conversation about it one day with Jackie, my friend from the hotel, it all became clear. 'It's your address, that's the problem Liz'. It had not occurred to me that the single lights displayed in the front windows of just about every other house along Derby Road, bore any significance. But it had in fact long been infamous as the Red Light District of the city, situated as it was close to the docks and perfectly placed for sailors on shore leave to find relief.

Once it was explained to me it all made sense, as did the odd occasion when I was followed by a kerb-crawling car. No one ever harassed me and in any case, I was resolute in my conviction that I would never be afraid of another man. The 'girls' themselves were quite a community. Meeting together in the laundrette across the street and taking turns to look after each other's children. I didn't envy them and I had no problem with them, in fact I really admired them and the way they apparently supported one another.

Eventually, I was invited to interview to be trained as a Dental Nurse, responding to an advertisement by phone rather than letter and so not having had to disclose my address. I had no desire to be a dental nurse. When I was a child, I'd had regular visits to the School Dental Clinic due to a calcium deficiency and had hated every minute of the treatment. So much so, that I ran away on one occasion, leaving my Mum sitting in the waiting room by herself. But I needed a job badly, so........

The Practice took up the ground floor of a huge old house on the Portswood Road which was divided into four surgeries, a reception and a waiting room. There were actually five dentists working at different times and I was interviewed by the owner and senior clinician, who lived in the flat upstairs with his wife.

The interview went well, I was attentive, polite and enthusiastic. He explained that a condition of the job was attending night school classes and gaining a DSA qualification, he would fund this but asked for total commitment. I needed a job and I gave him my word. I was surprised to find myself unperturbed by the dental smells and thought I could probably do it.

He was a pleasant and decisive but austere man. He offered me the job there and then but when he asked me for my personal details, I knew instinctively that if I told him the truth, he wouldn't employ me. In need of the work and knowing from past experience that lying was a justifiable means to an end, I re-invented myself again. I told him I lived with my parents in Chandlers Ford and made up an address and a telephone number. These were days long before everyone checked each other out on the internet and he simply believed me. I thanked him, promised I would work hard and returned to the hovel on Derby Road to tell Jon my good news.

The pay was a pittance, but to be busy and out of the grim house more than made up for it and to my surprise, I soon found that I enjoyed the work. Chairside assistance really was just that in those days, everything was mixed by hand apart from amalgam which was used for practically all fillings back then, and even for that, we had to literally pour mercury into the 'Amalgamator'. It was good to feel useful and I picked up the routines for different treatments quickly. Patient records were kept by hand on cards and the admin the responsibility of the nurse, so all round it was actually quite an interesting job.

I worked at first for a young Irish dentist but after six months or so he left to set up on his own and I was assigned to his replacement. He was a middle-aged man who had established a practice in partnership with a couple of others but had run into some difficulty. He came to us simply wanting to practice dentistry, without the added burden of management. We hit it off from the outset and worked together well. Bryan was encouraging and friendly and interesting, and our conversations between patients extended way beyond dentistry.

Although by this time, lying was becoming a way of life (I had increased my age by a couple of years to all of our friends and Jon's work colleagues and lied about my personal situation at work), I was not a clever liar. Bryan was so friendly I thought it unreasonable not to be honest with him and I soon told him the truth about our circumstances, whilst failing to let him know that I had invented a story to secure the job. We made friends with him and his wife Wendy over the next few months, and they became almost like surrogate parents to me, which was wonderful as I was soon to need them badly.

Jon and I had thankfully vacated the house on Derby Road when the students whose room we had taken, returned for their new term. We rented a bedsit in a large converted house in Shirley, owned by a very elderly couple who lived in the basement. We had a bedroom and separate kitchen and a bathroom which we shared with the other tenants on our floor. For its time, it was quite a nice place and I enjoyed getting to know the owners, who would often ask me in for a cuppa and regale me with their stories. I am saddened that I can no longer recall their names but I remember them well.

It was here that once again I did something that caused Jon to go silent and again, I was never to find out what it was. This time was much worse and went on for weeks, in the end I could stand it no longer and poured my heart out to Bryan at work. He and Wendy literally scooped me up and invited me to stay with them whilst   Jon sorted himself out.

Too relieved to think about any possible implications, I accepted and actually really enjoyed being with them for a couple of weeks. It all came crashing down around me though, when Bryan, in conversation with Peter the owner of the practice, mentioned that I was staying with them temporarily due to problems with my partner at home.

Peter hit the roof. I had now been working for him for over a year and he felt that he had been thoroughly duped by me. Which he had of course. He came to see me at the end of afternoon surgery and said that he had to ask me to leave with immediate effect. It was a shame he said, I was the best nurse at the practice, but he wouldn't be lied to and that was that. I pleaded my case, justifying my lie by explaining that I knew he wouldn't have employed me if I'd told him the truth, he was regretful but adamant. I was out.

Shame hit me like a ton of bricks and this on top of the current situation with Jon, just felled me. I was invited to go upstairs to the flat by Peter's wife, to compose myself and use the phone in private. I hadn't spoken to Jon for days, but as shocked as I was by my news, he agreed to meet me at home to talk things through. In a way, it did us a favour. Jon was kindness itself when he saw the state I was in and I moved back home that day. Bryan and Wendy were also kind, explaining that he had fought my corner with Peter, but to no avail.

Jon's response was also to fight, but when we visited a solicitor at the Citizens Advice Bureau, who put me through my paces and explained that there would inevitably be coverage of any tribunal in the local press, I lost my heart for it. It would have compounded every other lie, including the one that we were married, which we had told our dear elderly landlords in order to secure the lease on our rooms. It could even be that being referred to by them as 'hubby' was the thing that had tipped Jon over the edge and caused the silent treatment. I'll never know.

So, I had lost my first job in disgrace but I was home and Jon was once again communicative and we were healing. I was to remain very close friends with Bryan and Wendy for many years, and they shared with me, much later on, that the solicitor we had seen had been a personal friend of Peter's and had deterred us on purpose for his benefit, privately telling him that he'd been a fool, that my circumstances at home were none of his business, and my exemplary work for him would win me any claim for unfair dismissal I might make. It was bittersweet, but it helped a little.

The shame of being sacked intensified when, in need of money, I had to visit the DHSS offices and register for the dole. There was a mass of forms to be completed and an interview with a Dole Officer who required chapter and verse about what had rendered me jobless. I didn't fare any better than I had in my last brush with authority a few years earlier but I did tell the truth.

After receiving a lecture about being a responsible adult and the importance of transparency and accountability with any future employer, I was 'invited' to 'sign-on' to receive state benefit whilst I sought another job. Being well aware that I had brought all this on myself, did nothing to help me shrug off the shame I felt, which was only compounded by queuing each week at an appointed time and having to wait to be called forward to sign the register. It made me feel grubby, and one day, giving myself another talking to in the mirror, I determined to grit my teeth, set my sights higher and look for employment that would give me opportunity to better myself.

Bryan had long been encouraging me to train as a dental auxiliary or hygienist and I did visit the college and scope out the courses, but both took two years to train and I needed money. Looking to the immediate rather than the future, which had already become an established behaviour pattern and was to remain so for many years, I decided to look to pastures new.

Jon talked little to me about his past, but there was fond mention of a previous long term girlfriend, whom he'd had a relationship with back in his university days. She was an early 'foodie', a qualified Home Economist who'd been quite successful with preparing food for photography. Scanning the situations vacant section of the Daily Mail one day, an advert for trainee Home Economists caught my eye, and I figured that perhaps this might be a way to secure my relationship with him and also improve my prospects and maybe even my cooking. I wrote a letter, asked Bryan to give me a testimonial to include with it and applied.

The job was with Bejam, then a pioneering freezer food and white-goods chain, swallowed up eventually by a rival takeover in the late 1980s. I felt I was pioneering in making my application and didn't tell Jon about it in case it came to nothing. Amazingly it seemed to me, I was invited to London for interview, which was an adventure in itself. Travelling up from Southampton on the train and then navigating my way by tube to an office in Edgware was the equivalent of crossing a continent, having never really been anywhere by myself up to that point.

It went well and a few days later I received a letter offering me a trainee placement at the Reading store, which would last for three months. At the same time, Jon had been offered a promotion which meant relocating to a new branch of Carrefour, soon to open in Bristol. It felt like a timely opportunity for a new start and to say goodbye to Southampton. It had been an odd year. We had both made some good friends, but neither of us left with any great affection for the place and we weren't sorry to move on.

Thanks to a generous relocation package for Jon, we both had an almost free month to explore the city. We loved it and when it came time for me to leave for Reading, I wasn't at all sure that I wanted to go. Although I had by now been 'left home' for practically three years, I had never actually been by myself, but Jon reassured me that we would meet on our free days and the time would soon pass.

I had been found a room in a house owned by an elderly lady called Mrs Dean, who regularly took in Bejam trainees. I call her elderly, which she seemed to me then but she was probably not much older than me now. She had been widowed some years before and liked the company of a lodger and the security of the Company guaranteeing the rent. She was lovely. Motherly without being interfering, but always interested. It was a good fit and having her there gave me an immediate sense of belonging which was really helpful in the first few days.

There was a full programme at work and although it soon became clear that 'Home Economist' was a very loose term in this context, I didn't mind. I was busy and learning new things and it felt good. I was also determined to prove to myself and to Jon that I could be independent. In an attempt to carve out a bit of a social life for myself, I checked out the meetings for the local branch of CAMRA and discovered they met on Tuesday evenings in a back street pub near the prison.

They welcomed me as a bit of a novelty which I suppose I was, an eighteen-year-old girl, pitching up to drink beer with a bunch of strangers. But when it became obvious to them I actually did know something about real ale and that I could put quite a lot of it away, they gave me a grudging respect. Jon actually wasn't best pleased when I told him and I didn't go there for long. Bejam Reading was a flagship store and also took management trainees, so it wasn't long before I started to make friends with colleagues nearer my own age. This was a wholly new thing for me and I found that I actually quite liked it. My social life picked up and for the first time extended further than the local folk club or sitting in dreary pubs, or both simultaneously, which was often the case.

The next three months caused me to re-evaluate my life. Until that point, I had allowed myself to enter a persona completely of my own invention. Believing myself to be independent and avant-garde, leaving home so young, living with an older man, independent, strong and self-sufficient. The realisation that none of that was true slowly began to dawn on me.

Swinging from one extreme to the other, I began to view Jon less as my saviour and more as my jailer, and found myself making excuses for spending less and less time in Bristol. When my training period came to an end and I was assigned to a Bristol store, my heart sank at the thought of leaving my newfound friends and although I did try, once there I just couldn't settle.

Without discussing it with Jon, who had only ever been good to me, even in difficulty, I made an application to transfer back to the South East. There happened to be a vacancy at Maidenhead and I leapt to fill it, presenting it all to him as a fait accompli once the details were finalised. I would like to be able to say it was the cruellest thing I've ever done, sadly I doubt that's true, but it certainly comes close.

I had arranged to move back to Mrs Dean's and commute the two stops on the train to work. Being the gentleman that he truly was, Jon drove me and my few belongings up one Sunday afternoon and helped unload me to my new life. We said very little and when he drove away I didn't stand and wave him off. I was stepping into my future which I felt was my right and I had no concern whatever for my callousness, or the hurt that I was causing to someone who had looked after me so well.

Launching myself into a new job, new friends and very quickly a new relationship, I didn't give a backwards glance to what I'd left behind. Spurred on by a rush of self-belief and powered by the pretence that all was well with me, I became the 'party girl', burning the candle at both ends, living 'the life', no limits. Except that there were. After about six months of this, I crashed one day and realised that I had never before been so empty. The new relationship was nothing but froth, the work mostly unrewarding and the money spent. With complete disregard to my heartlessness, I rang Jon.

He wasn't unkind and although he didn't want to, he agreed to see me. He met the train at Bristol Temple Meads and we drove to the house in Portishead that should have been our first proper home but which I'd left before the boxes were unpacked. I confessed I'd made a dreadful mistake, I was sorry, I asked for another chance. He took my face gently in his hands and told me no. The last six months had been dreadful for him, he couldn't go back.

He'd hoped I would leave it there but I didn't. I pleaded, I cried, even tried to seduce and at that point, he told me he'd met someone else. A secretary at work. Older, divorced with two children. I crumpled. He put me back on the evening train and until it left the station I hoped against hope he'd call me back, but he didn't. I leaned my head against the window and for the 69 miles of the journey I wept as I had never wept before.

It came like grief. For the first time since I was thirteen I let my heart break for all the loss. My innocence, my home and relationship with my parents, and my hopes and dreams. And now Jon. I was alone and hopeless and it was my own fault and I had no idea what to do about any of it.

Many years later, in my mid-thirties, I was to be given a piece of sage advice that has helped me through many a dark night of the soul since. What do you do, when you don't know what to do? The answer, do what you know to do. It was offered to me by a dear Christian friend who touched my life very deeply, in the context of navigating through the 'desert times' that come to challenge every believer at some point. And in that context, it has helped me greatly. However in the context of an eighteen-year-old girl, devoid of hope and with no moral compass, it was less helpful, but unwittingly, it was precisely what I did.

In arrogance and out of ignorance, from the moment I closed the door back at Mrs Dean's, I determined to build my walls higher, make my heart harder and simply carry on. The next day I got up, went to work and got straight back on the party train that had already threatened to de-rail me in the first place. And there I stayed for the next fourteen years.

Chapter 8

They were not glory years. There was some fun and one beautiful friendship that endured everything and still does. There was a measure of worldly success, the acquisition of lots of 'stuff' and a bit of 'high flying' but mostly there was simply a vacuum.

I tried to fill it of course. Alcohol was already a staple and I changed my drink from beer to spirits with ease. It left more gaps than it filled but it was a great way to ease the pain for a night. Of course, it meant mornings were harder but an introduction to the superpower of 'speed' took care of that, and a supply of little blue tabs was not hard to come by. There was a string of failed relationships and many, many liaisons that didn't even get that far. In counselling much later I shocked myself by failing to remember them all by name. At the time I felt no need to justify myself, I had gone beyond that, I simply didn't care. Outwardly I was regarded as a tough cookie who held it together well; it was an image that I worked hard to cultivate but it was far from reality.

My time as a 'Home Economist' didn't last long, and I shifted sideways into management but soon lost the heart for retail and weekend working and left. However, it did provide one encounter that left a lasting mark and is worthy of mention.

One of the team at Maidenhead was a young school leaver who was simply different to the rest of us. Sixteen and gangly, with big square spectacles, Stephen always wore a brown suit and a tie even though he spent most of his days emptying the huge cold store and filling freezers. He refused to be drawn into any banter and certainly would not engage in gossip or anything remotely base, and there were opportunities for plenty of both.

Part of my job was to arrange and present talks and microwave cookery demonstrations to promote the food products and ovens, and I was always on the lookout for invitations. Stephen picked up on this and arranged for me to meet his mother, who lead a ladies group at the local Methodist church. She booked me to do an evening meeting which went well and gave a real boost to my performance stats.

Stephen later explained that his whole family was deeply involved with the church and that this was the reason there were some things he felt unable to join in on. The three of us in the office ribbed him mercilessly about this and more than once he walked away from us, hurt to the point of tears by our mockery. Our behaviour towards him was reprehensible and yet he never retaliated, always turning the other cheek. One day I asked him why and he answered me simply, 'because of Jesus'. At the time I shrugged and walked away, but I have never forgotten it.

I left to join an IT training company in the telesales department and discovered that I was quite good at it. It wasn't hard to learn a script and I could fall into character every time I made a call. It was low salary, big commission territory and there were celebrations when targets were hit. Performance meetings involved lunches and brandy, as did strategy meetings, team meetings and Friday afternoons. How we ever achieved anything remains a mystery to me and in the end, we didn't and the whole thing collapsed into receivership. So I lost my third job as I had my first, but at least there was no disgrace in this dismissal and I had now discovered that sales was an environment in which I could succeed.

From there I joined a pharmaceutical marketing and distribution company, where I really cut my teeth and learned how to sell. I was also schooled in the art of negotiation. Being able to fall easily into character helped me to overcome any natural remaining shyness and to find an ease, whether I was meeting a board member or a junior manager. It was valuable and stood me in good stead for my next move four years later.

Eschewing the tabloids and setting my sights higher, I began to scan The Times appointments section and landed on a vacancy for sales executives at a local computer hardware brokerage. I knew nothing about computers but I did know how to sell and was able to convince my interviewer that I would be able to learn whatever else I needed. They offered me a substantial increase in salary, opportunity for career progression and a BMW. Status symbols ruled, the car clinched it. After being there a month and yet to achieve anything in terms of sales, I was approached by the International Director and invited to join his new division, essentially fulfilling the same role but with travel and overseas clients. The package was the same and I got to keep the car, so I said yes.

This was the early eighties, money was to be made and spent. Success was measured in acquisition and I acquired a lot of 'stuff'. My 'all expenses paid' business trips were now overseas, my luggage expensive and my tickets business class. Image was everything. We wore designer labels on the outside of our clothes and checked into four and five-star hotels throughout Europe. We caught early morning flights and drank complimentary champagne, we courted clients with long boozy lunches and lavish dinners. Excess was expected and we delivered it well, and somehow in the midst of it we negotiated lucrative contracts that held water.

Looking back it was a surreal time but I don't remember ever questioning how I got there, surely it was all just my right, life having dealt me such a cruel hand early on. The chip on my shoulder grew with the size of my shoulder pads (and believe me, they were huge) as I stormed ahead careless of my bitterness or what people thought.

It must have been an incredibly tough watch for my parents. By now we were on reasonable terms and I visited them for a weekend every two or three months. I'd swagger in, bearing ridiculously expensive gifts and wine and food, shamelessly flaunting my belief that I had elevated myself out of their humdrum existence and done so completely without their help. They took it all on the chin but they must have been appalled, and I am sure I was insufferable.

Working away so much, often two weeks out of every four, gave me the excuse I needed to believe that finding any meaningful relationship was impossible. I worked hard at maintaining a social life without attachments, often arriving back at Heathrow and driving straight to the pub or a party. I gave myself very little breathing space to rest, and was sustained by rich food and alcohol and a little chemical help from time to time. The treadmill raced so fast I didn't have time to think and if I hit a problem, I simply found a way to skirt around it, which occasionally worked but more often compounded it.

On the surface, by the age of twenty-five I'd done well. I had a high flying job and all its benefits, my own flat, a wardrobe full of designer gear and a life that took me to the best restaurants, clubs and hotels. But inside I was dying. All my colleagues were men and I worked hard and was accepted by them on pretty equal terms, but my heart broke a little every time they told me stories of their families, a new baby, a son or daughter's birthday, a holiday. I resented their happiness and was acutely aware of my own loneliness and my body clock, and the realisation that neither alcohol nor drugs helped either situation.

Just before midnight at a New Years Eve party in 1985, a mutual friend introduced me to Alex. We were both worse for wear. We woke up on New Years Day in a hotel room and stayed together for the next few years. It was not love at first sight, it wasn't even lust. It was simply convenience. He was twelve years my senior, a successful hotelier bound to his business and in his own way, as lonely as I was.

We rubbed along well together most of the time, he ran with a fast social set and we drank our way through the seasons. I moved out of my flat and into his substantial house just outside Windsor. I sank my life into his, neglecting the very few friends that I had and pouring my heart into being accepted by his, which I was for the most part.

The most significant memory I have of our relationship is that I don't remember that much of it, yet it lasted for years without either of us attempting to change it. It helped each of us to be half of a couple and on the surface we looked good together, but it was mostly veneer. It was probably clear to us both that we weren't actually going anywhere very early on, but we just kept on going, nowhere in particular.

Long-standing tensions between Alex and his elder brother, with whom he owned the hotel, came to a head after we'd been together for a year or so, and Alex eventually sold his share in the family business. It cost him dearly emotionally, he was very close to his parents who were also involved and he was saddened to see them disappointed. For months he was listless and not helped by me or his friends who encouraged him to fill his days in a never-ending whirl of socialising, seeking solace in easy company. One friend held a private pilots licence and they would fly to Le Touquet or Jersey for lunch. Hedonism is not a good helpmeet.

He was 'saved' by a couple of friends who had moved to Somerset a few years earlier to open a hotel and now wanted to establish a restaurant business. They invited Alex to form a partnership with them for that venture and bored to tears with doing nothing, he jumped at the chance. I encouraged him in it, despite the hundred or so miles that would separate us.

Around the same time, and becoming tired of the constant travelling now that I had someone to come home to, I was coaxed away from my own job by one of my clients. Octavian was a middle-aged Yugoslavian, living in Vienna and making his money supplying computer hardware to companies in the Eastern Bloc. He had lived and worked in Moscow for five years, had many contacts and knew how things worked.

It was a lucrative business that very few people were willing to get involved in at the time, due to the complications of obtaining export and import licences. He wanted to form a UK company as a staging post for shipping from the US, as it was practically impossible to get licence approval from there for direct shipment to Eastern Europe.

Unbeknown to me, several of the deals that I had arranged for him had been for onward sale and even when he explained it to me, I was too blinded by the incentives he offered to see what I was exposing myself to. He offered me a huge commission, the promise of very few working days each year, and minimal travel. It was too good to resist, so I didn't and resigned on short notice. My employers were none too pleased when they knew what I was going to do but I had never been asked to sign an exclusivity contract, so they had no redress.

Although I was now working from home and was unable to justify the need for one, Octavian bought me a car for my own use and set me up with everything I needed to run an office from my study, which in those days was nothing more than Amstrad pc, a printer and a telex/fax machine. The work was ridiculously easy and demanded of me only a few office-based hours a month.

Occasionally he invited me to travel with him, which I willingly did although I never felt I contributed anything of value. There was never any impropriety between us and he was quite candid about his 'needs'. He was divorced, had a daughter Lilly who was only a couple of years younger than me and studying in Italy, and he had no desire to be in any sort of relationship. If he needed sex he paid for it and he never asked it of me.

Lilly had a self-contained apartment at his house in Vienna and when I visited him I stayed there. We drove in his Porsche from Vienna to Budapest, where we stayed in five-star luxury in a swanky hotel on the Buda side of the river. He ordered champagne and pate de foie gras for lunch, and I am ashamed to admit that I ate it. In the evening, we crossed the bridge to Pest and ate in a Romany restaurant where he wept as a gipsy trio played an old Slavic song. He pointed out bullet damage left over from the war in the walls of houses in the city.

We spent a long week in pre-glasnost Moscow staying at the Hotel National just off Red Square, where I developed a hatred of caviar and a love of Russian champagne. We had a series of meetings, one at the Mongolian High Commission, which seemed to consist of nothing more than vodka and bawdy jokes. There was a lot of vodka, meetings began and ended with it and there was often some consumed in the middle if any agreement was reached. Between meetings, he showed me sights not revealed on the tourist map, like the KGB headquarters, and also encouraged me to explore on my own. I wandered around G.U.M. the nearest thing in Moscow at that time to a department store, but where it was impossible to buy a toothbrush. I had been raised with the USSR portrayed as the ideal state and although I'd never really bought into that, I was astonished at the poverty of the place and the huge divide between the obscenely rich and powerful and the rest.

In the hotel, one of the most expensive at the time, the bedroom was stark. A rickety bed, a couple of rugs on the dark hardwood floor. A shower room with a mouldy curtain and bath towels more suitable for drying plates than people. There was indeed a babushka on every floor and the atmosphere was hugely oppressive. But the restaurant service was hilarious. Surly waiters would bring everything ordered quickly and efficiently, but never, never clear anything away. At the end of a four-course meal, whether it be breakfast, afternoon tea or dinner, the table would be literally piled high with a mountain of dirty dishes. By the end of the week, I wasn't at all sure what I thought Moscow was, but it certainly wasn't an ideal. Most of the people seemed sweet though.

After taking a bus tour alone into the countryside to see some sights, I was so appalled at the living conditions of the farmers and the state of the villages that I bought a metallic cast bust of Lenin and a china samovar to take home as gifts for my parents, as some sort of ironic statement. It totally backfired on me. Lenin took pride of place on the display cabinet in the living room and the samovar in the kitchen/diner, and both pieces remained in situ whilst Mum and Dad were alive.

It was the oddest trip I ever made and I felt a little stunned when I said goodbye to Octavian, parting to catch our separate flights home. Mine was an Aeroflot to Heathrow and onboard was an ITV camera crew returning from filming footage for a documentary. When we touched down safely on the tarmac in London, they all clapped. It was a relief to be home.

Octavian also sent me on a couple of missions to New York, one to collect a disk drive to send on to him in Vienna. The trips were great, I loved the buzz of New York and the zoo and the trip on the Staten Island ferry, the Empire State Building, all the sights. I loved the shopping and the brusque friendliness of the New Yorkers. I recall one lady approached me in the hotel bar, after hearing my English accent, to offer her condolences over the tragic death of Laura Ashley following a fall. She was from the Deep South and was convinced that I would know Laura Ashley personally, England being such a small country. I was astonished at her naivety and her own accent which I thought truly bizarre at the time. She was super friendly though and we enjoyed each other's company for a short while.

After a year or so of working this way, I came home from meeting a friend for lunch and some shopping (I was doing a lot of shopping) to find a handwritten note on the doormat. It informed me that I had been visited by two Inspectors from HM Customs and Excise and asked me to make contact urgently to arrange a meeting. In my own shallow naivety, I really had no idea of what this could specifically be about although I did feel a frisson of unease. My call to the number on the note was answered by a pleasant woman who 'invited' me to assist them in their enquiries at a meeting to be arranged in their offices in The City. She would give me no further information but it was clear that refusal was not an option, so I agreed.

With some trepidation I visited at the appointed time and was escorted into a small, stuffy interview room containing a table, four chairs and a tape recorder. There was no window. She came in with a male colleague, clearly her senior, who explained to me that I was not at this point under arrest, but that this was an interview under caution regarding the activities of Extopin Limited and its Directors, namely Octavian and myself.

Trepidation quickly turned to fear as the realisation hit me that I had no idea where the disk drive that had been delivered by courier to my hotel in New York, had come from, nor where it was ultimately going once received by Octavian in Vienna, which is where I sent it on my return to the UK. It was a tricky couple of hours and they must have thought me very stupid (which I was in this respect) but thankfully they did find me credible. Once they were satisfied that I had no further information to disclose they let me go, but told me that I should expect to hear from them regarding any action that might be taken against me.

At the end of the interview and once her colleague had left the room, the female officer was gentleness itself. She said that she found her job really difficult when she had to be so firm with someone she warmed to, and she was sorry that it had been a tough meeting for me. I was very grateful to her but desperately ashamed of myself for my carelessness. I clearly remember hailing a cab to take me to Paddington and once there heading straight for the Station Hotel bar and a very stiff gin and tonic, uncaring of what anyone might think, and I was practically hysterical when I rang Alex who was understandably not very sympathetic.

Octavian was more circumspect, he told me not to worry, there would be a fine, nothing more and obviously he would meet the cost. It was a relief and also a wake-up call, seriously, who on earth would expect to earn so much and work so little, to enjoy international travel and expense account benefits without a little risk?

A letter arrived a couple of weeks later and Octavian's theory was proved right. The company received a hefty fine for non-compliance with regulations and providing incorrect documentation. He was as good as word and forwarded me the funds to clear it, but I never felt completely sanguine about the business after that.

Coupled with this unease was boredom. Alex was now in Somerset from Tuesday to Saturday working on the new restaurant and I was kicking my heels at home. I began to scan the situations vacant sections again to see if I could find something that would work in tandem with Extopin and perhaps provide a way out if I needed it.

My eyes lighted on one of those small, mysterious box ad's that offer the possibility of being your own boss, working from home or office and deciding your own hours and salary level. I rang the number and after a quick chat with the very well-spoken and pleasant man who answered the phone, was invited for further discussions to an office in High Wycombe.

Chapter 9

And so began a five-year stint in the insurance industry. At the start I found it interesting, financial services was a complete diversion from anything I'd done previously and there was much to learn. I enjoyed the bustle of a busy office having been out of one for a while, and I was indeed able to manage the little work I had to do for Extopin alongside that of 'Sales Associate', without any interference.

There were several 'Branches' of the company working out of the same office and a male to female ratio of about 90%. In the main it was a noisy and brash place and hugely competitive. Each branch posted personal daily sales stats on a board outside the manager's room and any name that appeared too regularly at the bottom soon disappeared. It was a very polite but quietly cutthroat environment.

There was something distinct about Wheelers' Branch which struck me at the outset but which I had no understanding of for quite some time, and revolved around a core of three of the highest performing Consultants and the Manager who had recruited me.

They were good friends rather than simply colleagues, they looked out for each other. They were smart and friendly and encouraging and always willing to give help and advice where needed, which was unusual in that climate. In no way did they hold themselves aloof, but neither did they get caught up in the gossip which was rife throughout the whole office. They were happy to party and celebrate and there were frequent Friday afternoon drinks, but they always knew where to draw the line and politely did so. These four colleagues became my friends during what was to become the most tumultuous time of my life to date.

Through all of this Alex and I trundled along, he would come home at weekends or occasionally I would go to Somerset. We always packed the time with social commitments and it passed quickly, so we never really had to get in touch with the truth that we were drifting further and further apart, in fact we barely noticed it. Or rather, I didn't. One particular weekend, friends were due to come to us for Sunday lunch and Alex was travelling back that morning rather than the usual Saturday night. Wanting to make sure that he left in good time, I called him at the flat in Somerset first thing, hoping that he would already have left. My heart sank when the call connected and even more when the voice that answered was a woman's.

Already knowing the truth in my heart but desperately not wanting to believe it, I apologised explaining that I must have the wrong number, and was about to hang up when she, sensing her opportunity I suppose, asked if I was calling for Alex. She went on to triumphantly inform me that they had been seeing each other for months and that they had plans for when I was out of the way, Alex was simply waiting for me to leave. I was speechless, astonished that I could have been so blind, I responded with something innocuous and then hung up.

A few minutes later the phone rang. Thinking it would be Alex calling to let me know he was on his way I answered it, but it wasn't. It was the cuckoo, practically hysterical and in floods of tears. Alex had tried both numbers during our call and hearing them both engaged, joined the dots. He had then called her and in no uncertain terms told her to pack her stuff and leave, threatening her harm if she didn't. The poor girl was terrified and shamed too I imagine, that her device to bring things into the open hadn't gone the way she'd hoped. Somewhat magnanimously, she told me 'I was welcome to him' and slammed down the phone.

Then Alex did call me and we had the first of many difficult conversations that we were to have that day. I rang the friends who were due to come for lunch and cancelled, poured myself a large brandy and waited. Amazingly, I didn't pour myself another and by the time he arrived I had pulled myself reasonably together. He was solicitous and sorry, but I suspect more in that he'd been found out, rather than for what he'd done, but at least he was honest. He had been seeing her for some time, she was there, willing and available, very young and pretty but absolutely no, they had no future and on his part at least no intention of one. I believed him.

In retrospect, I have come to understand that at the time, I had so little belief in the hope of a truly 'right' relationship, I was prepared to settle for 'partly right', and having convinced myself of that, was determined to hang on to what I did have. In any case, as far as I was able, which wasn't far, I forgave him and it was akin to swallowing bile.

Alex was close to both of his parents and especially so to his mother, and we all got on well and spent time with each other regularly. Unkindly, I confided my hurt to her, hoping for support but she leapt immediately into lioness mode, dismissing his straying as inconsequential and to be expected of 'these men', I must toughen up and shrug it off. I imagine that she had been confronted with similar situations throughout her marriage and 'toughening up' had been her way of dealing with them.

I lifted my head, stuck out my chin and did my best, but really the damage was done and it was only compounded by the fact that my response was completely duplicitous. Years before I had a fairly tumultuous affair with a man I worked for and although all the intensity had long died, we did still occasionally meet. Whilst Alex was finding company in Yeovil, I also had found it elsewhere, with this man. To my shame though, I never confessed it, and even when we eventually separated sometime later, I continued to let Alex believe he bore all of the responsibility for our failure. Worse even than that, I duped myself into believing that I was protecting him from hurt by keeping silent.

We kept going, him feeling somehow bound to me by his guilt. His mother, now widowed, had hopes that we would marry, and we did consider it, but fortunately both realised that we would be doing so for wrong, if differing reasons. Neither pleasing a parent, or maintaining a certain lifestyle is a basis for an enduring marriage, and to this day I am thankful that at least divorce does not appear in my litany of mistakes.

We kept going in fact for quite a while, but how is a mystery. I let myself become bitter and proudly showed it, never missing an opportunity to jibe or ridicule. It must have been a nightmare for Alex, who actually had behaved no worse than I had myself, and I am grateful that he put up with me, as nightmares of my own, rooted in my history, were about to overtake me.

They seemed to come out of nowhere and with no quantifiable trigger. Night after night I would wake in a sweat from a replay of my rape in 1973. Literally a replay. All five senses engaged. I saw the cycle track and the nettley hedge that bordered it and that I was dragged through, the construction site and the shell of the house he pulled me into. I heard the voice of my attacker, felt his hand around my neck and the taste of his nicotine-stained fingers as I bit down on his hand. Felt again every violent moment of the ordeal. But the worst was the smell. It assaulted me again and again and I simply couldn't shake it, I smelled him everywhere.

This went on for weeks and eventually Alex, still only around at weekends and so only seeing in part, in sympathetic but no uncertain terms directed me to the GP for help. Having reached the stage where I was frightened to go to bed, I reluctantly agreed.

The treatment I had received all those years before at the hands of the Police Surgeon and then the lewd behaviour of our family doctor a couple of years later, had firmly put visiting the GP at the bottom of my list of favourite things to do, and even though at this point my doctor was a really lovely lady, it was still not an easy appointment. She was very patient and kindness itself when I finally managed to stop trying to fudge and broke down in tears in her surgery.

She diagnosed a reactive depression and referred me to a psychotherapist who specialised in sexual trauma, and was desperately apologetic that it was not a service provided by the NHS. Fortunately, this was not a problem for me and immediately feeling better that she had taken me seriously and that I could now 'do something', I pulled myself back together and waited for my appointment.

Counselling was not something that I'd consciously avoided, it had simply not been on offer, or even recognised as necessary, at the time when I most needed it. Subsequently, I convinced myself that my coping mechanisms of deeply burying my feelings, building a wall around and hardening my heart and employing what I convinced myself was a healthy mistrust of everybody, were enough. I could manage without help and excluding the self-medicating with drugs, alcohol and ambition, I had pretty much done that, until now.

Congratulating myself on having made it this far on my own, I pulled up in the Clinic car park feeling slightly nervous, but full of expectation that a few sessions would get me 'fixed'. A residential psychiatric facility on the outskirts of Windsor it was a beautiful old house in even more beautiful grounds. Reception was in the huge entrance hall and a peaceful atmosphere pervaded the place, I was quickly at ease.

After only a few minutes I was collected by the therapist, who lead me through a large hall where a couple of guys were playing snooker, up a staircase to the first floor and into a tiny, softly lit cubby hole of a room, with a couple of chairs, a small side table and a box of tissues. My initial ease began to dissipate. She sat and invited me to do the same and I remember being a little surprised at it all. I'm not sure what I'd expected, but I was pretty sure this wasn't it, and I remember grappling with my emotions from the outset.

She sat with a clipboard on her knee and explained that she would make notes as we talked and then she asked me a few questions. I talked, and every now and then she'd interrupt me with that hackneyed question, 'and how did that make you feel?'

By the end of the prescribed hour which was brought to an abrupt close by the buzz of an alarm clock on the table, I was agitated and unhappy but I reasoned that it was simply a process I had to go through and booked another session for the following week. This went on for five weeks, me getting more uptight and exasperated at each appointment. I wasn't feeling better, I was feeling worse and the nightmares whilst not now nightly, had not yet ceased.

In the middle of all this, in an effort to treat myself and with Alex's somewhat reluctant agreement, I had bought a puppy. We had taken in a rescue kitten a few years earlier but I had always wanted a dog and I felt making the commitment now would somehow cement our crumbling relationship.

My closest friend, was and is a huge dog lover, and when I told her I was looking, she immediately went into bat for me and located a reputable breeder. She found one in Chatham, Kent and we drove out there to see the litter of English Springer Spaniel pups.

At her recommendation, I had read up on the breed and agreed with her that we'd be well suited. I'd chatted with the breeder who described the litter and made an appointment to see a particular tri-colour dog. There is an old adage that says you never choose a dog, a dog chooses you, and when we arrived and all the puppies were running around our feet, it was a cheeky black and white bitch who plonked herself on my lap and looked into my eyes. It was love at first sight for me and we arranged to return and collect her at eight weeks.

Back at the insurance company office, I had confided some of my troubles to Neil, my manager who had become, if not at that point a friend, certainly more than a boss. He was easy to talk to and a very good listener and he seemed genuinely concerned for my welfare.

He'd listened patiently as I'd confided my woes about Alex and was careful not to pass any judgement. I didn't tell him about the nightmares until I'd begun the counselling, which seemed to be exacerbating the trauma rather easing it and again, he'd listened and remained impartial. I was thankful for his support and found myself increasingly opening up to him, somewhat surprised at my desire to do so.

Each of the four appointments I'd had so far with the therapist had been traumatic in its own way. She'd offered little in the way of guidance, other than to assure me that my feelings were normal and that facing my fears and reliving the incident would help me recover from it. She was insistent on detail and none of it was pleasant to recount, it left me feeling sad, vulnerable and even frightened.

The imminent arrival of Winnie, the spaniel pup, lifted my spirits enormously and I checked in for my fifth appointment, upbeat and excited. It was obvious to my counsellor that something had changed and instead of the usual, 'let's go back to that night' opener, she asked what that change was. I told her that I'd put a reserve on a puppy and would be collecting her in a few weeks, that it was a lifelong dream for me and I was really happy about it. I'd have gone on to give her every detail of visiting the litter but she cut me short and unbeknown to her, the response she gave was to be the catalyst for a life change for me. She said bluntly, 'life isn't about buying puppies Liz, life is about taking responsibility for yourself'.

It was our most uncomfortable appointment to date. Generally, I accept she had a point, but I was deeply offended that she should think me irresponsible. I argued that by making this commitment to an animal at this point in my life, I was in fact taking on responsibility not running from it. She argued back. I was paying her for this and indignant and made my feelings known. We did get back on track but it wasn't good. I remember weeping as I drove home, completely deserted by my earlier ebullience.

A week later I arrived for my appointment, as usual a little early and sat in my car. After a few minutes I realised I was shaking. With every fibre of my being I did not want to go in, but I sat there trying to examine the alternatives. As unsatisfactory as this counselling seemed to be, all my hope for finally overcoming my hurt and fears was in it, and I reasoned that if I walked away now there was nowhere else for me to go. But even knowing this, I simply couldn't face it and I did walk away, or rather drove, without making my presence known.

A wreck when I got home, I harangued myself for my own cowardice and wondered what on earth I was going to do now. The memories that had surfaced so vividly before only in my nightmares, were now with me at the forefront of my mind, all the time, dredged up by the counselling but not in any way treated or dealt with. It seemed to me that I had spent my whole life, since that fateful summer night in 1973, battling to be free of my demons, I had tried everything I knew and here I was at 32, in a worse state than ever. I could not find within me the resolve I needed to plan further, and after nineteen years of falling, I finally hit the ground. Hard.

Somehow I dragged myself into the office the following day, bleary-eyed from lack of sleep and at a loss as to how I would manage to work. Neil's door was open so I went in and without thinking about any of it, out came the whole sorry tale.

He offered no platitudes, he simply listened, occasionally asking the odd question for clarification. He was not critical or judgmental, he was respectful and kind and compassionate. And intensely practical. My expectation was that I had probably talked myself out of my contract, seeing no conceivable way that I was fit to work. But rather than telling me to take time out, he suggested that focusing on and putting my energies into work might help me find my way out of this abyss. I couldn't see it myself, but I was so grateful to him I agreed to try, and then as I was about to leave his office, he offered me what I didn't see then, but now know, was my lifeline.

He'd remembered from my C.V. that I had described myself as an avid reader and asked me whether I'd ever read a book by C.S. Lewis called Mere Christianity. I hadn't but I had absolutely adored the Narnia books since I was a child and read the series many times, so when he pulled a copy out of his desk drawer and suggested I read it, I happily took it. 'Let me know what you think', he said. The appeal of curling up in a comfy chair and reading was far greater than that of making appointments and although I had accepted Neil's advice to try and apply myself, I left the office soon after and went home. I made coffee, settled myself on the sofa and opened the book. That I had claimed myself to be an avid reader was true but my preference had always been for escapism rather than education, I read more literature than pap but very rarely did I turn my attention to anything other than novels.

Mere Christianity is not a novel, but it was the same voice that narrated the children's adventures with Aslan that I heard speaking from its pages. In it, Lewis describes in a series of broadcast notes, his own journey from scepticism to salvation, in a reasoned and simple way. Remarkably I felt as though I was somehow journeying with him, as I read from cover to cover in one sitting.

I had given Christianity no thought whatsoever since years before, when I asked dear Stephen Foster at Bejam why he didn't react to all the cruel ribbing we gave him and he'd responded, 'because of Jesus'. In fact, when I'd considered that remark afterwards I dismissed it as weakness and chose instead to see his vulnerability as a flaw rather than the beautiful strength that it was.

My 'informed' opinion of Christians, aside from the negative parental input, was that they were, by and large, weak, unattractive, and appallingly dressed. The men sporting ill-kempt beards, corduroy trousers and open-toed sandals and the women devoid of make-up, with dreadful untreated hair and flowery frocks. Their speech sugary and their handshakes limp and their time spent hosting table sales and handing out tracts. It was most definitely not for me.

My only experience of Christians had been those childhood encounters described earlier, that at the time had touched me deeply but that with time, I had buried somewhere way down in the recesses of my mind and had left undisturbed since.

This book disturbed all of it. I reasoned that if it was good enough for C.S. Lewis there must be something in it, and why had Neil given it to me to read? It certainly had my attention and I eagerly went into the office the following day with questions aplenty. There was a wry smile on Neil's face as I declared my interest, which only the day before and at the end of my hope, would have been impossible to capture. He went on to explain that there was a small group of Christians in the branch who met for breakfast every Monday morning, simply to share a little time together; he extended an invitation for me to join them the following week, when they could perhaps help with some of my questions. He told me who they were and I, somewhat churlishly, thanked him and said I'd give it some thought and get back to him.

I gave it some thought. These four men were the highest achievers in the branch, and they'd had my attention from the start. There was something about them that was impossible to quantify, that went way beyond their appearance which was smart indeed, no open-toed sandals here. They each had a confidence and an air of assurance beyond the norm. They were the ones the rookies like me went to for advice and they were always more than generous with their time and wisdom. Without doubt they had something that I didn't and I was intrigued. Covering myself by asserting my reluctance to 'join' anything, I accepted the breakfast invitation and met with them in Neil's office for coffee and croissants the following Monday, and every Monday thereafter for the next three months.

During that time I read more books, asked questions and argued, resisted and argued and then argued some more. They were patient and kind and honest, never claiming to know the answer to any impossible question but always asserting their own faith and implicit trust in the God of the Bible.

It was this trust that grabbed my heart and would not let go. Asked once by Neil who would I trust in any given situation, I said 'no-one' and meant it. My survival had been constructed on the premise that not trusting was the only way to avoid betrayal and crushing disappointment. When push came to shove, I believed the only way was every man for himself. And yet here were these four men, whom I had grown to respect hugely both professionally and personally, placing all of their trust in an unseen God. They were not stupid or gullible, they weren't members of some cultish group preying on the vulnerable. They were intelligent, smart, successful individuals who at some point in their life's journey had made an uncompromising commitment to the triune God.

On the day when my questions had come full circle, I stormed into Neil's office, sat down without invitation and said, 'I don't understand what it is you've got but here I am, still at the end of myself and I know that whatever it is, I want it too. Can you help me with that? What do I have to do?'

He smiled and responded with words that seemed to slip easily into my very soul, 'If you really want to know Jesus Liz, all you have to do is ask Him to come into your life. If you do that, then, although I can't promise you when, I can absolutely promise you that He will'. Astounding myself, who until that point had only taken advice with an unhealthy dose of cynicism, I believed him. I simply believed him and left him with my heart set on course.

For the rest of that day and into the evening I worried about what on earth I would do if I took this step and got no response. I almost worried myself out of it, but again, surprised at the strength of my conviction, reminded myself that Neil had 'promised' and that he was a man of his word and I had, in spite of myself and my history, decided to trust him in this.

In retrospect, I have no idea why I felt it necessary to wait until I went to bed before asking God to make Himself known to me. It seems ridiculous thirty years on but that is what I did, waited and worried, until I finally laid myself down and turned out the light.

I had prayed to an unknown God when I was seven and struck down with acute appendicitis, shouting out that I was too young to die. And again at thirteen, in the violent grip of a stranger who stole my innocence but spared my life. Both had been raw cries for help rather than eloquent prayers and this was no different.

'God, I don't know whether you can hear me. I don't even know if you're real but if you are, I am crying out to you, would you make yourself real to me. I want to know you for myself, I am at the end of myself and recognise that you are my only hope. Would you please come into my life and help me. Amen.'

That was it. I lay there, expecting I knew not what and waited. Within a few seconds my whole body started to shake, it was like electricity passing through me, not violently but with increasing intensity. There was heat too. I had no idea what was happening and remember thinking, 'this is it, I must be dying' but in that thought experiencing a deep, deep sense of peace and no fear whatsoever. I heard nothing and saw nothing, simply lay shaking, enveloped in this warmth and peace.

Minutes passed and the trembling passed and the heat passed and the peace blissfully stayed. I had absolutely no idea what had just happened except that I knew something had and when I woke from undisturbed sleep the next morning, I knew that it was something irrevocable and that I was changed.

At the first opportunity, I went in to see Neil and slightly embarrassed that he might think me fanciful, gave my account. Again he smiled, affirming that he thought that Jesus had indeed answered my prayer and that what I had experienced was a touch from Holy Spirit. He suggested that it would be good to pray together with the others, a more formal prayer, to help me begin my Christian journey.

And that is what happened. They lead me through the prayer of confession which I prayed now with all of my heart and the best of my understanding.

My understanding was limited. My experience the night before enabled me to pray the prayer with conviction and without baulking at asking for God's forgiveness for my wrongdoings. But in truth, the chip that I carried on my shoulder had grown to such huge proportions during the previous nineteen years, that I didn't really recognise that I was responsible for any of the things that had gone wrong in my life. My prayer was not insincere and my desire to commit my life to God was total, but it took some time for me to realise and accept that in terms of my mortal life, what I had been saved from largely was myself.

It was easier for me to see the bigger picture and I did understand that by choosing to surrender my will to God, my eternal destiny was secure. In fact I grasped this so well, that in the first few months following my conversion, my desire to bypass my earthly life and head straight to my heavenly address was significant. Thankfully I was counselled wisely by my colleagues and helped to find a local church, where I spent my 'nursery' year and was nurtured well.

My colleagues, now very much my friends, encouraged me to share my story, explaining that this would not only help me to root my faith but would also be a blessing to anyone else who was perhaps exploring the Christian message and help them make their own commitment. This became the first real challenge of my Christian life.

It seemed to me from reading about and hearing other people's testimonies of coming to know Jesus, that my greatest and most burning desire should be that everyone else come to know Him too and that I should be the one to tell them. In actual fact, the complete opposite was true. I didn't want to tell anyone what had happened to me, not because I was embarrassed or scared or frightened of their judgement, but simply because what had happened to me was so precious, so beautiful, so completely unsullied by anything, that I imagined sharing would somehow dilute it and that was just too unbearable a thought. This was mine and I wanted to keep it that way. Quite honestly, I was afraid that in sharing about God, I would also have to share my portion of His love and I wanted all of that for myself.

The accrued hurts and abandonment of my childhood and adolescence, coupled with all the subsequent years of disastrous choices, self-deprecation and abuse had completely depleted my love tank and I had simply been running on empty.

No one rushed me and I am so thankful for that. If they had, I may have bolted and so missed out on the process of transformation that is still in progress; and is the most wonderful and exciting journey along the most excellent way.

Part Two

Chapter 10

My world had indeed shifted on its axis and I was seeing things generally through a very different and much brighter lens, but all was not yet crystal clear and in some ways, it was difficult to slip from what had been my old life, effortlessly into the new.

Trying to explain to Alex what had happened to me, was the first major hurdle. Initially, he was pretty incredulous and then very cautious, and made it clear that whilst he wouldn't try to stop me from pursuing my new-found faith, I mustn't expect him to follow. However he was surprisingly magnanimous about me going to our village church on Sunday mornings. He even went so far as to say that he thought it was a nice thing to do, but he did seriously object on one occasion. For reasons I can't remember, I had failed to get to a particular service and had received a call from the pastor that afternoon to check all was well. Alex thought this a huge intrusion and interpreted it as control rather than care, which was both unfortunate and untrue. By and large though, he was supportive and I was thankful for that.

Within a few days of praying the salvation prayer, my friends at work had explained how important it would be for me to be part of a church family going forward. They also explained how not all churches are the same, and that I needed to be somewhere where there was 'life'. My past dalliances with church in my childhood, had not prepared me at all in terms of understanding how it should fit into everyday life, and I was sincerely grateful for their wisdom and guidance.

In the meantime, they suggested we go together to a communion service at a nearby church which they sensed might be significant for me.

I remember being a little nervous and not really knowing what to expect, or indeed what might be expected of me, but I caught their sense of urgency and agreed. The five of us went to a lunchtime service at Gold Hill in Chalfont St Peter, the first time I had ever been to a Baptist Church. I understood nothing of denominations, and as my friends each belonged to a different one, it seemed of little importance. They explained it as in the main, being a matter of style and finding the best fit, and that was good enough for me at the time.

It was a simple service and I recall little of the content of the short message that was given, but I do remember being deeply affected by both it and the act of partaking of the bread and wine. I also vividly recall feeling ridiculously stupid as I sat there and wept throughout. I was powerless to stop, the tears simply flowed and it was sometime after the whole thing was finished before I regained my composure. My friends seemed to completely understand and gave me space without adding to my awkwardness, afterwards explaining that again, this was a touch from the Holy Spirit and very probably a healing one at that. That day, I think I began to appreciate for the first time, the gravity of the commitment I had made, if it cost me my composure it was a very small price to pay.

There were three churches in our village, Catholic, Anglican and Baptist. Clearly and for reasons I understood even back then, the Catholic Church was discounted and the Anglican, although not 'high' was very traditional. Whether this rendered it 'dead' I didn't understand but guided by Neil who had made investigations on my behalf, I decided to pay a visit to the Baptist Church. We went to meet the Pastor and discovered that he had a vague connection with Neil's father, which in itself it meant nothing really but the connection put us at ease.

Philip welcomed me from the outset, although there may have been a few occasions when he wished that he hadn't. I certainly wasn't the easiest member of his small congregation, I questioned almost everything and was very vocal if I disagreed or didn't understand; I turned up at his office on more than one occasion demanding to know why something had to be done in a particular way. He was patience personified and although ultimately firm, so gentle in his guiding that I was never made to feel inferior or stupid.

The congregation was mainly elderly, although there were enough families to warrant a small Sunday School, but aside from myself and the lovely Linda, who had been a Christian forever and was soon to be called to China as a missionary teacher, there were no single, younger people. For all my brashness, I was thirty-two, reasonably intelligent, desperate to gain understanding and obviously looking for somewhere to get stuck in, and I suppose that made me an exciting prospect for the church. Back then, my unregenerate cynical self would probably have said this was the reason for the amount of time and input I received from Philip and his wife, but in truth, it was simply because they cared deeply for their flock. And there was so much more than that, it was in a very real sense 'a family' and during the time I spent there, I learned lesson after valuable lesson about what being in a family actually meant.

Still one of the most wonderful discoveries of my Christian walk has been to find that a group of completely disparate people can come together, work together, serve each other, stretch each other, and really love one another well. I have often looked around the room in a house group setting and realised that without the common bond of salvation, the folk gathered would probably not give each other the time of day. And yet with Jesus at the centre, all differences can easily be set aside and deep bonds forged between the most unlikely of people.

That Baptist Church became my nursery, I was loved, taught, challenged and encouraged, and grew quickly in my relationship with God through the ministry of Philip and his team. It wasn't an overtly 'lively' church, and Sunday morning services always followed a set pattern. Between notices, readings and sermon, we sang songs from Baptist Praise and Worship to accompaniment from a single out of tune piano, played by one of the congregation. The evening service was slightly less rigid, sometimes we even sang three songs in a row, but still it was all very undemonstrative, just the occasional hand lifted demurely in praise. However there was a refreshing degree of informality in the overall order, and we were encouraged to participate and contribute where we could.

Watching Philip preach from behind the big lectern on the small stage, stirred something in me and as I learned more from the bible and experienced God at work in my life, I discovered that I very much wanted to share these new-found truths from that stage too. To be brutally honest, at that point it was probably the stage that called me rather than God, but I hope there was at least a spark of Holy Spirit fire in the mix.

Philip was a good, solid teacher and a careful and methodical man. On one occasion, he drove me to a meeting in Reading in his Ford Escort and didn't once exceed fifty miles an hour on the M4. It was excruciating to me, and I had to seriously bite my tongue to withhold merciless criticism, as we were constantly overtaken. But it was a measure of the man, unhurried, unruffled, safe. It was amazing, given his disposition, that he would trust me to preach early on, but for all his caution, he was a determined encourager and that is what he did.

Having been deeply impacted reading a book on forgiveness, and naively believing that by the simple act of conversion I had completely forgiven anyone who had ever hurt me, I deemed myself a bit of an expert and managed to persuade Philip that I had something worthwhile to share. I imagine with some trepidation, he invited me to bring my message on a Sunday morning, in what would normally be his preaching slot. I agreed of course, feathers puffed and full of confidence. It wasn't a disaster but it wasn't the wonderful thrill I had imagined it would be. I read huge swathes of text from the book, interspersed with my own opinions and some testimony. I doubt anyone was particularly blessed, but they were all very kind as I took my place with Philip at the church door, shaking hands as they left at the end of the service.

In truth the whole episode terrified me. As I took my place behind the huge lectern, where I had so longed to be, and prepared my notes, my mouth had dried completely and I was doubtful I would be able to utter a word. When I did start to speak, my top lip seemed to stick to my teeth making coherent speech impossible. After taking a pause, a deep breath and a sip of the water that some kind soul brought me, I began again and doggedly slogged through my notes to the end. It was a salutary lesson in pride coming before a fall and thirty or so years on, one I hope I am nearer to learning!

In a debrief a few days afterwards, Philip had generously shared a few of his own less than laudable attempts at the pulpit, to relieve my embarrassment at what now felt like abject failure, and had then encouraged me to persevere. He went on to counsel me gently, explaining the dangers of 'zeal without understanding' and the importance of seeking only the audience of One. I am indebted to him indeed.

Over the next few months, my journey with God deepened as did my involvement with the church. In fact I got involved in things that I would previously have ridiculed others for. I served tea at a family fun day in the church grounds and borrowed a huge gas barbecue for the day from a friend Alex and I socialised with, who, when he found out why I wanted it, was too flabbergasted at my request to refuse. I knocked on doors handing out evangelistic tracts and issuing invites to church events, unconsciously avoiding the houses belonging to people who knew me. I went to bible studies and house group, and attended a course on evangelism and by and large, although I invested much of myself into it, I kept my church life separate from everything else.

During this time, it became apparent, even to me, that something was not quite right. Although I didn't hide my new-found faith from those I knew who I thought wouldn't understand it, neither did I display it, and no acquaintance would have been able to recognise any discernible difference in my outward behaviour apart from a slight tempering of the extremes. Inwardly I began to sense my own duplicity and discomforted by this, knew that the time had come for me to make some changes.

For the first few weeks at church I had let everyone believe that I was married, simply by not contradicting anyone when they referred to my 'husband', but this was so clearly wrong, that I soon met with Philip and explained my circumstances. Whilst he was very clear about the Church's standpoint on this and that it would be an impediment if I ever sought a position within it, he was hugely understanding, recognising I believe that I was on a journey of discovery and that enlightenment about my personal circumstances would come at some point along the way.

Much to his relief I'm sure, it came quite quickly. As I went to God in some confusion about what I should do, He in His kindness made it clear almost immediately with that same all-pervading peace that only He can bring. In my heart, I had known that my relationship with Alex had been built on sand from the outset and although now, after years together, we did have love and respect for one another, we were not the match either had hoped for. It was a horribly difficult conversation. Mistakenly thinking it would be easier in a neutral environment and at my suggestion, we went out for a meal that neither of us was able to eat. It is hard to leave, it is even harder to be the one who is left and Alex was desperately hurt. Not so much at our separation, but more that he didn't see it coming and that it didn't involve anyone else. It was impossible for him to understand that for me it was simply no longer right, and as there was a tacit understanding between us that we would never marry, there was no option. He left me in the restaurant and the next day returned to his business in Somerset. Our subsequent discussions were by phone, and civil and sad. He would stay full time in Somerset and I could stay in the house until he decided what to do with it in the long term.

It seemed to me, that making this huge change in my life cemented my commitment to following Jesus and I allowed myself to believe that any other lifestyle issues were secondary, barely registering on the 'need to be addressed' scale. I was still drinking way more than was good for me, although I cut out the spirits and limited myself to wine. With my new Christian friends I would also limit my consumption, but in other company I was far less disciplined. Discipline in any area has been a constant challenge throughout my life and until I met Jesus I had managed to avoid it almost completely. Implementing strictures on my behaviour for the first time at the age of thirty-two, was a real battle and one I lost more than I won for years. It is testament to the kindness of a loving Father that He never once gave up on me, as I time and again chose a very temporal pleasure over His eternal reward.

There was though a significant change that occurred almost immediately I was saved, for which I can claim no credit whatsoever and only give God the glory, which I do willingly and thankfully. It came about almost without my recognising it but it was hugely noticeable to my friends.

Never frightened of an expletive, my Mother had been very liberal in her own language throughout my childhood, and swearing became a normal part of my vocabulary from early on. Until my early twenties it was mild, the odd 'b' word when something went wrong, and the occasional 's....' but it rapidly deteriorated when I began working in the transport company environment and grew steadily worse from there. By the time I met Alex, I doubt I spoke a sentence without swearing and I was, as my mother had also been, always inclined to blasphemy. Once I was saved, all trace of blue left my language, as though every filthy word had been erased from both my vocabulary and my memory. My friends at work were delighted, as was I when it registered. Truly it was a miracle, not least because not only could I now no longer utter these words myself, I also couldn't bear to hear anyone else utter them.

And with that came a challenge, especially with Mum. Although our relationship was still testy we were by now on better terms and I saw my parents every other month or so for a weekend.

Usually, I would visit them at my old home in Nottingham but occasionally they would head south. They were never at ease though, the house too grand, the people too posh, but bless them, they tried.

The most difficult conversation I had to have with them was to tell them of my conversion and to say that they initially were appalled is an understatement. Dad was particularly vehement in his opposition and eventually could only sanction it by believing that it provided me with an emotional crutch, which he obviously felt I needed. As it had been for them in the past, the way forward was denial, pretend nothing had happened and hope that in time it would all resolve. I was hurt but also glad to be spared debate, which I loathed, so went along with it as best I could.

The language was a problem though. Mum punctuated every sentence with an 'OMG' or 'JC' or 'for the love of.....' and I couldn't bear it. Actually I didn't really know why I couldn't bear it, it simply offended my spirit, going in like a sharp needle. I asked my friends for advice about how to broach the subject with her, painfully aware of the fragility of our relationship. I also prayed, asking God for help and wisdom. The advice I received was sound and good, and the grace I received to effect it was even greater. Mum's response was completely out of character for her. I had braced myself for a barrage of abuse, her accusing me of being all high and mighty and superior, wanting to shame her for being herself, that sort of thing. She was inherently manipulative and well able to make everything about her, always putting herself at the centre as a victim. She did none of that. She apologised, she said she didn't really understand but she would make a concerted effort to try not to offend me. She was not easy to love, but I knew in that moment that I did love her. She was not always successful in her efforts but she tried, it was enough.

After a few months, despite my continuing struggles with discipline, I felt a strong pull in my spirit to be baptised. I had been neither christened nor baptised as a baby, so there was no preclusion to full immersion baptism now, and I duly went to see Philip to express my wishes. Always the encourager, he was thrilled, but we ran into difficulty when he explained that there were a couple of the children who also wanted to make this rite of commitment. Still not good at the concept of sharing, I had imagined that there would be a baptismal service for me, an opportunity for me to make my statement of faith before the witness of others. I didn't want to do this with anyone else and certainly not with a couple of kids.

As ever, Philip was patience personified. He tried to explain it to me in terms he thought I would understand, proffering that heating the baptismal pool was an expensive undertaking, an unreasonable thing to do for just one person. I was so obviously crestfallen that he suggested a compromise, if I would agree to the same date, the children could be baptised at the morning service and then me at the evening. This was wonderful, I desperately wanted Neil to be there and knew that the morning would be impossible for him because of his commitments at his own church. We agreed and a date was set, both of us relieved at a hurdle overcome.

I never fully appreciated quite what a stretch this arrangement was for Philip. Baptisms were never held at the evening service and he had to stand his corner with the elders, who were less inclined to tolerance, discerning probably rightly, the diva in me. Looking back I am amazed and humbled at his forbearance and very thankful for it.

Then came hurdle number two and if we had been in a steeplechase it would have been the water jump (pun not intended). I was about to get my first lesson in the might of 'denominational establishment'. Somewhat sheepishly (I think he would consider this a fair statement) Philip went on to explain that baptism marked entry into full membership of a Baptist church. I bridled at the word 'membership', had I after all joined a club? And I bridled even more, when he told me that to be accepted for baptism, I would have to be interviewed by two of the senior church members, who would determine whether or not I was a fit candidate. Although my bad language had miraculously been obliterated, I had not yet learned to tame my tongue and I expressed my absolute disgust at this formality without restraint.

What had the last few months been about if it hadn't been to bring me to this point of making a public confession? Was he seriously questioning my sincerity? He allowed me to vent, sitting quietly with a resigned expression on his face, and when I finally ran out of steam he assured me that it was simply a formality, the way things were done and a leap too far to expect a break with tradition. Then he asked me with humility so great even I could see it, to agree to submit to the process for his sake. Selfish to the end I continued my argument, I simply wanted to be baptised, I wasn't even sure I wanted to become a 'full member', what was that all about anyway? Did membership come with entitlements? He took me through it all slowly, step by painful step and eventually, seeing no other way and probably realising I was testing even Philip's patience, I agreed.

A date was set for my interview, which would be with two ladies who were pillars of the church, with the baptism to follow a couple of weeks afterwards. The ladies came to my home on a chilly Tuesday evening in November. I didn't know either of them well but we had passed the time of day at the end of a service and were familiar with each other. I felt distinctly nervous, even though I was in my own home and in spite of Philip's assurance that this was, in effect, a 'rubber stamping' exercise. My only grid was to understand the process as a test, and I knew that tests were pass or fail, and also that I was prone to failure. But they were gentle and kind and quickly put me at ease, welcoming me officially to the church family and simply asking me to share something of my journey to faith with them. I had by now begun to really enjoy recounting my testimony and had done so publicly several times, so once in my stride all of my nervous angst and antipathy dissolved. They closed our meeting by praying for me and I think satisfied that despite my crusty exterior, I was sincere in both desire and belief and my motive sound. I had passed the test and the water jump was crossed without incident.

The baptism service itself was wonderful. Philip's kindness knew no bounds and having agreed to my demands, he went an extra mile, asking me if there were any particular inclusions I would like.

There was a Welsh lady in the congregation who had a voice like a nightingale and I asked her if she would sing. After an evening spent leafing through Baptist Praise and Worship I found a song that reflected my heart. It was not one we normally sang, but she learned it and accompanied herself on guitar as she sang it out. Each verse ended with the words, 'let forgiveness flow'. I read from Psalm 139 with all of my heart and shared a little of my testimony. Neil had agreed not only to be there but also to take part, and he and Philip were the ones to climb into the pool with me, lowering me into the water and lifting me out. A cheer went up at that, probably the loudest from Philip who must have felt himself to have come through some sort of test. He kindly gave me a card to mark the occasion and in it generously wrote the words 'I have never known someone so young in the faith, to have such a deep understanding', I was hugely touched and also slightly confused, as in my less arrogant moments I knew full well that I understood very little.

Carried home on a wave of euphoria, I closed the door behind me and gave myself some time to reflect. Sitting silently and alone, I felt myself overwhelmed by the enormity of what had just happened. This really was it. It was deadly serious. As I had been raised up out of the pool I entered a new life. New. This sense of newness floored me. What had just taken place had not been about restoring the old, very broken me, it had actually been the birthing of the new me. I looked at my skin, almost expecting to see it appear like baby skin, all fresh and pink and plumped. It didn't of course, but I remember just staring at myself as if in wonder that here I was alive, and this was my second chance. I wept, maybe a tiny bit for the loss of the old, but so much more in gratitude for the new. For the first time in my life I was truly humbled. And it was all good. It was before My Lord and Saviour in whom from this point on, I would live and move and have my being.

It was November and I had been at the church since March, and separated from Alex since May. We had met once during this time when he came up to see his mother, who was now living alone following the death of his father from a stroke a couple of years earlier. Somewhat wistfully he said that she had cried when he told her of our parting, he was deeply affected by this, showing emotion was not something she was prone to. We talked very, very vaguely about trying again, marrying, but we both knew it was over. We parted amicably, accepting that it was time for each of us to make independent arrangements for the future. Alex decided to shift his life permanently to Somerset and the house was put on the market. Although I knew this was inevitable, it left me in a bit of a quandary. The house belonged to Alex and I had no claim to any of the substantial capital that would be raised by its sale. I owned a small flat in Reading which was let on a short lease but even had I been able to, I had no desire to move back there. I began to sense in my spirit that it was time to move on, relocate away from the village and cut ties completely with my previous life there. It was a strong sense but it did confuse me a little. What about church? I had settled in there, was being nurtured and discipled well by Philip who had by then, together with his wife, become both my mentor and friend as well as my Pastor. The thought of leaving them all was almost horrifying, but it felt inevitable.

My friends at work were helpful, suggesting that I visit a couple of churches nearer to High Wycombe where the office was situated, and scope out the surrounding towns and villages. It would be geographically close enough to maintain my existing church relationships, whilst also giving me the opportunity to stretch my wings. With this in mind, Neil suggested visiting St Andrew's Church in Chorleywood for a Sunday evening service and he and a couple of the others, knowing the place by reputation, offered to go with me. Grateful for their support, I readily agreed and was eager with anticipation. St Andrew's is a large Anglican Church situated in the heart of a quintessential Home Counties village. Back then it was known as a vibrant and charismatic community, recommended highly as a spiritual home by many. I was used to Sunday evening services being more informal than the morning but it seemed to me that St Andrew's was positively wild. I was so thankful to be accompanied as had I not been, I doubt I would have stayed long. The worship was lead by a band, and the people stood in the pews, moving to the music, hands raised. Both hands, and not tentatively either, but purposefully, proudly almost, in concentrated and overt praise to God. Some folk even stepped out of the pews and danced in the aisles, and not simply stepping from one foot to the other, but expressively, bending, running, sweeping the air with arms outstretched and bowing low, all graceful and beautiful and reverential, and way, way too much for me. I stood there with both arms pinned to my sides as I quietly sang the words that appeared on the overhead screen as best I could, unfamiliar with most of the songs. The remainder of the service was equally uncomfortable as different folk came forward to share prophetic words and words of knowledge, many of which were responded to by the congregants, who also went forward to be prayed for by the Ministry Team, who seemed to have appeared out of nowhere at some point. All this was way beyond my experience and I sat there dumbfounded throughout. Certain that they would be as bemused as I was, I didn't even look at my friends to gauge their responses, and so was absolutely astounded when we left the building to discover their enthusiasm and delight at the whole thing. The following day at work I told Neil that I didn't think it was for me, it was too big, too lively, too vibrant. He looked surprised but didn't try to persuade me otherwise, reminding me that Gold Hill was also close by and not to be discouraged.

Forced out of any reverie by the rather quick sale of the house, I began to look at rental properties. Another work colleague introduced me to a letting agent in Chesham and she quickly came up with a house for me to view, which was a relief as I would be moving with a dog and a cat in tow and that did somewhat limit my options. Chesham wasn't completely unknown to me, as I'd had a friend who'd lived there years before, but initially it did feel very far away from all that was familiar, and the property itself was far a cry from the house I'd shared with Alex. It was a small three-bed terrace built in the 1970s, not dissimilar from my parents' home in Nottingham, with a tiny garden in the back. It bordered woodland to the front so there would be easy walks with Winnie, and it was situated on a small private road which helped me feel confident that Minnie, the little tabby, would be able to negotiate it reasonably safely. In all honesty, the thought of living there made my heart sink a little, but needs must, and anyway who knew what the future would hold now. After discussions with my trusted friends, I decided to go for it. The landlord kindly agreed that I could paint throughout, which was almost a deal-breaker for me as the whole place was pink and very flowery. With the house decorated and new curtains hung at the windows, I felt I had put my mark on it and made a conscious decision to go forward with my best foot and God.

The hardest part of the whole episode was letting Philip know, and it was hard to shake the feeling that in moving away I was somehow letting him down. He was, as ever, wonderful, releasing me both as a friend and also before the church into this new chapter of my life, and 'blessing me out' as he had blessed me in a year before.

What a year it had been. One in which I had learned to embrace loss and change in equal measure, and had found at last that which would sustain me through whatever was to come. Everything had changed, and with it so was I changing. I had no idea just how much more was to come.

Having spent a week or so wrapping and packing, moving day finally arrived and the lorry showed up first thing to clear me out of one place and install me in another. I'd hired a small but reputable firm and the removal men were, quick, efficient and kind. It didn't take a degree in rocket science to work out that this was a downward move in worldly terms, but they were sensitive and asked no questions. The lorry loaded with furniture and clothes and essentials and my car with the most fragile bits, together with a tabby cat and a springer spaniel, we set off to pastures new. It was a strange leave-taking and in the moment I felt quite alone. I was aware of a jumble of negative emotions simmering just below the surface, disappointment, loss, failure, anger even, but in recognising them, I was flooded again with that peace that passes all understanding and knew that alone I was not. This was going to be a good move and with that thought in mind, I drove away.

Boxes all unloaded, the removal men left but not before the owner, a good looking guy with a beautiful Irish lilt had asked if he could give me a call once I'd settled in. Never finding it easy to say no, I didn't, and after they'd left wondered if I'd dug myself into a bit of a hole but then I reasoned letting him down on the phone would be simple and satisfied myself with that. There was much to do and never good at living in a mess, I wanted to get on with it. It was Friday and I was determined to be reasonably straight by Sunday as I was eager to venture out and visit Gold Hill Baptist for the first time from my new address. Many friends had sent cards to welcome me to my new home, and there were flowers and a tin of handmade cupcakes delivered and phone calls aplenty; the neighbours either side knocked to say hello and I was swept along on a sea of good wishes. By the time Sunday rolled around I felt that I had indeed 'moved in' and set off, in eager anticipation to find what I believed would become my new church home.

It has never been difficult to navigate from Chesham to Chalfont St Peter by road, even in the pre SatNav days of the early '90s. I had spent years by then driving all over the country in the course of my various jobs and was well used to reading a map and planning a route, it was easily within my capabilities. It was a glorious spring morning and I drove off full of its joys, heading out along the leafy Chess Valley, everything bursting with promise. Forty-five minutes later, I was still driving and completely confused about where I was. It was only an eight-mile journey, how hard could it be? Recognising I'd have to surrender and look again at the map, I pulled up on a hill. It was almost 11:00 o'clock and the Gold Hill service began at 10:30. I was going to be seriously late, which was a huge problem for me, having an almost pathological hatred of tardiness. Disappointed but not deflated, I decided to try again the following week and spend the day exploring the area instead. I pulled out and drove a little further down the hill and there on my right was the entrance to St. Andrew's Church. Somehow I was in Chorleywood, I smiled to myself and kept going. The next week and more familiar with my surroundings, the directions I was sure, firmly in my mind, I tried again. And again but by a different route, I found myself outside St Andrew's and too late to go on to Gold Hill. At the third attempt, and unbelievably in the same position, outside St Andrew's, it occurred to me that maybe God was trying to tell me something. This time I parked the car and went in.

Nervous at the prospect of being mobbed by over friendliness at the door, I tried to sneak in close behind the family in front of me. I shouldn't have worried, the Welcome Team were well versed in spotting the reticent, and after offering a simple warm hello and a news sheet they left me alone. Inside the sanctuary I shuffled into one of the back pews, making sure to sit firmly at the end in case I needed a quick getaway, and buried my head in the news sheet to avoid having to talk to anyone. The church quickly filled, packed with folk of all ages, and there was much chatter as people recognised and greeted one another. It was very much a family service and whilst the worship was much like it had been on the Sunday evening of my last visit, there was less of it and somehow I didn't feel quite so intimidated by the expressiveness of many of the congregation. There was an invitation to stay for coffee at the end of the service and somewhat reluctantly I did, but again I wasn't mobbed by anyone and surprisingly found myself relatively at ease. The following day at the office, Neil smiled when I told him where I'd been and suggested that I give it a try for a few weeks. I had to accept that this was good advice, especially in the face of my inability to locate Gold Hill, and anyway, I reasoned, it was always there as an option if necessary. I spoke to Philip too who was slightly less enthusiastic at the possibility of my deserting the Baptists, but he also knew St Andrew's by reputation and was happy to endorse it.

God has such a wonderful way of straightening our paths and guiding our steps, and He was to go further than the little nudge He'd given me a couple of weeks before. The work colleague who'd introduced me to the Letting Agent in Chesham, also lived there himself and had overheard me talking with Neil about St Andrew's. Confirming with me that it was the St Andrew's in Chorleywood, he went on to explain that his next-door neighbours were really involved there, that they were lovely and that I should say hello next time I visited, mentioning his name. So the following Sunday, I did just that. Easily identifying them from Michael's accurate description, at the end of the service I screwed up my courage to introduce myself and they welcomed me with open arms. I felt all the tension of not really knowing where I should be, simply dissolve in that moment and although I didn't understand it at all, felt that I was 'home'.

I never did go again to Gold Hill, although I was to become good friends with several people who did, and my then future husband was baptised there a couple of years later. As God had lead me to the village Baptist Church through a coincidental connection, so He lead me to St Andrew's, through some navigational misdirection. I was a little confused about whether this made me an Anglican, but some wise counsel from my friends helped me to recognise that church was more about a gathered group of believers than any particular doctrine, and that was enough for me.

Settling into the new house was not as difficult as I'd imagined it might be. The move had coincided with a spell of really beautiful weather and I enjoyed some wonderful walks with Winnie in the stunning Chiltern's countryside. Dog walking is a great way to meet people and I soon got to know my neighbours and other local dog owners. It was a friendly road, with children often out in the street playing and there was a real sense of community. This was new to me and I really warmed to it. It was also conveniently much closer to the office and so, although the house was not mine or remotely palatial, it felt like a win.

The first awkward moment came after a couple of weeks, when I received the promised phone call from the owner of the removal company. He asked me out for dinner, I hesitated, he was persistent, I agreed. He picked me up at the arranged time and we had dinner at a nice restaurant in a nearby village. It was a pleasant enough evening, and when he dropped me home, he pecked me on the cheek and said he'd like to see me again. He had my number. He called and a second date was arranged. Again a nice restaurant in a nice village. He was a sweet man and I liked him but I was very wary, and when I told him of my faith, so was he. He was Irish, he had been touched too by all things church but not in a good way, and not by God. My old self probably would have wanted to take him on as a 'project' (which is a terrible thing for one person to do to another), my new self just instinctively knew that this was a relationship that wasn't meant to happen, and I finally did what I should have done at the beginning and declined his invitations. He was gracious but a little bitter and I was sorry for that. In itself, this short episode doesn't seem that important but in fact it was hugely significant for me. My history with men up until being saved lacked any propriety at all. A date had meant bed and that just wouldn't do anymore. Although I was yet to learn to value myself, I had learned to value my commitment to God, and I was adamant that I was going to keep it. Saying no was a massive step for me and this experience taught me early on that it was far better not to get myself into compromising situations in the first place. It felt like a victory to have stood my ground.

The next time I went to St Andrew's I was encouraged by my new friends to also return with them for the evening service. They were unaware of my first visit a few weeks earlier, or my discomfort at it. It is primarily a worship service, they explained, less time spent on family matters, more informal. It seemed churlish to refuse the invitation to accompany them, especially as they had given me a lovely lunch and company for the afternoon, and so I did. The service was everything it had been the first time, but my reaction to it completely different. The worship somehow now seemed wonderful and so too the varying ways it was expressed. I even raised an arm at one point, though not for long, frightened in my self-conscious conceit, of looking foolish. Finding myself more able to enter in, rather than simply observe, I realised that in fact this style of service suited me well. This pleasant surprise was only compounded when Neil and Liza introduced me to a whole host of their friends at the end, who were all as welcoming and inclusive as they had been. As I turned the key in my new front door that evening, I knew unequivocally that God had indeed directed my steps and although the path may not have been exactly straight, had lead me to my new spiritual home.

Chapter 11

Prevarication is something I have always been prone to, but once a decision is made, my investment is wholehearted. It was not long before I made an appointment to see Brian who was the vicar responsible for pastoral oversight of the church. He welcomed me like the loving father that he is and I found myself immediately at ease with him, at least to begin with. Having chatted for a while he said that he knew exactly where he thought I'd thrive best in the church family, just the place for me, I'd be a real asset he was sure. I had no idea what I was expecting but it certainly wasn't what he said next. 'I'd like to connect you with Will & Caroline, he is our full-time Youth Worker and they work closely as a couple with our teenagers.' All my ease left me in that sentence. I was thirty-three, had no experience whatsoever with children of any age, and was acutely aware that I had pretty much missed my own adolescence, how on earth could this be a good fit? He urged me to be open-minded, suggested he get Will to call me, just see how it goes. The twinkle in his eye, which I was to discover was ever-present, won me over and I agreed eventually, if somewhat sceptically.

Quite what Brian had seen in his twinkly eye, I'll never know, but whatever it was, he saw clearly. Meeting Will and Caroline soon after changed my life, and although to begin with I went almost kicking and screaming, the following Friday evening found me for the first time ever at a Church Youth Club. Friday nights for as long as I could remember, even at their tamest, were spent with wine and food and friends, and simply agreeing to go along and observe felt like a huge sacrifice initially. Little did I know that it was to become one of the most pivotal things in my life, healing, restoring and preparing me for what would be my future. The youth group was called 'Breakout' and it did indeed fling wide a prison door that had long been locked shut on me.

That first evening in some ways was a little bewildering, it was an established group and team, but I was made so welcome by leaders and young people alike, that I found myself agreeing to join almost without realising it. These 'new look' Friday nights became one of the highlights of my week, as I steadily got to know both the other leaders and the young people themselves. Even the leaders were considerably younger than me but my grand age was no impediment to forging good relationships. This was helped by a weekly leaders home group, which allowed us to share freely with one another as adults, and so strengthen our budding friendships, as we also grew together in our relationship with God. Brian hadn't known of my earlier connection with Neil and Liza when he directed me to the Youth Work, but the fact that they too were both involved as Leaders seemed hugely confirmatory to me and helped me to feel less of a newcomer. He must have been blessed knowing that God had orchestrated this connection.

Over the next two years, I got more and more involved with Breakout and the Young People and I loved both it and them. Friday nights quickly became a joy, not a sacrifice, and before too long I reduced my working week to four days in order to give a day to the church helping Will however I could. I received far more than I was ever able to give. There were film nights and games nights and girly pamper nights and fondue nights. I remember watching the chick flick 'Clueless' and one of the girls exclaiming 'flipping heck actually!' at the drop-dead gorgeousness of one of the actors, and for a second being quite blindsided by it. She was fifteen and so very young and sweet and innocent, as were all the others, who thought she was being a bit explicit in her appreciation. So very, very different from my own fifteen-year-old self. However, it wasn't all laughter and frivolity. Chorleywood by any standards was then (and I imagine still is) a very white, middle-class suburb, but that didn't preclude these young folk from problems and for some, there were real difficulties to be worked through. There were family breakdowns, physical problems, emotional problems and for one family the worst possible tragedy and trauma. Being able to come alongside them was a huge privilege.

We also went for the occasional weekend away, usually involving decorating something, but not always. We once visited an outdoor pursuits centre near Tunbridge Wells purely to spend the weekend enjoying being together, and being with God together. It was a wonderful time, but my overriding memories are feeling terribly inadequate not being able to summon up the courage to abseil down a tower, and that the place was freezing. I spent a lot of time in the kitchen that weekend, but fortunately wasn't harshly judged. I think my 'great age' gave me an excuse! These weekends also provided great spaces for the young people to take their time and work through things and there were always wonderful testimonies of God's healing and releasing that followed.

The highlight of the year was the trip to the Soul Survivor summer festival, which provided the opportunity for us to spend five uninterrupted days together, joining with hundreds of other young people from all around the country to worship, listen, learn, grow and receive from Holy Spirit. Will's predecessor as Youth Worker was Mike Pilavachi, who having laid the great foundations we were now building on, had gone on himself to lay even deeper ones, birthing Soul Survivor as a ministry from the upstairs office at St Andrew's. It was a remarkable venture. The God-given dream of one man that became a reality through the vision and faith of another, and a growing team that gathered momentum quickly to pioneer the work forward. I arrived on the scene too late for the first summer festival but was there at the second in 1994, and was absolutely overwhelmed by all of it.

We arrived en masse at the Royal Bath & West Showground, which had been divided into 'villages' keeping church and friendship groups together. From the gates we were directed to our pitches by the wonderful and tireless volunteer stewards, who welcomed everyone with a smile and a kind word. There were a few caravans but in essence the showground became a campsite for the duration. My only reservation had been about camping, something I had not done since the Woodcraft days and for which I held no fond memories, but I couldn't find any way out of it so I gritted my teeth, it was only five days after all. Fortunately one of my work friends was able to lend me a tent which turned out to be the same type I had owned back then and I even remembered how to pitch it without too much difficulty. Amazing after so long.

The festival drew young people from churches across the nation and all were encouraged to bring along non-Christian friends, resulting in a huge and diverse mix. I was deeply impacted by the realisation that despite this and with over four thousand gathered on a relatively small site, there was very little trouble. There were strict rules prohibiting alcohol and drugs, but still, rules are made to be broken. Even so, the few incidents that did occur were negligible and swiftly dealt with. Only God. What an amazing few days, there was salvation, restoration, healing, deliverance and freedom. Extended times of uninterrupted worship provided the backdrop and release for much of this, and the power of God in the aptly named 'Showering Pavilion' where we gathered, was tangible. We were literally showered day and night with His presence and this was amplified often by the sound of real rain hitting the corrugated iron roof.

1994 was a special year. In March an outpouring of the Holy Spirit had begun at a relatively small church in Toronto; night after night folk came and were mightily touched by the power of God and word spread quickly around the globe. Those who were thirsty, tired and weary, broken, burned out or physically sick were literally overcome by His presence. Many Pastors on the point of giving up were restored, refreshed and re-envisioned.

Broken lives were mended, marriages restored and sicknesses healed. And it seemed infectious, as those who met deeply with Holy Spirit became anointed to release this same healing fire in their own places. The mission statement became, 'Receive God's love and give it away'. Our dear Vicar, who was actually the 'Right Reverend' David Pytches, having previously held the office of Bishop of Chile, Bolivia and Peru, flew out together with a few other leaders, to experience what later became known as the 'Toronto Blessing' for themselves, and returned so full that we were soon holding nightly meetings at St Andrew's with the same results. What a truly precious time it was, and Soul Survivor took place in the power of this amazing prevailing atmosphere.

Whilst Soul Survivor was unashamedly aimed at the under 25's, it ran alongside New Wine, an already established summer family gathering and the God-inspired brainchild of Bishop Pytches himself, who had also given his full backing to Soul Survivor. It provided the perfect opportunity to stay and be ministered to personally, relieved of responsibility once Soul Survivor was over.

It is fair to say, we all returned home from that summer deeply enriched. As the young people took their leave of one another, many expressed their fear that they would be leaving the 'real thing' behind and going back to churches that operated more in tradition than in faith. It struck me then for the first time really, just how ridiculously blessed we were at St Andrew's and how easily and quickly we can take things for granted. I determined from that point on, to be very intentional in counting my blessings. I hope I have managed at least in part, to do so, there are very many.

It was a source of much joy and a great privilege to be part of the Youth Team. Reflecting on it from this distance, it is overwhelmingly apparent to me that I received so much more than I ever gave. There is a wonderful verse in the book of Joel (2:25) where God speaks to Israel about restoring the years the locust has eaten, He did just that for me during this time. Through Breakout and those young people He restored to me the adolescence that I had been denied, as I experienced the wonder and excitement of growing up with Him through their young and largely innocent eyes. He restored to me also the joy of simply having silly fun, which was delightful. I will never forget playing my first game of 'chubby bunnies' at the age of thirty-three, it was totally hilarious and completely devoid of any dignity whatsoever. Walls of self-consciousness were demolished by laughter in one moment of trying to recite a phrase with a mouth crammed full of marshmallow, and realising that everyone was laughing with me, and no one at me. Again, only God. But still there was more. There is always more with God. What He knew and I couldn't possibly know at that point, was that a few years on, two very special young people would come into my life and stay, and without this experience, I would not have had an ounce of the capability needed to relate to them. He directs our steps indeed.

Breakout was a huge part of my journey to healing and I will forever be thankful for it and everyone in it, not least Brian who saw something in making the connection and pursued it. In so doing he set me on a life-changing course that yielded wonderful friendships that endure to this day, and almost thirty years on I continue to be nourished by the very special memories of those times. Although perhaps not the camping. I have to confess that subsequent years at Soul Survivor, and there were many, found me either in a local B&B or a hired caravan, and if there truly is any joy to be had in sleeping under canvas, I am yet to discover it!

Returning home from the summer festivals was, I imagine, akin to re-entering the earth's atmosphere for an astronaut. However I was determined not to land with a bump, and so full of all I'd witnessed and also experienced for myself, that one of the first things I did was contact Philip my previous Pastor. We spoke for over an hour on the phone, him listening patiently and me jabbering excitedly. I doubt I was that coherent, but he caught something of God in it nonetheless and invited me to share at a meeting with the church leadership. I blush remembering my response and can only hope that it came more from Holy Spirit than my arrogance, 'I'd love to come Philip but there is a condition. You must give me the freedom to minister in the power of Holy Spirit, I am not prepared to simply share my own experience'. I remain seriously embarrassed at the memory, this man had been my first pastor and baptised me and not so very long before either, but he was a truly humble man and although perhaps a little hesitant, did not take offence. With my friends at work and my friends from St Andrew's all covering me in prayer, I pitched up for the meeting both nervous and expectant and well aware that I hadn't any idea what I was doing. God is so faithful when we acknowledge our weakness; after sharing for a while, we stood together and I simply asked Holy Spirit to come, and He did. Philip especially was touched and felt the power of God knock him back down in his chair. This was something completely new for them and when I left the atmosphere was a little subdued and even a little sceptical. I went home feeling somewhat deflated, questioning whether I had even been right to go, perhaps truly I was just too arrogant.

The following morning sitting at my desk, I got a call from Philip. Bracing myself for criticism and probably correction, I took a deep breath and listened. He explained that after the meeting he was praying and felt he should contact Linda, previously one of his elders, now working as a missionary in China, and share the events of the night before. He admitted that he was seeking some sort of confirmation that this was indeed of God and not some flesh induced hysteria. She had replied immediately, having watched a live broadcast from Hong Kong the previous night by Nicky Gumbel one of the vicars from Holy Trinity Brompton, who had also recently been to Toronto and experienced first hand this outpouring of Holy Spirit. Philip valued her wisdom and of course our accounts complemented one another, so coming through Linda such a trusted friend, Philip had the confirmation that he had been looking for. In turn Linda was also blessed, hearing an account from what had been her own home church. God is so good at managing the details and then some.

This little episode was to give me the first opportunity that I actually took, to get out of my pew and share publicly at St A's. Up until that point, intimidated by the numbers and also perhaps the memory of my not so laudable attempt at preaching, I had stuck firmly to my seat when testimonies were invited from the congregation. At the service the following Sunday evening it was as though I was jet-propelled. I was at the front so quickly, I almost didn't register what I was doing and handed the microphone, was able to recount the whole episode with humour and eloquence and without thinking about it. There was a wonderful audible response from the room, praising God and renewing in me a desire to use my voice to give Him glory. He is so very kind. Unbeknown to me a friend of Phil's, one of our Christian group at work, was at that service. He had been so affected by it all that he called Phil afterwards to tell him about it, including the story of a young woman who gave an 'amazing testimony' (his words). When Phil shared this with me the next day, at our Monday breakfast meeting, he did so with a knowing smile, 'I think probably that was you Liz, was it?, you need to know it must have been a very powerful testimony for him to call me like that, he said that you spoke with real authority'. At the time I didn't really know what that meant, but I received the approbation gratefully and humbly I hope.

This lead to a further opportunity to share my testimony from the summer, when I was invited to join a 'faith sharing' trip to a special service at Wells Cathedral. The place was packed, every seat taken and folk standing at the back, and I vividly remember being seriously nervous. Knowing that I was to be 'interviewed' by one of the team, rather than standing up on my own helped, but still I was quaking when my turn came. However, when I was handed the microphone and opened my mouth to answer the first question, my fear deserted me and the words simply tumbled out. It was as though, in that moment, I was discovering what I had been made for, to 'receive God's love and give it away', that infectious anointing out of Toronto and via Chorleywood to Somerset, had indeed infected me!

Being part of the Youth Work was a wonderful, inclusive but not quite all-consuming thing and adult life went on. Never managing to develop a real interest in financial planning (something that evades me still) I found it hard to apply myself as I should have done to my day to day work. I was helped along by my Christian colleagues, all great encouragers, but it was soon apparent to me that this would not be a new career, and I always had a sense of biding my time, despite having no idea of what for.

Since finding Jesus, I had been in more frequent contact with my parents who although still sceptical were beginning to accept that perhaps there really was something more to my faith than a crutch or belonging to a new club. We still weren't really able to discuss anything easily, but they saw a difference in me and I think were intrigued by what they saw. My witness to them was to be a steady drip, drip over time and with each drip there was a softening between us that was precious. In fact even I was aware of a softening in myself, as brick by brick God gently demolished the walls I had built around myself over years and years. It was in this process that the nightmares began again. They weren't the same vivid horrors that had sent me seeking help before, but hugely disturbing nonetheless. My initial reaction was desperate disappointment, naively I really thought that everything had been erased at the very beginning of my Christian journey, and for a short while I allowed myself to believe the lie that it was hopeless. But not for long. Finding myself too frightened to go to sleep at night, I cried out to God and as He promised He would, Holy Spirit quickly came alongside to help and gave me direction.

St Andrew's was well known for its Prayer Counselling Ministry which was available to anyone who sought it and I sensed that God was directing me that way, so I did. Deeply discouraged by my previous experience with secular counselling, I was cautious but very aware of two of the team, who I'd often seen minister during services. I knew without a doubt that it was to them I should go. However, I discovered there was a protocol to be followed when I approached the administrator and asked for an appointment. Firmly, but not unkindly, I was told that who I saw was completely dependent on who was available and that it was not possible to request anyone in particular. Momentarily I was taken back to my experience at the staff room door at Clifton Hall, when my form teacher had dealt with me so harshly for suggesting that I was now ready to sit an exam. This in itself was a stark indicator of how much I still needed healing, but at the time felt like a poisoned dart from the enemy. So anxious about going through counselling again, I had set my hope on seeing these particular ladies and wasn't sure that I would be able to face it with anyone else, but I went away meekly, saying that I'd wait to hear.

God just knows. A few days later I received a call to confirm that Mary and Prue would be able to see me, and a time was arranged for the following Friday morning. It was going to be alright. My relief was palpable, and the healing process began immediately as I realised that the response I'd received from the administrator was not admonishment or judgement, as it had been from my form teacher, but simply an explanation of how the system worked for everyone. The victim mentality was something I was to learn quite a lot about going forward.

When they ministered together at church services or conferences like New Wine, which they did frequently, these dear ladies often referred to themselves as 'the two old bags', they are both now very well on in years and yet neither of them could reasonably be described as old, and old bags they most certainly are not and have never been. Mary Pytches and Prue Bedwell have been used by God to turn around the lives of countless men and women over many years and I am very, very happy to say that I am one of them.

Fridays happened to be the day that I spent helping Will at church, so I was there anyway which helped me to overcome any anxiety about the first appointment. I soon discovered there was nothing to be anxious about, Mary and Prue both oozed with the honey of Holy Spirit and almost instantly and instinctively, I knew that I was completely safe with them no matter what happened. The counselling room itself was a prayer soaked space, tastefully and simply furnished with nothing to distract and only a simple painting adorning the wall, of Jesus as The Good Shepherd holding a lamb under his cloak. There was peace in that place. What happened during that first hour set the tone for what would continue to happen practically every Friday morning for well over a year. Mary described the process as like peeling an onion, layer after layer coming away, each with its own stinging tears, until finally........it was a big onion. Over the weeks I shared my life with these women, detail after often stinky detail, knowing that if I truly wanted to be free I had to be prepared to completely unmask. Listening always for the prompting of Holy Spirit, Mary and Prue worked seamlessly together, taking me back through my life and settling on relationships and events as He lead. They coaxed and comforted me through deliverance after deliverance and gently 'counselled' me when I struggled to understand, or kicked against something I thought unfair. Their utter dependence on God to act created a prevailing atmosphere of peace, even in the midst of violent struggle, and absolutely nothing phased them. Because of that I was completely at peace in my spirit, even when the demons held tight, somehow knowing, even without understanding, that freedom was coming.

Two particular memories stand out, one almost frivolous, the other definitely not. After each session, they suggested I took a little time out to rest and Prue kindly opened up her home, so that I might have a little private space to do this. One time when I was leaving, I caught a glimpse of my reflection in the hall mirror and was stopped in my tracks. My neck was completely covered in what looked like a violent red rash, it didn't hurt, it wasn't itching but it looked terrible. Desperately wanting reassurance I hurried back to church and fortunately bumped straight into both of them crossing the car park. Not quite hysterical, but seriously worried, I blurted out, 'Look at my neck. What is happening to me?' Of course they both knew straight away and weren't in the least concerned, lovingly explaining that the demons hadn't been fleeing easily that morning and that I'd popped a few blood vessels in the eviction process. Neither batted an eyelid, they'd seen it all before and assured me that the marks would go in a few hours. They did, but now understanding the cause I wore them almost like a badge of honour throughout that afternoon, and if anything, they increased my desire to get completely free whatever the cost, so a total 'own goal' for the devil!

In the counselling room I sat facing Mary and Prue, with the wall bearing the painting of Jesus the Good Shepherd in front of me. In one session, towards the end of this journey, as we sat waiting on the Lord together, Jesus appeared in front of me not as a painting, but in person. He stood there looking straight at me, smiling, and with liquid love pouring from His eyes. There are no words. Simply Jesus. That moment changed my life, again. He was real. Really real, and I knew that from then on, all my trust, all my hope, all my heart, I could give to Him. Not mental assent, not even a heartfelt conviction, but an absolute revelation. Blessed assurance was mine. Afterwards, I shared as best I could with Mary and Prue, who had also both been deeply touched knowing His presence in the room.

A few weeks later just before the summer festivals in 1995, they felt it was time to stop. Go and fly they told me, and whilst that still felt like a huge ask, I too, knew that the time was right. Prue told me later that it had been a joy for them to minister to me because I had really wanted to be free and was prepared to go wherever Holy Spirit lead in order to be so. It remains true that I shared more with those two wonderful women than I ever have with anyone, and is a testament to their own integrity that I never once felt their disapproval or judgement. I will always be indebted to them both. Later Mary was to write to me and ask whether I would mind if she included part of my journey in a new book she was writing, not referring to me by name. Of course I said yes. In it she describes how they watched while 'God did open-heart surgery on this girl'. It is a testimony in itself, that I was so delivered I wouldn't have minded one iota if she had used my name. What freedom. Only God......with a little help from the 'two old bags!'.

So that summer, I 'flew' to Soul Survivor and New Wine, full of expectation and excitement. Neither festival disappointed. Soul Survivor numbers increased dramatically from the year before and the young people arrived on site ready to receive. And they did. Holy Spirit loves a party and He was ever-present, saving, healing and restoring. It was a joy. As was New Wine, if perhaps a little more sedate. Never would I have ever have dreamt that I would spend my holiday time at Christian Summer Camps and enjoy it. Except I didn't, camp that is. After the previous year's experience under canvas, contending with rain and no sleep, I stayed with a friend in a local Bed and Breakfast which was delightful. We had been concerned that we would miss out on some of the atmosphere being off-site and perhaps we did a little, but a hot shower, clean sheets and not needing to find shoes to pop to the loo in the night, won out. It was a wonderful two weeks and even though towards the end I picked up a slight cold, nothing could diminish my enthusiasm when I shared about it back at work with my Christian colleagues.

September has always felt like the beginning of the year to me, and never more so than this year. Living in a new-found freedom and complete conviction, I wondered what the next step in God's plan for me would be. Whatever it was I was ready to embrace it, if only I could shake this jolly cold.........

Chapter 12

Always of the opinion that it was better to 'battle through' cold symptoms rather than give in, I did just that for the first couple of weeks but instead of improving, I got worse. The sore throat and runny nose eased off but every bone in my body ached and my head felt as though it was about to explode; all this came with debilitating tiredness, and one morning when I couldn't even manage to walk Winnie to the end of the road, I knew it was time to see the Doctor. My usual GP was away on maternity leave but I'd hardly had occasion to consult her, so had no problem with seeing the stand in Locum, especially when the receptionist told me it was a woman. My early experiences with medical men had left a deep scar and even though I knew now that I was free, it was a relief not to have to test myself when I was feeling so awful. The Doctor was my age, very personable and concerned, I had now been feeling really quite ill for a month or so and that clearly was too long for a simple cold. She did all the usual checks but couldn't identify anything seriously amiss and so diagnosed a viral infection, which would work itself out with time and rest. She 'signed me off' work, which initially meant nothing as I was on a self-employed contract, said I should put myself to bed for a week and take ibuprofen for the aches as required and then return to see her if necessary.

The only time I had ever taken sick leave of any length was when I contracted chickenpox at age 19 and had to isolate for two weeks, and I was not enamoured with this advice, but it was all I could do to get myself to the surgery, so reluctantly I took it. Two weeks later I was back to see her, no better and actually worse. The pain in my limbs was acute, especially my legs, although it seemed like I was aware of each individual bone in my body. Everything hurt. I couldn't sleep, and even despite doing absolutely nothing, I was dog tired, all the time. She was sympathetic but had nothing new to offer, time and rest and review was all she could prescribe. At six weeks, we reviewed, me again worse rather than improved. At this point she said that she thought my condition was now post-viral and proceeded to talk to me about the probable ramifications of that. It was crushing.

A few weeks before in a conversation with Neil, the context of which I can't remember, he'd mentioned a friend of his from university who'd struggled to recover from flu-like symptoms. She was eventually diagnosed with ME/CFS (Myalgic Encephalomyelitis/Chronic Fatigue Syndrome) which had then lasted about fifteen years. I was reminded of this as I listened to the Doctor and my spirit plummeted. She was gently telling me that this same sickness was my own likely diagnosis and that this was something I would be in for the long haul. We could try various ways to manage the symptoms and that was really all we could do. She prescribed a stronger pain killer and advised that I consider taking an anti-depressant which would help to regulate my sleep, and hopefully ease some of the tiredness. I hated the idea, mainly because I was not depressed, but reluctantly agreed when she assured me it would not be addictive and might be the best help available in terms of managing my energy levels. Issued with a prescription and a few self-help leaflets, I left the surgery if not depressed, then certainly downcast.

Just a few short weeks before I was in the best place I had ever been in my life and now here I was absolutely floored. All my hope, not in God Himself, but in my own future and how He might use me, started to drain away as from a dripping tap in my soul, and with each drip, my physical condition deteriorated until I found myself to all intents and purposes a prisoner in my home. The next few months were by and large a complete nightmare, except that I was so totally depleted that I didn't really engage with that much of it. Once she returned from maternity leave, I saw my regular GP, who was a little more proactive and switched the med's I'd been prescribed to ones she thought more appropriate. She had me see a neurologist who visited the surgery, to rule out MS as a diagnosis which thankfully he did, and then referred me to a Consultant Immunologist at St Bart's in London. In the mid-nineties, ME or CFS as it is also known, was still considered by many as 'yuppie flu' and disregarded completely by some of the medical profession. It seemed to be the term arrived at when all other possibilities had been excluded and that was the process I went through. Although the experience wasn't pleasant, I was aware of my good fortune in being taken seriously by these Doctors. Even in the midst of it all, the irony was not lost on me, that I should be struck down by an illness that was so widely believed to be a sham. The fear of not being believed, birthed in childhood with a grumbling appendix and cemented in a police interview room in 1973, had remained with me always, and was the single biggest issue to be dealt with in my time with Mary and Prue. Whether it had indeed been dealt with was severely tested in all of this. In fact sitting in the waiting area at St Bart's with the friend who'd driven me, I was given pause to question myself whether I was actually ill at all. The Consultant I was referred to spent most of his time treating HIV infected patients, many with full-blown Aids, and there were some seriously sick folk in that waiting room. Nonetheless, the Consultant treated me with compassion and in all seriousness, and he did not for one moment make me feel as though I was in any way a fraud. I was to see him several times and he always treated me with the utmost respect. He helped me to see the way forward in terms of management rather than treatment, but he was careful also to manage my expectations and keep them always within the bounds of possibility. I understood that this would serve to help me keep a positive attitude, at the same time hating the idea of congratulating myself on achieving the most basic of things, like making myself a cup of tea for example.

An Occupational Therapist came to see me at home to advise me on ways to organise myself to make day to day life easier. My still very independent spirit caused my hackles to rise at what I saw as an intrusion rather than assistance, but actually she was amazing. Up until then I had never given any thought to arranging a kitchen, other than for appearance, but by re-siting the kettle and the toaster in closer proximity to the fridge and rearranging a couple of cupboards, she showed me that it was possible for me to make myself tea and toast from the comfort of a perching stool, which she also organised the supply of. Along with that and a few other gadgets came a full-length stair rail and grab rails in the bathroom. I have to confess I wept when the lovely man who'd come to fit them left, only seeing that my house now resembled an old people's home and not the wonderful helps that these simple things were for me. And they really were. Especially the stair rail. Using it and the bannister opposite I was able, albeit very slowly, to drag myself up the stairs to go to the loo a couple of times a day. Perspective is everything.

Once diagnosed officially by the Consultant, I knew that I would have to let my parents know that all was not well. It was a surprisingly difficult conversation and I couldn't help feeling that I'd somehow let them down by becoming ill. This was ridiculous of course and not in any way attributable to them, but the devil comes to steal, kill and destroy and this was certainly an opportune time for him to try to claw back some of the ground that he'd lost during my time with Mary and Prue. He tried hard. Mum's reaction to my 'news' was histrionic, 'we feel so helpless love.....what can we do for you from this distance......I feel so awful, I should be able to look after you.....' unwitting, but hugely manipulative concern that somehow made what was happening to me, seem more about her. And Dad's wasn't much better, after quizzing me about what treatment I was being offered, he said, 'they'll probably refer you for some sort of counselling, they seem to treat everything with counselling these days.' He practically spat the word counselling, and I suspect that initially he imagined CFS a less than credible illness and thought that I'd suffered a breakdown. None of us was blessed by that particular call. The next day, Dad rang back to say that they thought I should go 'home' for however long it took to get well. For a moment I was too stunned to reply, I hadn't been back to Nottingham for longer than a weekend since I was sixteen and it had not remotely entered my mind that they would suggest this. God is so very kind. Following our disastrous call the night before, I had rung friends in London who suggested I spend a few weeks with them and arrangements had been made, so I was able sincerely to thank Dad and also assure him that I was being taken care of, much to the relief of us both. We agreed to stay in close touch and ended our call well and lovingly. In fact Mum and Dad were both amazingly supportive going forward and we grew closer than we had ever been in the process. Another own goal for the devil!

Bryan, the dentist that I had worked for all those years before in Southampton, and his lovely wife Wendy had remained firm friends throughout all my ups and downs. They relocated to Rotterdam in the early eighties and I had often stayed with them when business took me to The Netherlands, which it did frequently for a time, and when they returned to London we saw each other regularly. Over the years they became like surrogate parents, always ambitious for me, encouraging me to strive and achieve, and ready with consolation went things didn't go to plan. They were less than enamoured when I told them of my decision for Jesus, having both been hurt badly by the church establishment many years before. However much I tried, and I did, to help them see that they had been hurt by people and not by God, they were never able to disassociate the two. However they didn't hold it against me and when I asked them for help, they'd agreed without hesitation that I should go and stay with them for a while. Not only did this provide me with invaluable support, it also served as a little respite for my church and work friends who had all rallied around providing help where I needed it, which was with just about everything.

Bryan came to collect me the following evening and I remember wondering fleetingly, as we drove away from the house, if I'd ever be returning. Despite being so grateful to them, it felt a bit like defeat. A little bark from Winnie on the back seat pulled me out of my reverie and I gave thanks that they loved her too and had simply assumed that her welfare came with mine and she would be with me. The next few weeks with them were precious, they were kind and solicitous and ultimately only concerned for my welfare. I returned home much strengthened in mind if not in body, and more able to cope with receiving the help that I needed. I remain hugely grateful to them both.

The next seven years were to be both the best and worst of times. At my lowest, although never at the point of wanting to take it myself, I seriously thought that my life was over. I fell victim to the lie that my inner healing had been for the purpose of eternal preparation and let go of all my dreams. Put simply, I was just waiting to die and my only hope was that it would be soon and my misery would be over. I developed quite a capacity for misery and am deeply indebted to wonderful friends, who whilst always sympathetic and always helpful, absolutely refused to join me in my pity parties. However without question, I was in need of a great deal of help, which for the first few months came almost exclusively from my fellow Youth Leaders. They were totally amazing but it was a heavy load, and eventually an SOS was sent out through the church home group network for available volunteers.

Throughout all of this, one of my biggest concerns had been for Winnie, who was about four years old and a bundle of energy. Springer Spaniels are high maintenance on the exercise front, ideally they need to run for a good couple of hours every day and without this stimulation can become sullen and irritable. This little dog deserves a book to herself. Almost from the outset, it was as though she knew instinctively that something was wrong and saw her role as to be by my side as my comfort. Day after day, I lay on the sofa and she lay on the floor beside me, only standing if I changed my position, seemingly to check I was ok with a soft nuzzle of her nose. That I was sick, soon became known by the other dog owners locally and often someone would call and kindly offer to take her out. I was immensely grateful for this but there was no regularity to it and I worried that it was completely unfair to Win and not sustainable in the long term. At a time when it felt like she was all I had left, the prospect of possibly having to re-home her was unbearable.

One afternoon I answered the phone to hear a voice I did not recognise. When the man introduced himself, explaining that he was from church, I vaguely recalled having heard the name but I still couldn't place him. He explained that at his home group the previous evening a notice had been given about my needing help, and he was calling in response to that. His work was flexible, he was often around during the day, he thought perhaps he could help with walking my dog. He was an answer to prayer, though I doubt I told him that at the time, but I hope that I thanked him before we arranged for him to come round later that day and ended the call. We were both surprised when confronted with each other. It wasn't the most dignified of introductions, I had to roll off the sofa and practically crawl to the front door but when it was finally open, I saw someone I recognised and I found out later that he didn't see the person he was expecting. Winnie greeted him as if she knew that he was to be her saviour, and for me he was certainly an answer to prayer, in more ways than one as it turned out.

On Easter Saturday the year before, a group from church had arranged to go for a morning walk in the Chiltern's, culminating with lunch in a lovely old pub in the village of Sarratt, and one of my youth leader friends had asked me along. I dipped out on the walk, having set my heart on going to buy a new slouchy sofa, which was being sold on special offer that weekend, but said that I'd love to join them for the lunch. As we sat down to eat I noticed an attractive guy sitting at a table by himself but who seemed to be part of the group and asked my friend who he was, to be told he was married to the organiser of the walk. I didn't give it another thought.

The sofa in fact turned out to be an even better buy than I could possibly have anticipated, as to all intents and purposes I pretty much lived on it for a couple of years. The attractive guy was to become Winnie's dog walker and so much more than that. Mike turned up faithfully every weekday and Winnie was always waiting and ready for her walk, showing her gratitude with exuberance and waggy tail. They'd return after an hour or so and depending on his schedule, Mike would come in, make coffee and give me company for a short while. It turned out that we had many church friends in common and it was good to catch up with what they were all doing. He was a great help to me and knowing that he would be arriving at some point each day, was often the only thing that gave me the impetus to move myself from bed to sofa.

Around the same time the Spring Harvest annual Christian conferences were about to take place. A group of friends were going to the Minehead venue and asked if I would like to join them. Initially, I couldn't see how it was remotely possible but they kindly volunteered to take care of everything and assured me that all would be well. They felt strongly that a change of scenery would be really beneficial for me, even if I didn't manage to get to any of the conference, and were happy to take care of all the arrangements and provisioning required. The conference was held at the Butlins holiday campsite and they had booked several apartments to accommodate us all. Their thoughtfulness was extraordinary and they were insistent that I took a large room in a ground floor unit so that I would be comfortable and able to get around. With the aid of sticks, I was able to 'walk' a very short distance before needing to rest and they were solicitous in ensuring I could sit down anywhere if I needed to. Amazingly I made it to the main morning meeting each day, inspired by the wonderful teaching of R T Kendall. I was deeply affected as he expounded grace over law from the book of Galatians, even though my ability to concentrate for more than a few minutes was so compromised that I couldn't take most of it in intellectually. I bought all of the tapes so I could listen again at my own pace later. It was such a huge blessing to be able to get to these daily meetings, that any disappointment I may have had at not being able to do anything else was completely cancelled out. But it did take all of my energy, so when one evening a few of the group decided to go off-site for an hour to a pub in Porlock and encouraged me to join them, I wasn't keen; however, they were doing so much for me it seemed churlish to refuse, so eventually I agreed somewhat reluctantly. Little did I know that during that hour God was to speak to me directly.

Settled by my friends on a comfy chair facing the bar, I sat and listened as they shared their experiences from the day, laughing and encouraging each other, but found my eyes were drawn to a couple just arrived and in the throes of a very loud and nasty argument. I was riveted by them. He was smartly but not subtlety dressed, labels on the outside, shirt unbuttoned at the neck revealing a huge medallion, and she was something else. Leather-clad in short skirt and black jacket with shoulder pads that gave her an American footballers silhouette, knee-high boots completing the ensemble. She was dripping with statement costume jewellery. Her foundation was peelable from the neck and her eyes daubed in sparkly shadow, but it was her language that arrested me. It was vile, way bluer than her eye make-up, every other word an expletive, and she was loud. My attention completely diverted from my friends, I just sat staring at these two, somehow transfixed at how awful it all was, and as I stared I heard the voice of God speaking to me loud and clear. Not audible exactly, but as close as it could possibly be without sound. Very firmly but gently, and without condemnation He said, 'That was you, Liz'. And I realised that it was, I was looking at a picture of the woman I had been, so many times and in any number of situations, before I met Jesus.

For the past few days through the anointed teaching of RT Kendall, I had been learning about the grace of God, and here I was in a pub in Porlock being overwhelmed by it. I sat and cried quietly, comforted by my friends who, not knowing any of this, were concerned I had simply overstretched myself. In fact, my tears were those of someone humbled in the moment by the realisation of the outrageous grace of God in her life. Not seeing any reflection of myself when I first looked at that woman, and judging her without mercy, God in His, had gently reminded me of where I'd been when He found me. He had lifted me out of the miry pit, planted my feet securely on His rock and washed me whiter than snow, and although I was there on that day, winded by an illness that was threatening to rob me, He spoke, and in those four words reminded me that He was near, that He had promised me a hope and a future, and to show me just how much He had already done in my life. It was not over yet. When we were preparing to leave, I hauled myself up on my sticks and walked out of that pub as someone with purpose. Only God.

A couple of days later, I was safely installed back at home with my spirit lifted and my previously ebbing hope restored, if not my body, which whilst it was no better at all, was not worse, and that in itself felt like victory. Having been so blessed by RT Kendall's teaching, I later wrote him a short letter in the spirit of Galatians 6:6 to thank him for his ministry and to let him know how deeply I had been impacted by it. Completely unexpectedly I received a reply a few days later thanking me for taking the time to write, 'you must know what a blessing it was for me to receive your note'. His humility opened my eyes to how much we all need encouragement, irrespective of our status. Kingdom work indeed. The trip to Spring Harvest had been a glorious adventure, proving to me that what had become my very small world didn't have to be quite as limiting as I imagined, and that Gods plans for me were still being worked out, despite the state of my body or any diagnosis pronounced over me. In fact it gave me enough confidence, even though I was no better, to accept an invitation to join a family for Soul Survivor and New Wine a few months later, at which I was also thoroughly blessed.

There was no way I would have been able to manage the summer festivals independently but again, dear friends came to the rescue, offering help and accommodation in their huge caravan throughout both Soul Survivor and New Wine. I was thankful for the change of scenery but had to deal with my pride at not being able to contribute anything at either event, and hated hobbling around the site with my sticks for support. Encouraged by everyone to simply rest and receive, I was able eventually to let myself relax and do both. But God just knows. At my weakest and feeling so very useless, I happened across one of the lovely young girls from Breakout who was visibly deeply upset, even angry about something. We had been really close and when I asked her what was wrong it all came out; I listened but there was little I could do practically for her other than that and to be an outlet for her tears. We prayed and hugged and she went off with her friends. They were a close-knit bunch and I was so thankful that she had that support, but I returned to the caravan feeling even more useless if anything. Everyone else was at meetings so I was alone in the van and I sat myself down thinking through what this girl had shared with me, and as I thought, it was as if all of her pain fell onto my shoulders. Awkwardly I knelt on the caravan floor and began to cry out to God on her behalf, both in my own and heavenly tongues. It was as though I could feel the very weight of His heart for her and her family and I wept like it would break apart at any moment. This lasted for probably thirty minutes and then, as quickly as it had begun, it finished, the weeping stopped, the weight lifted and I breathed deep. Astonished at the peace I felt after all that and also the absence of emotion, I spoke to my friends about it as soon as they returned from their meeting. Fortunately for me, they were both great prayer warriors and were able to explain that God had released to me an intercessory burden, literally praying His heart for my young friend. So even at my weakest and least able He was still teaching me, and that afternoon I learned something about travailing in prayer. I also learned that we are never, ever useless to God no matter how depleted we may be. Both valuable lessons indeed.

Over the year that I had been ill, I had been on the receiving end of so much prayer and I was grateful for all of it. But although I had seen much in other areas, like provision, there was no progress in my physical healing and I had reached a stage where I almost felt guilty for not getting immediately better when someone laid hands on me. With all my heart I wanted to be 'leaping and jumping and praising God' like the healed cripple at Gate Beautiful (Acts 3:8), but my body did not respond and often times the pain in my legs became so acute that they would go into spasm and reduce me to tears. I keenly felt the disappointment of the pray-ers at the lack of improvement, and couldn't shake the feeling that I was failing somehow. I desperately needed to hear from God for myself. On the penultimate night of New Wine, there was an altar call for the sick and for the first time and for all of the above reasons, I would not allow anyone to help me to respond. I sat in my seat feeling miserable and unexpectant, head down and probably selfishly hoping that there wouldn't be too many wonderful healing testimonies to endure at the end. Sad, but true. And right there in my faithless sullenness, God spoke to me. That beautiful, still small voice, that only whispers but has the impact of the loudest roar, 'You will get better Liz but it will be in My time, and it will be gradual but it will be complete, body, soul, mind and spirit.' It was an awakening in the truest sense. I was in His hands, it was going to be alright, it really was going to be alright. There was no physical leaping or dancing but with every ounce of my being, I praised God for his goodness and for restoring my hope.

Chapter 13

Before all that, and back at home after Spring Harvest, I settled again into some sort of rhythm. There was very little I could accomplish and it had become obvious early on that I would not be able to resume my work anytime soon. It was an irony that I was too ill to actually worry about money, but also true that my reserve of funds was practically depleted and bills and rent still needed to be paid. In these months I was to learn much about God as my provider, as week after week and in many ways, my needs were abundantly met. One friend spent hours researching the different state benefits that were available to me and then as I could not make head nor tail of any of it, more hours with me completing the application forms. As a result of her patience and diligence I received every benefit I was entitled to and more. When assessed by the council for housing benefit which would cover my rent, I was deemed under their criteria to have too many rooms for a single person living alone to qualify, but was immediately told to appeal the decision and was awarded the full amount at the case review. Financial gifts arrived regularly, some anonymously, and I would often find an envelope on the doormat when I eventually made it down the stairs in the morning. One time I was greeted at the door by Brian the twinkly-eyed vicar from St A's who pressed a bulging package into my hands and simply said 'from us all, be blessed'. It was stuffed with notes which when counted came to the exact amount bar a couple of pounds, that I had paid myself each month from my now empty drawdown account at work. He, nor anyone else who had contributed, had any idea how much that was. But God did. My car was useless to me, my concentration was too poor to be safe and the pain in my legs made driving impossible anyway. A friend in need of transport took over the lease payments for me, using the car whilst I was unable to. This blessed me so much as I actually felt like I was helping someone else for a change. The bible refers to a gift of 'helps' in 1 Corinthians 12:28 and truly, I was in receipt of all of them. Everything was taken care of for me as I needed it, meals, shopping, cleaning, transport to doctors and physio appointments. I was ill for sure but I was never once in need. It was overwhelming and very, very humbling and through it, God did some more much-needed work on levelling my pride and teaching me to receive with grace and gratitude. I can only hope that all knew just how grateful I was and still am to this day.

In all the 'helps', Mike calling every weekday to faithfully walk sweet Winnie probably warmed my heart the most. His dependable reliability eased the huge guilt that I felt about her much-reduced lifestyle and my complete inability to make it better for her. She never once showed any sign of frustration or impatience and simply spent most of every day lying at my feet by either bed or sofa. But she was always glad to get out and burn off at least some of her pent up energy. Mike would sometimes come in for a coffee on their return if his schedule allowed, and I valued this as it broke the monotony of my days, which could be overwhelming at times. Our conversation was often limited by my compromised concentration and inability to understand and I'm sure I spouted a lot of gibberish, but he was always patient and we shared some laughs along the way. Never once did I think beyond the obvious, Mike was a help and I was grateful.

However, I was hugely surprised when he turned up unexpectedly one Saturday afternoon in late September, totally out of routine. And even more so at the wry smile that spread across the face of the dear friend who was, at that moment, vacuuming the landing. Winnie had actually already been for a long walk with a neighbour and I was wondering how to say she didn't need to go out, but Mike got in first and explained that he'd had some unexpected free time and wondered whether I might enjoy going out for a drive, he'd been struck that day by all the seasonal colour and had thought that I might like 'to go and look at the leaves'. It seemed a strange proposition to me, but Donna gave me a nod of encouragement from upstairs and I had no good reason to refuse. Getting ready was a slow business, but once helped into the car we set off up the hill and out into the beautiful autumn countryside. The leaves were indeed stunning and we drove through village after village, sometimes chatting and sometimes in what was for me at least, companionable silence. I was aware of Mike looking at me from time to time and thinking it simply concern for my comfort, paid no mind, until at one point his eyes left the road for too long and he drove onto the kerb. He chauffeured for a living and was acutely embarrassed at his mistake, but we laughed about it and carried on. At one point we were exchanging salvation stories and Mike shared that during his journey to Jesus, he had spent time in a psychiatric clinic near Windsor being treated for severe clinical depression. I volunteered that I too had received treatment at a Windsor clinic as an outpatient and he asked which one. As I pronounced the name, he let out a sort of odd groan and then 'Oh Liz', I hadn't got a clue why I was getting this reaction and just babbled on regardless.

The plan had been to stop in one of the villages for tea and we found a likely place and parked the car. It truly was a beautiful autumn afternoon, the sunlight was golden in the valley, there was a green with a duck pond with and an olde-worlde tea room. But it fell apart when Mike realised he'd forgotten his wallet, I hadn't thought to bring a handbag or purse, and having no money scuppered it. Again Mike was horribly embarrassed and again we laughed and got back in the car to head for home. When we arrived Mike asked somewhat sheepishly if we could have tea there, he had something he wanted to talk to me about, and although I was by now at the end of my energy, I couldn't refuse him. Being at the end of my energy also depleted my curiosity and I doubt I offered him much encouragement to talk at any length about anything. In fact, he abandoned whatever it was he'd been trying to say after the first few minutes and made a fairly hasty exit. I confess to being a little bemused by it, but at that point was too tired to give any thought to what it was all about. Mike returned on Monday to walk Winnie as usual, as pleasant as ever and without mention of Saturday. I was simply relieved that there was clearly not a problem. But a few days later, returning from a walk, he asked if we could chat over coffee. It was a strange request, he often came in and we often chatted, even to me it was obvious he had something on his mind and my concern was that he might be unable to continue with his help. I couldn't have been further off the mark.

Over the next couple of hours, Mike laid bare his heart and soul as he shared with me more of his journey and how God had been speaking to him recently. His marriage of nineteen years had not long ended in divorce, following a gradual breakdown that culminated in his wife meeting someone else. They had since married and Mike harboured no bitterness, recognising that their relationship had become irretrievable. He was living in digs and had settled into a stable if unremarkable routine. There was no animosity around the situation and he saw his two children, aged eleven and thirteen, practically daily without problem. He was living very much in the moment, and in so doing was able to maintain a level of acceptance of the situation that made it workable, if not ideal, and he had given little thought to the future. He was thrown off balance somewhat, a few months before, when the notice had been given at his home group about a woman with chronic illness, who needed some practical support. His initial reaction had been relief, that there was always someone (else) who was willing and able to help so that he didn't have to, but to his surprise he felt himself immediately challenged by God. Holy Spirit often nudges in a way that is so gentle but at the same time absolutely insistent, and when Mike heard 'I'd like YOU to help with this', he surprised himself by agreeing to without hesitation. When God receives a 'yes' there is always more and the still small voice went on to whisper to him, 'this lady is for you'.

Mike, having heard, then completely forgot, as though this last phrase had been erased from his memory. For a while at least.

Over the months that he had been faithfully coming to walk Winnie something had been stirring in him that he was unable to quantify, until one day a few weeks before. He had been walking to his car on his way to me, when he found himself outside an estate agency. He stopped to look at the property details displayed in the window, not such an unusual thing to do for a man living in digs, but he was brought up short when he realised that what he had been looking for was bungalows, properties that would be manageable for someone with limited mobility, namely me. And then it hit him full force and seemingly out of nowhere, 'I am in love with her, I want to spend my life with her'. And afterwards, from the deep recesses of his memory came that whisper he had heard in the home group, 'this lady is for you', which he had so promptly forgotten at the time. Mike is a deeply wise man, not one ever to be caught up in flights of fancy, and his reaction to this revelation was to pray and enquire, calmly consider and seek wise counsel. Having done those things and settled in himself that he had indeed heard from God, there was nowhere else for him to go except to me and here he was, after one shaky false start, laying bare his heart with all humility and gentleness. When he'd said to me that he wanted to talk, nothing could have been further from my mind than this and yet, even though completely unexpected I remember no sense of shock, in fact it was more a case of pleasant bemusement than anything else. This man had only ever seen me ill. It was not a pretty sight, pale, gaunt, pretty much immobile, I was compromised on just about every level and here he was declaring his love for me. More than that even, he gave me a box from his pocket which contained the most beautiful sapphire and diamond ring, this was not a mere statement, it was a proposal. However compromised I might have been, I wasn't so detached that I couldn't feel empathy and knew that I needed to give some response, so I blurted out, 'well, I'm not completely averse to the idea but you're going to have to give me a little time.......'

It still embarrasses me now when I remember it, but Mike was, as he is, gracious indeed and he left quietly saying he'd be back the next day as usual for Winnie. He'd left the ring with me and after he'd gone I looked at it for hours. The whole thing was ridiculous of course, and yet, was it? Despite all the words I had received about healing and despite even having heard for myself at New Wine, as my condition gradually worsened over time, I had completely let go of all of my hopes and dreams for any sort of family future. But family had been my dream, and I knew also that my Heavenly Father knew that.

Mike returned the next day as promised, walked Win and then came in for coffee, but with no reference to the previous day's revelations. It was friendly, a little strange perhaps but not awkward or difficult. However, the following day made up for that. This time, walk completed, my invitation to coffee was sheepishly declined and standing politely in the hall Mike explained that he had been way too precipitous, had gone mad for a minute, he was sorry but it was just all a horrible mistake. Somewhat confused I gave him back the box with the ring which he put in his pocket, and then he left without saying if or when he'd return. Now I was shocked and a little shaken but not remotely panicked, except perhaps about the very possible loss of my dog walking help. Always a man of the utmost integrity, he did return the following day, which must have taken huge courage. He was embarrassed and contrite and asked if we could put it down to a momentary aberration and continue as we were, though perhaps more slowly. This was completely fine by me, still reeling somewhat from his original confession and the unexpectedness of it all. Mike breathed a visible sigh of relief at my acceptance of his apology and as ever, hooked Winnie to her lead and headed off for the woods. Panic over, I had time to reflect on Mike's gentleness and the kindness of God in it all. Walk complete and sitting down to coffee, we agreed to take it one day at a time and continue to seek the Lord for direction. Well, I would continue, Mike was very, very sure and the

162

wobble of the previous day seemed only to strengthen his conviction. He held on to the ring though, it seemed the right thing to do.

It was now for me to seek some wise counsel myself and I talked to the friends who pastored the church plant that Mike was now part of and who had been a huge help to me over the months. St Andrew's had planted several satellite churches and theirs, based nearby, was the newest. Unbeknown to me, although I should have realised as they were his Pastors, Mike had also sought their wisdom and so they were put in the unenviable position of guiding both of us! They did this unflinchingly and admirably, helping us to dream whilst keeping our feet firmly on the ground, and of course they prayed with us and for us continually.

In the three months since the summer festivals, my health very slowly began to improve. Most days now included a short walk and I was able to manage more things for myself at home. I hung firmly on to the words I had heard so clearly at New Wine, my hope for a future very slowly returning, and as I sought Him myself for direction, He re-connected me with some of my dreams. Long before becoming ill, in one of those 'wish list' conversations with God (that we all have but are reluctant to admit!) I had asked for a man with a beautiful voice. Whether a hangover from my very early days at the theatre or a reaction to the monotony of the flat and hard Midland accents I had grown up with, I don't know, but the sound of English well-spoken has always been hugely appealing to me. When Mike first called me, I had been struck by the kindness of his voice and the clarity of his speech. I was moved as Holy Spirit gently reminded me of my earlier request, as if to say, 'here he is'. And then I remembered that Mike had caught my eye in the pub at Sarratt, at the lunch that felt like a lifetime ago now. I had been drawn to him then and subsequently completely forgotten about it, on discovering that at the time, he was married. It all came back. I had actually noticed him too at St Andrew's, helping with the sound desk at the services, and thought what a good looking guy he was. Gradually the thought of a future together didn't seem quite so ridiculous. However, I was acutely aware of my limitations and determined not to fall into a commitment simply to get my needs met, which would have been disastrous for both of us. But the more I sought the Lord, the greater my peace, and against all my reasoning which screamed at me that the timing was wrong, I was ill and Mike on the rebound, and seriously beyond all understanding, that peace deepened with each day.

Mike was flying out to Toronto to a worship conference towards the end of October and we had made arrangements for me to visit my parents in Nottingham. I hadn't seen them since I was diagnosed and was even excited at the prospect, which was amazing in itself. By the time he was due to leave we both sensed decision time was upon us. Well, on me really as Mike had remained resolute throughout, which was hugely encouraging, him having got know me better in these last few months. Believing wholeheartedly that I would be able to, I promised I would give him an answer when he got back from the conference. He settled me into the train at St Pancras and we said our goodbyes, both wondering how final they might be.

It was good to be with Mum and Dad who knowing how much I hated being fussed over, were really cautious around me. It must have been hard for them to see me so compromised, but apart from my Mother's deep intake of breath when Dad arrived with me from the station, they were careful not to let it show and by and large they let me be. I was deeply touched by this, especially as I had been so averse to their suggestion of 'coming home' when first diagnosed. However, the week went by very slowly and as each day dragged on I realised that I was acutely missing Mike, and soon was absolutely longing to see him again. Lovesickness hit me out of nowhere, and in all my other sickness it gave me the clarity I needed for going forward. It helped me to talk about him, so I regaled Mum and Dad with stories about Mike being the best of helps. I've no idea what they thought at the time, but it primed them well at least. I left them on the day Mike arrived back and he drove straight from the airport to St Pancras to meet my train. As he helped me onto the platform it seemed the most natural thing in the world that he should be there, and at that moment I just knew this was right. We were both tired from our travel though and this was not the time for discussions, so once we had collected Winnie from her sitters, he settled me back at my home and then left for his.

Surprising myself, the next day when Mike came for Win, I said that I would like to walk too. It wasn't really fair on her as it seriously curtailed her exercise time, but it was almost like she knew what was happening. Fortunately, there were beautiful woodlands right on the doorstep and in only a few minutes we were on a footpath surrounded by trees and bathed in autumn sunshine. We stopped for a rest and Winnie, ever knowing and ever discreet, scampered off, after a squirrel probably. Turning to Mike I remember saying, 'Ask me again' and I also remember his slightly questioning look, 'you know, ASK me, AGAIN........' I persisted, smiling. I will never forget the love in Mike's eyes as the realisation of the moment dawned on him. It was the very end of October, it was cold and muddy, he didn't go down on one knee but he put his arms around me and asked me that question I never thought I would live to hear, 'Liz, will you marry me, will you be my wife?'. This time there was no bemusement on my part, but the peace was there, in immeasurable depth, and with absolute and irrevocable certainty I gave him my 'Yes'. And from there we didn't look back. We became officially engaged on November 1st, Mike having retrieved the ring from the inside of Tom & Donna's piano where it had been placed for safekeeping in the interim. I have worn it every day since; it was of course, the perfect fit.

Neither of us saw any reason for a long engagement, my health was improving only at a snail's pace and although we both believed healing would come, we had no idea when, and decided three months would suit us well. So the church was booked for 1st February 1997.

David P had retired some months before but we went to see him and Mary anyway and were absolutely thrilled when he agreed to conduct the service for us at St Andrew's. They in turn were both thrilled for us and we spent a joyful couple of hours together telling our story. Mary agreed to bring the address and Prue to share some testimony. It was perfect. We were so aware of God's abundant grace over us, smoothing out the bumps and coating us with a protective layer, that any possible disappointments simply ran off, as water from a duck's back. David had to explain that as Mike was divorced we would also need a civil ceremony to precede the church celebration. It marred nothing for us, we were able to view it as a formality that might even add something to the day, rather than a religious slight robbing some of our joy. And there were a few other little trials but nothing of significance.

There was however one hugely significant thing that had to be settled and settled well, and again we were simply showered by God's grace in the settling. Mike arranged to take his children Michelle and David out for a steakhouse 'early bird' meal one Saturday afternoon. As I had until so recently been, they were completely unaware of all that had been happening to their Father in the last few months, and he was braced against any disapproval that might come his way. It wouldn't have been unreasonable, they had no idea of my existence and they had already endured a hugely tough time, they would have been justified in baulking at another bombshell. But they were, and remain, generous and amazing, and even so young, their main concern was for Mike's happiness rather than their own welfare. They were excited as he shared the story with them and received the news as unequivocally good, which was indeed a measure of their generosity. As soon as he'd taken them home and also explained the situation to his ex-wife, he raced back to let me know all was well and we thanked God for that wonderful grace and probably also breathed a huge sigh of relief. Certainly I know I did, it was unthinkable that we would be able to proceed without their blessing and we have never had to, they have been blessing us ever since. We got on famously from the outset and it was an absolute joy getting to know them, both together and separately, and it soon became blindingly obvious that my time as a Youth Leader at Breakout which had been so restorative in other ways, was also preparation for such a time as this. Without it, I would have been absolutely clueless in respect of relating to my soon to be young family, and my faith grew in leaps and bounds as I revelled in God's goodness and marvelled at His planning! He knows, He knows......

So we were all set. Arrangements made and invitations sent. We were hugely blessed by offers of help on every front, the invitations and order of service cards were designed by a church friend, whose understanding and vision helped him create something completely unique. The invitations were designed as postcards and photo of Winnie was featured as a postage stamp, she being 'the dog who brought them together'. It was great fun and reflected so well the celebration that we wanted our wedding day to be. Another dear friend agreed to head up an army of 'caterers' who'd generously volunteered to give their time preparing and serving a huge buffet after the service, and we were given leave to simply remain in the church throughout the day, which meant there was room for everyone who came to the wedding to stay for the reception. Another friend lovingly took care of all the flowers, and created the most beautiful arrangements for us throughout the church, together with bouquets and corsages. During those three months, we were continually overwhelmed by goodness as we somewhat tentatively began our life journey together.

Unconventional though our courtship was, we thought that we should probably go on our first 'date' before we actually got married, and so Mike asked me out for lunch one Sunday after church. He explained that he'd booked somewhere but wouldn't say where, wanting it to be a surprise. As we headed up the M40 towards London I remember a feeling of slight trepidation about where we were going, afraid I suppose, that it might be too challenging and knowing how much Mike wanted it to be special. However I was reassured by his casual dress, he was wearing smart jeans and shirt with a sweater, so surely it wouldn't be anywhere too formal. He would give me no clue, but as we headed into the centre and the traffic slowed to a crawl, he became concerned about the time, and when we came to a complete standstill heading down Berkeley Street he finally gave in. Straight ahead of us was The Ritz in all its sparkly splendour and he told me that was where we were going. Although we were only about 500 yards away, it may as well have been 500 miles gridlocked as we were. Actually the traffic was a gift, the delay meant we were far too late to make our table reservation, which in turn saved Mike the embarrassment of being turned away. In all his thoughtfulness and desire to bless me, it hadn't occurred to him that there might be a dress code. I had been in a situation before in the days of expense account entertaining, when a corporate guest had been completely affronted by an officious Maitre De who, having explained the policy, went off to find him a tie and jacket, and the thought of Mike getting similar treatment filled me with horror. That we were going to be too late was the perfect escape and I suggested we just relax, let the booking go and do something else. Knowing Mike as I do now, I realise I completely underestimated him and he would have handled the situation with aplomb. In truth, it would have been me who was embarrassed, but I was so still full of pride, I was incapable of admitting that to myself at the time. Any disappointment Mike may have felt he was too gracious to show and ever the pragmatist, he was already thinking ahead and hatching 'plan b'. We waved The Ritz goodbye, vowing to return and celebrate something there at some point. Instead we spent a lovely hour or so at St Mary's Rose Garden in Regents Park, enjoying the late autumn afternoon sun and sipping steaming tea from styrofoam cups, watching the world go by. Lunch came very late and in the form of a takeaway pizza, which so very hungry by then, we ate with relish at my place in the evening. We have never made it back to The Ritz and nor are we likely to, we are both much more at home in a rose garden!

Time, which since I had been ill, had passed so interminably slowly, now seemed to be flying by and in an attempt to always keep track, I bought a little notepad using it as a countdown of days until the wedding. On each page, I wrote out a line from the Psalms to steady me and the day number, and one day I screwed up my courage to share my little effort with Mike. He flicked through smiling and nodding his encouragement and then at one point, threw back his head in laughter. At day number thirty-six I had obviously lost my concentration and started counting up instead of down! It is a testament to Mike's resolute faith that he didn't make any comment about subconscious belief and simply saw it for the error that it was. Over the years he has become very familiar with my lack of attention to detail and my inability to count, which has always been the subject of much mirth, especially considering that I first met Jesus whilst working in financial planning where numbers are everything! Whatever my mistake, the countdown was on and we sailed into the Christmas holiday time full of joy and anticipation. My only concern about the wedding day itself was having enough energy to get through it, and I also desperately wanted to be able to walk down the aisle unaided by a stick; I couldn't see how it would be possible. But God.....

Chapter 14

Between Christmas and New Year I was to experience one of the most profound encounters with God I have ever had. On consecutive nights for three nights, I heard His voice so clearly that He must have been at my bedside speaking directly into my ear. And each night He asked me the same question, 'Do you trust me?' to which my answer was always yes, and with my yes, He gently impressed on me that I should discontinue the medication I was taking. Three nights running this same thing happened. My initial waking reaction was to deny that I'd heard anything at all but as day followed night, again and again my spirit was disturbed, and I knew that denial was not an option. Sharing this with anyone, even Mike, didn't seem an option either and on the third night, what had been a simple question followed by an instruction from heaven, became a conversation with my Heavenly Father. My daily drug intake was a huge cocktail, analgesics, anti-inflammatories, antidepressants, and then more to counteract side effects, and with them life had grown gradually more manageable, if limited. In my spirit, I knew that I was being challenged to place all of my trust for healing in the hands of my Heavenly Father, who had already promised it to me. I also knew that psychologically, if not physically I had become dependant on swallowing this cocktail daily and that was not good on any level. However despite my heartfelt yes when asked if I trusted Him, I was terrified of going backwards, of being in acute pain again constantly, and reduced to immobility and inability, and so I asked a question of my own. I asked God to promise me that my condition wouldn't deteriorate without the drugs, crying that I simply wouldn't be able to bear it if it did, it would have to be the end. To which unsurprisingly there was no audible reply, external or internal, but there was a powerful and unequivocal response. I was flooded again with that deep, deep peace that passes all understanding and when I woke the next morning I knew without a doubt what to do. Consulting no one first, I flushed every pill away and cleared the corner of the kitchen work surface which by then resembled a pharmacy counter. When Mike arrived later I told him what had been happening and he, quietly confident and full of faith, simply gave his affirmation, and with that, all fear left me.

Over the next days I noticed no change in my condition whatsoever, I hadn't been expecting instant healing, God had already told me that it would be a gradual process, so I wasn't disappointed; in fact as each day went by the fact that there was no change became a cause for excitement. True, there was no obvious improvement, but neither was there any deterioration at all. Not only that but there were also none of the common signs of drug withdrawal. There was simply no reaction whatsoever. Then after a couple of weeks the chemical-induced fog that I had been living in started to lift and my thinking to sharpen, my concentration levels improved too and everything seemed brighter somehow. It was wonderful. And there was more to come.

A week or so later, and again in the night hours, I heard God once more, this time impressing on me to put away my stick and lean on Him to steady me. My faith bolstered now, again I gave Him my yes, but the following morning I realised that this was going to be a harder call than simply flushing the pills. No one saw the pills but everyone saw the stick. I remembered once even being described as the 'lady with the stick', and over time that is actually how I'd come to identify myself. Yes, it was a practical help and kept me upright and steady, yes it gave me needed support if I had to stand for any length of time, both great positives, but I had also allowed it to become part of who I was, almost like an extra limb. The thought of being without it made me feel naked and vulnerable, and it also fed into any remaining fear I might have of not being believed. That without the visible sign of the stick, people would think me to be completely well and even possibly to judge that I may never have been unwell. It really threw me. Mike was as supportive as ever and pragmatic, suggesting that rather than dispose of it, I simply put the stick in a cupboard. He poured cold water on my fears, and some hot truth into my spirit as he reminded me of all the help people had given and how much everyone wanted me to be well. I was reminded too of my desire to walk down the aisle unaided, surely this was God answering that prayer, He would get me through. The stick went into a cupboard and the first time I went out without it, no comment was passed by anyone. More of that amazing grace.

A scheduled appointment with my GP around this time was less positive. She had been incredibly supportive and was astounded and even offended that I had taken myself off her prescribed medication without first consulting her. I felt a bit of a heel but couldn't restrain my excitement at what God had done for me, and she was unable to refute the fact that I had experienced no ill effects and my condition was no worse. However, she cautioned me against being too hopeful and warned me of the probability of a quick relapse, but also kindly wished me well and gave her assurance of future treatment should I need it. We invited her to the wedding but she couldn't make it, it was a shame, she would have been blessed I'm sure.

So, January rolled by. We had visited my parents to introduce Mike and they couldn't have been more pleased, but as the wedding itself drew nearer Mum pulled attention back her way and prevaricated about whether she'd be able to make the journey, her nerves were so bad. Dad had already agreed to walk me down the aisle on the understanding that he wouldn't be called upon for any speeches. I was so touched that he'd agreed to see us married in church, knowing that it went hard against his avowed principles, that I put up no fight, although he would have been a great speaker. Mum came through in the end and looked lovely on the day, even enjoying being 'Mother of the Bride', and Karl travelled down too which was an added bonus and a real blessing to me. I had never dared to dream that one day I would be married in church, with the whole of my family around me.

It was surreal waking on February 1st knowing that this was the day my life would change forever. The Registry Office was booked for 11:00am, with the church ceremony following at 1:00pm. We had decided to treat the civic proceedings as the formality they were and reserve all our celebrations for the church, so my making ready would happen in between the two. Mike was due to pick me up at 10:15 and when he had still not arrived at 10:30, I became a little anxious. He showed up not long after and it turned out that he'd had a few anxieties of his own. Wanting his car to be immaculate, even to get to the Registry Office, he'd put it through an automated car wash where it had become waterlogged and refused to start. Fortunately, we are both pathologically punctual people and even despite this mishap we made it to the Council Offices at Beaconsfield with minutes to spare and were shown into the waiting area. When the Registrar came to meet us, her face seemed to fall slightly, but she was polite and friendly as she took us into the hall. Treating this as a formality, neither of us had made any effort to dress well and we had no invited witnesses, all we wanted was to get the papers signed and go home and get ready for the 'real thing', we didn't even exchange rings. Totally self-absorbed and focused on what was to come, I made it abundantly clear to her that we just wanted to get the proceedings over as quickly as possible and go, and she graciously, if somewhat quietly, acquiesced. Afterwards she wished us well and thanked us, explaining that ours was the first wedding she had conducted as a Registrar. We felt absolutely terrible for her, that it should be so lacking in anything other than formality. If we were to do it again now, we would still view it the same way but I hope I would be much kinder in my attitude, it was after all, a big day for her too. A life lesson for me and one I hope she has laughed about since.

From there it was back to our homes to get ready for the church. I relished the short time I had by myself before friends and family arrived to see me off. I changed carefully into the beautiful dress which had been a gift from my parents and a double blessing from God. Before I bought it and wondering how I would be able to afford to, I had been given an unexpected financial gift by my work colleagues who'd taken a collection for me. It was very generous and it paid for my whole outfit. Then my parents gave me an unexpected cheque which also covered the cost almost to the penny, a double portion indeed! It was wonderful to be able to tell Mum & Dad that they'd bought my wedding dress, which seemed significant and really blessed them. The whole day was a demonstration of the abundance of God. When I made my entrance, coming upright down the stairs rather than bouncing down on my backside which was easier, there was an audible parental intake of breath, and I felt the love of my parents for me in that moment in greater measure I think, than I ever had before. And then the doorbell rang and our driver arrived and soon, I was being driven to my wedding sitting in the back of a white Mercedes with my father. As I glanced back to wave goodbye I marvelled that the next time I came home it would not be alone.

Arriving at St Andrew's was wonderful. David met us at the door and lead us in. Arm in arm with my Dad, which was amazing in itself, I walked down the aisle, with Michelle following behind looking absolutely beautiful in the emerald taffeta bridesmaid dress she had chosen for herself. The church was packed to the rafters with well-wishers who all turned in the pews to watch us, but my eyes were straight ahead, looking only at Mike who was beaming from ear to ear waiting at the front. David welcomed everyone to what, as the invitations had promised, would be a great day, and we began as we have continued ever since, with worship. The band comprised musicians from both churches, with my about to be stepson David on the drums. He is now a huge military man who has made his career in the army, but then he was still only a little guy whose head just about rose above the enormous drum kit. We sang our hearts out in praise to our wonderful Heavenly Father, and to the bemusement of most of our respective families, who apart from Mike's mother only ever visited a church for weddings and funerals, and possibly at Christmas. This was like nothing they had ever witnessed but witness it did, to God's amazing grace and goodness. Once the ceremony itself was complete we continued for the rest of the afternoon, right where we were in the church. The worship band played on throughout, with different musicians, including Mike at one point, joining in to allow others to mingle and eat. A stunning and lavish buffet was unveiled and served by a whole team of dear friends, many of them young folk from Breakout who had spent all the morning working to prepare it. Wine was poured and glasses raised in many toasts.

During the service Mary and Prue had both brought wonderful messages, testifying to all God had done in each of us to bring us to this day, and giving us valuable keys for living together well as man and wife. During the afternoon, instead of traditional speeches, other friends who had been with us on our journey brought testimony, as we did ourselves in the form of an interview conducted by one of our church leaders. I'd been a little concerned about this and my ability to speak coherently, but once I got started I couldn't stop and there is an embarrassingly funny frame on the video, that captured our interviewer raising his eyes heavenward at a point when he couldn't get a word in edgeways! It was all great fun and even the hardest hearts were softened a little I believe. The car arrived at 5:00pm to whisk us away, the timing perfect, I was thoroughly spent, but as we reflected on the drive to our London hotel, what had seemed an impossible ask only three months before had become a joyful reality. I hadn't 'survived' the day, I had lived it, and it had far surpassed anything that either of us could have asked or imagined. What a blessed way for us to begin our married life! Michelle had shed a few tears as we pulled away from the church and was comforted by my Mother, which was very sweet. Even sweeter was learning when we spoke to her later that Michelle had said her tears were simply an overflow of emotion at seeing her Dad so happy. No sadness, she was simply surprised by joy.

We spent the night at The Lanesborough Hotel off Hyde Park, which was ridiculously lavish but a fitting expression of the extravagant heart of God. Mike had booked us into a small suite and we were met at reception by a man in full livery, who introduced himself as our butler and showed us our rooms. There was personalised headed notepaper on the writing table and also a wallet containing calling cards in our names. The rooms themselves were lush, with triple aspect floor to ceiling windows overlooking the park. The commissaire met us at the hotel entrance and welcomed us out of the car, summoning a valet to take our luggage. He had been there forever and I am sure had seen everything in his time so was not phased in the least when out of the boot came my cases and two Tesco's carrier bags containing Mike's overnight stuff. Neither batted an eyelid, unlike me. I wanted the ground to swallow me, I was so embarrassed, and experienced a moment of wondering what on earth I'd done in marrying this man who clearly lacked any sense of propriety whatsoever. It was only momentary fortunately and we were soon giggling about it. The truth was and still remains that Mike is so completely devoid of vanity, that it simply didn't occur to him that plastic carrier bags might be a problem, he just needed something to hold his stuff and that was all he had to hand. He is über cool, my husband. To think that he wouldn't have been able to handle a disgruntled maitre d' at The Ritz was to do him a terrible disservice, I have since repented!

Some things are simply too precious to share, but suffice it to say that once installed in our suite, we didn't leave it until the following midday when we checked out. We may have both been around the block, but we were newlyweds in the truest sense and we were both so glad that we waited. There is a line in the very final episode of the tv series Poirot, which we love, starring David Suchet, and spoken by him, 'There is nothing in the world so damaged that it cannot be repaired by the hand of Almighty God......' He is the God of restoration and only ever true to His word.

Mike had asked where I would like to spend our honeymoon and I totally surprised myself when I answered him. He had been expecting me to suggest somewhere very warm with a beach, which ordinarily would always be my preference, but it was not my answer. 'I think I would like to stay in a cottage, in the Scottish Highlands......' is what came out of my mouth and he loved the idea, so the decision was made. After that he took care of all the arrangements, determined that it should be a restful time for me. So, following our night at The Lanesborough, an afternoon in Hyde Park and the evening service at Holy Trinity Brompton, we took a taxi to Kings Cross where we boarded the overnight train to Fort William. Even in first class, The Scot Rail sleeper was a bit of a comedown after the opulence of the hotel, but we were riding on such a high we thought it all a great laugh and took it well in our stride, and we woke to such an incredibly amazing view that more than compensated for any discomfort. The morning mist was hanging over Rannoch Moor, the sun just rising and the landscape seemingly endless, it was breathtaking and we were not even near to the mountains yet, their snow-covered peaks barely visible in the far distance. I had travelled but I had never seen anything like this, it was deeply affecting. We stopped at a station that was no more than a platform in the middle of nowhere and a lone walker left the train, no doubt he had good supplies in his rucksack, there was nothing but moorland for miles. And then, as we travelled further, came the first of the mountains and onward into the Highlands until eventually, we pulled into the station at Fort William.

Our final destination was Loch Lochy and a crofters cottage on the lakeshore. We took a taxi from the station and tired though we were, our friendly driver had us in stitches regaling us with stories of encounters in his cab over the years. He went the extra mile when he dropped us at the Croft, insisting on unloading our cases and the many bags of shopping we'd filled at the supermarket by the station.

I gave him a peck on the cheek as we said goodbye and I can still hear him saying, 'Och, it's a lang time since I been kissed by a Sassenach lassie!' As we'd expected the cottage was simple but very cosy, with thick walls built to keep out the cold. The back door opened straight onto the loch shore and a small motorboat for our use was moored alongside a simple jetty. We soon were unpacked, and banked up the open fire in its grate till it was blazing and we ate and sipped wine, and read and talked and relaxed.

February in the Highlands is not noted for its clement climate, but we were continuously blessed with good weather. Apart from one serious blizzard which caught us out on a walk to the local shop, the skies were blue and the sun shone, and although it was bitingly cold it was fresh and crisp and delightful. Most days the loch was still and glassy, mirroring the sky and the pine forest that rose from its banks, and turning its surface into the most perfect reflection. We wrapped up and ventured out in the boat and were astounded by the beauty of it all. Two weeks passed quickly and before we knew it, we were back at Kings Cross and being met by the same driver who had taken me to the church and then us both to our first night hotel. Within the hour he was dropping us at the door to the house I had lived in alone for six years to truly embark on the adventure that is married life. We spent the first few days unwrapping the mountain of presents that were piled high on the living room floor and then another week writing thank you cards. We were outrageously blessed by all these gifts and by the thoughtfulness of the friends who had delivered them and stocked the fridge, arranged flowers and made up what would now be our bed. It was a wonderful homecoming completed by collecting Winnie from her sitters the following day, she too had enjoyed a grand time and been thoroughly spoilt throughout. Lavished by love all three of us.

Reality did eventually take hold and our first two years as a married couple were roller coaster ones. There were many reasons for this, not least being that we were now married but didn't actually really know each other very well and there was a settling process to be gone through that at times severely tested us both. I had developed a very deep vein of selfishness living alone for the previous seven years, six of them in the home we were now sharing, and it took some time for us to find an even keel. Although it wasn't a constant state of tension, neither was it completely harmonious and there were many disagreements and a few dreadful and very loud rows. I once got so mad, I became mad myself and stormed out, slamming the front door so hard that it broke the glass panel. Mike was amazing, when I eventually calmed down and returned home, having simply driven a couple of miles and sat steaming in the car, he had already contacted a glazier and ordered a fresh pane, temporarily repairing the damage with a piece of hardboard. Although I tended to be more verbal and much louder in my angst, Mike was very capable of making his own displeasure deeply felt, with some choice cutting remarks and a long sulk. We were well matched, and as we got to know each other better recognised that we each were able to counter the others' behaviour as we needed to. Mike was able to help me to be more objective, see things less emotionally, be less reactive and more patient, and I, never able to handle a bad atmosphere or sustain a sulk was always willing to break any deadlock between us. He says I have helped him to be more forgiving which, if true, is nothing less than the fruit of knowing how much I have been forgiven by my Heavenly Father. There were some tumultuous times, but more often than not they were resolved eventually by laughter, a hug and a whispered, 'I love you'. It was actually a truly blessed and valuable time and one in which I learned finally that the way to solve a problem is not always to walk away.

Day to day life established its own pattern, Mike was based at home and in and out throughout the day, giving us time to do things together which was precious. My health would improve and then deteriorate for no obvious reason and we both got frustrated at the 'one step forward, two steps back' nature of my healing.

I succumbed to a pattern of believing that expending too much energy would cost me dearly and unwilling to pay that price, strictly limited my activities to what I believed was a supportable level, which often meant that I didn't do very much at all. It was stultifying, and desperate now to be fully well, we sought out ministries that seemed to carry a special healing anointing for immunodeficient illness and then travelled miles to attend meetings so I could receive prayer. Although we witnessed healing in others, it never came through for me which served only to compound our frustration and to feed my unhealthy and ungodly belief in disappointment as an expectation. I came to see my condition as manageable, let go of the promise of complete healing made to me by God Himself, and settled into the lie that I just had to make the best of the good days and accept that there would be bad days and cope accordingly. I became expert at managing my energy levels and pushed myself as hard as I dared to do as much as possible. I screwed up my confidence, severely dented during the time I was incapacitated, began driving short distances by myself and clawed back some of my freedom. I met friends for coffee, helped with various things at church and eventually took a part-time job, serving in a pub at lunchtime a few days a week. It was little but it was so much more than I had been doing and it felt like victory, so I settled for it. Driving myself around and no longer using sticks for support, the questions asked after my health understandably changed from 'how are you doing?' to 'are you completely well now?'. Always wanting to protect myself, my answer was guarded, I would admit to being hugely better but with the rider that if I did too much, I would pay for it and that I had to be careful not to overextend myself. This non-committal answer became like insurance, giving me leave to be sick if I needed to be. How ironic that I had placed my faith in Jesus whilst working in the insurance industry, and indeed it had been Him who had lead me there. You have to love God's sense of humour!

One glorious and blessed day the penny finally dropped. I don't remember what I was doing, or what prompted it, but the revelation that insurance and faith can't co-exist hit me out of nowhere and I saw clearly how I had been mitigating against the fulfilment of God's promise to me. This time I didn't 'hear' any whispers from heaven or even feel a gentle nudge, it was as if the weight of truth simply landed on me and the light came on. To be fully healed, I needed to be full of faith, irrespective of diagnosis, prognosis, energy levels, pain even, and when asked the question, 'are you completely well now?' all that was required was a simple yes. No rider, no insurance. I have never thought myself courageous but if not courage, taking this final step took all of my guts and then some. But it was so worth it. The results were immediate and extraordinary. By the words of my mouth I walked into my healing and it was done. It was like shrugging off a heavy coat that I had worn for years and that had weighed me down so hard I was unable to stand. Now I stood resolute, believing that I was healed, and with each step forward my strength returned and with it my confidence.

My greatest fear had been the complete loss of my self to the illness. In fact, I was so fearful that I embraced being referred to as the 'poor sick lady' rather than reject it, believing that at least it gave me some identity, and I would rather that than nothing. In fact I embraced it so well, that fuelled by fear rather than faith, I was reluctant to surrender it, and I am pretty sure that this reluctance was costly in terms of time. However God is wholly redemptive and nothing is wasted if we choose to learn. It was a seven-year journey and it was undeniably hard. At times, especially at the beginning, it was almost unbearable but even in the midst of the worst of it, such goodness shone through in the care of friends and strangers who became friends, one who even became my husband.

M.E. is a wretched illness and I would wish it on no one. It robs and destroys and at its most effective even kills, it is not something I wish to experience again. However, during the course of those seven years, my relationship with God developed, grew and was strengthened in the midst of weakness, as I relinquished my independence to acknowledge my dependence on Him.

Without this interruption my driver would have remained the ambitious pursuit of 'success'. It's true that 'success' had been somewhat redefined since giving my life to Jesus, and had largely lost its materialistic meaning but even so, the pursuit of it was still paramount. Fiercely protecting my independence kept me desperately running on the treadmill of busyness, and it was only by the complete surrender that came through incapacity, I was able to get off and really find my rest in Him. In that place of rest and in the midst of pain, wonderful things happened and nearly twenty years later, I can honestly say that they were seven very precious years indeed. I would not trade them.

Chapter 15

Ill or not, life continued on and the first few years of our marriage were marked by four separate and hugely significant 'events' concerning children and parents.

Despite not knowing each other well before we married, trusting wholly in God as our matchmaker, we had spent some time exploring our hopes and dreams for a life together, and we had talked at length about starting a family and what a blessing that would be. Having children had always been a longing for me but one that I had dismissed as a pipe dream, knowing that the way I had lived my life mitigated against it. Mike understandably believing his family complete years before, had undergone a vasectomy. Considering those things and the fact that as yet, I was far from well, we knew the odds were against us and agreed that the best course was for us to do what we could do and trust God for the outcome.

Mike saw our GP, who continued to be brilliant and advised him about reversal surgery which was duly arranged. The operation was deemed a success, although tests showed that a percentage of the sperms were swimming backwards. I thought this hilarious at first, well acquainted myself with 'swimming against the tide'. Despite this, the Consultant felt that we had a reasonable chance and wished us well as he signed the discharge form. Over the next six months we experienced the joy of trying and the disappointment of the twenty-eight-day cycle, and eventually returned to our GP. Although we had been trying to conceive for a relatively short time in fertility terms, she felt that some help was warranted because of my age. Mike and I had talked about IVF treatment and whilst he would have undertaken anything to make me happy, I felt very strongly that it wasn't for me. This was an instinctive reaction and had no basis in any solid reasoning and in the end it turned out to be a blessing, our doctor strongly advising us against pursuing it as an option due to my health history and the fact that I was still struggling with it. What she did suggest as a viable possibility for us was I.U.I. treatment, a far less invasive option and an easier process to deal with both physically and emotionally. It was not treatment available on the NHS in our area but she would be happy to refer us to the Alex Radcliffe in Oxford if we decided we would like to explore it further. After prayerful consideration and some wise and Godly counsel from trusted friends, we made the decision to try. Our GP had described it as a helping hand rather than an intervention and that sat well with me.

So began our journey into the highs and crashing lows of fertility treatment and what a journey it was. Our consultant and all the staff on the unit at the hospital were wonderful, down to earth and realistic, and whilst fully supportive, never ever giving false hope. The walls in the waiting area were adorned with success stories, photographs of bouncing babies and thank you cards, but for each one of those there were many disappointments and it was not unusual to see a crying couple being comforted by a nurse. I have debated whether to go into detail about the process here and decided against it, this is not a medical memoir after all, suffice it to say that it is not a desperately pleasant one for either partner but we couldn't have received better care and were always treated warmly and sensitively and with great humour when necessary, which it was at times.

We had a few laughs ourselves during the process, which involved daily injections for a few days prior to insemination. Issued with instructions and an auto-injector we decided that as we were in this together, Mike would do the injecting. The vial containing the fertility drug had to be thoroughly shaken before filling the syringe and we managed to get the hang of it quite quickly. However, on the day before treatment, he opened the vial before shaking it and knowing the shaking vital, simply covered the open end with kitchen-towel before giving it a thorough mixing. When he came to fill the syringe though, he saw there was only a drop of the drug left in the vial, most being absorbed into the kitchen-towel, which was ultra strong and had all the qualities of blotting paper. Mike knew it was essential that I received the full dose and whilst he admitted that it went through his mind not to tell me what had happened and just administer the little that remained, his integrity got the better of him and he somewhat sheepishly confessed. It was early evening but we rang the hospital and after a while were contacted by one of the on-call doctors who explained that without the drug the treatment could not happen. The urgency was compounded by the administration of the drug being time critical, and we had only a two-hour window. The doctor was amazing and arranged for a replacement vial to be put by at the hospital pharmacy for me to collect and inject whilst I was on the premises. Mike was working that evening and it was far too late to rearrange any of his bookings and drive me the forty-five miles or so to Oxford, so despite having only driven very locally so far, I found myself gunning down the M40 in the dark, to the Radcliffe, trying not to break the speed limit. Incentive is everything. When I got to the hospital, the next hurdle was finding the pharmacy which was nowhere near the unit and the hurdle after that was finding a pharmacist, their presence thin on the ground in the evenings. However at each point, there was help and even though the clock was ticking and the window threatening to close, the final hurdle was overcome in the ladies toilets with the auto-injector I'd taken with me, somewhere in the bowels of the hospital. I then had to find a phone and let the on-call doctor know that all was well and that the treatment could go ahead as planned. It was a horrid episode until the end and then it felt like triumph, and when we finally met together later at home it fuelled our expectation for a good outcome for what was our second cycle of treatment. The first had come to nought but we were advised that this was often the case and the odds of success were greater the second time around.

Sadly it was not to be so for us, and this time our disappointment was palpable. Mike assured me that we could and would try again after the summer holidays which were now upon us. We were going to spend our time at Soul Survivor and New Wine and although in some ways that now seemed like a cruel interruption, we were looking forward to both. During a ministry time at New Wine, there was an altar call for couples who were experiencing problems conceiving and it seemed to me like a gift designed especially for us. I grabbed Mike's hand and we raced to the front eager to receive the prayer that would be answered and negate the need for more treatment. We were prayed for by a lovely lady who was kind and warm and full of compassion, and we opened our hearts to receive the healing of whatever impediment it was that was preventing pregnancy. When she had finished praying, she took me by the hands, looked me straight in the eyes and said with authority, that when she saw us again the following year, we would have a baby in our arms. Mike was quiet but I was full of renewed hope. God works in all things for the good of those who love Him and I interpreted this word to mean that rather than negate the need for it, our next cycle of treatment would be successful. Oh boy.

So we began again. We paid the not inconsiderable fee and went through the build-up, the heightened hormonal activity that came with drugs, at least this time administered without mishap, the tension of tests to see if the sperm were swimming well and the tension on insemination day itself. And then came the agonising waiting. At our previous attempts my bleeding had occurred exactly when it was supposed to, and I was so very sure this time would be different that I did a home pregnancy test on the day I was due. There was the faintest blue line. I repeated the test the following day and the day after with the same result. I sat and looked in the little window on the stick for hours, convinced that I could see something, albeit very, very faint. Mike wasn't sure but he was tenderly cautious refusing to let me get too carried away. I rang our GP and explained and she immediately invited me in for a blood test which would be conclusive either way. She was herself married with four children and when she called to give me the test result I could hear the catch in her voice. There was no pregnancy.

I had been so certain that it took me a few days to believe it and with my emotions still raging from the hormone therapy, when I finally did accept the result I plummeted. It felt like it was my fault, like I had somehow been found wanting and had failed hopelessly. Kind friends cajoled me, rightly reminding me that all was not lost. One dear couple gave us a massive financial gift with no stipulation as to how we spend it, but it was enough to cover another cycle of treatment should we want to try again. We talked and we cried and we prayed, though not necessarily in that order and although it felt like letting go of our hope we decided that another round of treatment would be too much for me. Except that I didn't, let go of my hope. We had been given that word at New Wine, that we would return the next year with a baby. We had three months before that became an impossibility. Maybe, I reasoned, we weren't supposed to have taken the earlier treatment, maybe pregnancy would occur naturally. And we really tried, but there was no joy in the trying and only grief at each set of twenty-eight days. When December arrived and the deadline for a full-term baby in August passed, I even convinced myself that maybe there would be a premature birth to fulfil 'the word'.

It was an awful time for both of us, and in the end I tied myself into such a tangle of knots that I just couldn't get myself out. For the first time in my Christian life I began to doubt. Where was the goodness of God in this? I couldn't see it. I couldn't see anything beyond cruelty and I blamed God for all of it. What was the point? It took months, I was angry and sullen and broken and could only see myself as a failure as a woman and a wife. Only the patience of my wonderful husband and the wisdom of very dear friends finally enabled me to see my very costly error. Gently they helped me to understand that while God is not fallible, people are. Slowly, slowly I came to see that what the lovely lady who prayed for us at New Wine had offered was comfort, given as prophecy, and it was there the misunderstandings had begun. Her compassion had overcome her judgement, and in my desperation to hear what I wanted to hear I had allowed it to almost derail my faith. This was not her fault entirely, it is the responsibility of the receiver to test any word, but she would have spared me so much pain had she only resisted the urge to offer me false hope and instead blessed us to rest in and trust Him for our good.

It was a long journey back, but Father God walked every step with me and at the same time taught me one of the most valuable lessons in the prophetic that I have ever learned and which I now teach in my own ministry. It is never wisdom to attribute to God something that He didn't say, even with the purest and most compassionate of motives. It is neither wise nor kind and ultimately may even prove to be destructive. I am so thankful that again what the enemy used for harm, God redeemed for His glory, by empowering me to release others in their prophetic gifting with an understanding of the importance of good governance. Another own goal for the devil and his cohorts.

We never were to conceive and it has been a sadness, especially for me, although I have been ridiculously blessed by both of my stepchildren. And when I am brutally honest with myself, which I do try to be, I know that my disappointment is more to do with never having experienced childbirth, rather than raising a child. It is hard to explain and I imagine even harder to understand if you're a woman who has done so, and know the pain of it. It was an almost visceral longing and only when assailed by the challenges of menopause did I truly, completely let go of it. I am well aware too, that there are many who are robbed of any joy in childbearing for other and far more painful reasons, than simply the absence of conception. My heart goes out to you.

Twenty years on I can testify that I have and continue to experience 'the joy of the barren woman' as God has released me. As well as my wonderful stepfamily, I have acquired a large family of spiritual children whom I dearly love. He has also enabled me to see that the life we are living is His plan for us and to understand that His plans are the best. I can say with my whole heart that there is nothing missing in our family and I am so very thankful for that.

In the midst of all this life threw us a curveball concerning Michelle and David, which was hard to catch. A new job in California for their step-father, meant relocation for the whole family and once a suitable house was found it all happened very quickly. It was a huge wrench for everyone but after much discussion, we all agreed that it was an opportunity too good to pass up on and with all the generosity we could muster, we gave them our blessing and tried to embrace their excitement in all the planning. When departure day arrived we met them all at Heathrow and waited through the lengthy process that is checking in animals and excess baggage for travel. We had arranged to visit within three months and knowing this helped us to get past the awfulness of saying goodbye. But it was awful, and as we watched the children disappear through departure security, the floodgates opened and our tears poured. I will never forget Mike slumping against the car and almost howling with the pain of it for a few moments once back in the car park. It was desperately, desperately hard for him.

Thankfully time has proved it a good move. Now married, with families of their own and both holding dual citizenship, they have made the U.S. their home, and although they are now separated from each other by almost as many miles as we are from them, they remain as close as ever and are a great support to one another. We are hugely thankful for the technology that keeps us in touch and although the distance has had an impact on the way we relate, we feel no less close to them for all that. We are immensely proud of them both.

The remaining two significant events to occur in our early married years concerned parents rather than children and also involved separation, this time sadly, of a more permanent nature.

My parents, a year apart in age, were by now in their mid-seventies and had been retired for around fifteen years. Dad had taken early retirement at sixty, defeated by the changes and challenges of the school education system. He had bravely persevered through re-streaming and the amalgamation of two schools into one huge mega-comprehensive, but that together with numerous other trials eventually took their toll and he broke. He made a pragmatic and brave decision to go early on a reduced pension, but it took him a while to accept that he'd done the right thing and stop thinking himself a failure. Mum retired a couple of years later and her attitude was altogether more healthy. Spurred on by her zeal, they both enrolled for evening classes and pursued different and varying interests. They began to travel abroad and took to spending almost all of the harsh winter months in the more temperate climes of Spain or southern Cyprus. There was even talk of a permanent re-location at one point, although it amounted to nothing in the end, for which I found myself oddly thankful. Our relationship had continued to deepen and as forgiveness flowed between us, we actually began to enjoy each other in a way we never had before. They loved seeing me happy with Mike and although still not fully fit, I think through him they felt less responsibility towards me, this in turn lessened the intensity between us and helped us relax with each other. So I visited regularly and by and large we enjoyed our times together.

In the spring of 1998, Mum lost her footing whilst pegging out washing and fell, breaking her hip. It was a nasty break and surgery was required, it was to be the beginning of a long three months. Discharged from the surgical ward, she was sent to convalesce in a nursing home outside of the city. It was a long drive for Dad and daily visits took their toll on him, he also grew increasingly worried about his ability to be able to care for her when she was discharged and eventually he became fearful of her returning home. The care team handled it all well, several day visits were arranged to see how they managed, there were a few hiccups but eventually it was deemed safe to discharge her. Thankfully, back at home and without the supervision she blossomed, and Dad somewhat embarrassed by his reluctance to have her there, was galvanised into more action than he had been for a while. As she recovered, although not straying far from their home, they seemed to be growing stronger together and enjoying life and each other more.

So it seemed untimely, when one night that August we returned from a home group meeting around 10:00 o'clock to see the light flashing on the answerphone. I pressed the button and whilst I was hanging up my jacket heard my father's somewhat strained voice, 'Oh hello Liz, I'm calling to let you know that Mummy died this afternoon. Don't come this evening, tomorrow will be fine.' Stunned, I pressed play again. I had heard right. The message was brutal and businesslike and had the hallmark of my Dad's inability to communicate anything emotional all over it. I was reminded of the day many years before, when I returned home from school one lunchtime, to find a note on the kitchen table telling me that Mum was in hospital having suffered a heart attack, and my heart went out to him. I called him of course. She had been watching a favourite black and white movie on video that afternoon, and he had left her to go to the bathroom, when he returned a few minutes later she was dead. The initial shock rendered him helpless for a while and then he had dialled 999 and an ambulance had been despatched. With it came the police, alerted to an unexpected death, and the family GP was also summoned. Karl, who now lived in the city was contacted and he arrived as they all left. Dad was understandably shocked and exhausted. He was already worrying about the many and various arrangements that had to be made and reassuring him as best I could, I suggested that he try and get some sleep, we would travel up first thing the following morning and help. Karl of course agreed to spend the night and it was a comfort to me knowing that he was there. At that point, I could feel nothing, simply numbed by the finality. We had been due to visit that coming weekend and were looking forward to being together, the realisation that there would now never be an opportunity to do that was yet to hit home.

We let friends know what had happened, made arrangements for Winnie to be looked after and left very early the following morning. The hundred and twenty-five-mile journey to Nottingham was relatively quick given the hour, but had never before seemed so long to me. We arrived about 7:30, to find the house asleep and the front door locked but the lovely couple who lived next door and whom I'd known since childhood, saw us and asked us in to wait. They had seen the ambulance the previous day, but were not aware that Mum had died and had imagined that she had been taken ill and admitted to hospital. Knowing what an intensely private man Dad was, they hadn't wanted to intrude and were planning to call round this morning to see if there was anything they could do to help. They were sensitive and good friends and neighbours, I was so thankful knowing that they were just next door.

Dad looked dreadful, he was withdrawn and bowed down with shock and grief and tightly bound by the awful stoicism that dictated to him that he should betray no emotion. He might not have been able to cry but his despair rendered him helpless and I will never forget the tiny and quiet voice that asked me whether I would be able to take care of the arrangements, he simply couldn't face it. It had been and still is to some extent, a pattern in my life that whilst I can be completely floored by the smallest of inconveniences, I'm pretty tough in a crisis. On one visit to Mum in the care home, I had returned from a meeting with the staff nurse to hear her saying to Dad about me, 'Oh yes, she gets things done, I'll give her that', sadly it wasn't a compliment, she had been bemoaning the fact that when I visited her I was busy, and didn't spend time at her bedside. It was a valid criticism and it cut me to the quick. However, this was a time when the best I could do for Dad was to take the weight, so with Mike's invaluable help that's what I did. This also helped Karl, who was never the most practical of souls and found it almost impossible to offer anything other than his presence. And I was grateful for that, it was enough.

There is a lot to take care of following a death and we were blessed with much favour as we ploughed our way through the mountain of formalities. Not least was the acceptance by the Coroner of the GP's conclusion that the cause of death was a massive coronary. This negated the need for a post-mortem for which we were tremendously grateful and allowed us to make the funeral arrangements without delay. For all his incapacity, Dad was insistent that a simple, no-fuss cremation was what they had always agreed and that was what he wanted. He agreed that I should ask Tom our pastor if he would conduct it, they had met at our wedding and Dad had been impressed by his down to earth attitude, and I was much relieved not to have to accede the responsibility to a stranger. So caught up in all the practicalities, it didn't occur to me that I could have taken the funeral myself which was a pity, I think Mum would have loved it.

Dad's desire to keep things simple extended beyond the funeral itself, he was absolutely adamant that he didn't want to travel with the hearse or to host any sort of gathering after the event, fearing that he simply wouldn't be able to cope with it. I understood him completely, although felt a little sad on Mum's behalf, she had been a great lover of company and the idea of her friends giving her a good send-off would have appealed I'm sure. Actually several of the neighbours did get together afterwards to reminisce and raise a glass, and if she was aware she would have been blessed by that. She would also have understood Dad's reticence, she knew him very well and would have wanted to make things as easy for him as possible.

It was a good service. I shared as I was able and Tom spoke well and evangelistically of God's unfailing love and the glory of the heavenly eternity available to all who choose to believe. It was inevitably short and then it was over and Mum was gone. We went straight back to the house afterwards and after a while Mike and Tom left to return home. I stayed with Dad for a week or so hoping that it would help and it probably did in some ways, but I imagine he was slightly relieved when I'd gone and he was returned to his own company. After that, we kept in much closer touch by phone than we ever had and I visited a couple of times a month, as much for my sake as for his. Within only days of the funeral he'd asked if I would deal with Mum's things, their presence was no comfort to him and every time he opened a drawer or the wardrobe he was confronted again by his loss, he simply couldn't bear it. I thought it was too soon and was afraid that he would regret it but did what he'd asked anyway, praying that I was wrong. He was never to mention any regret, he didn't really have time.

Six months later, in the following March, I made my almost daily afternoon call to him and got no reply. Not unduly concerned by this, it was a pleasant early spring day and I imagined he'd taken himself off for a walk, I tried again an hour or so later, but there was still no response. This time I sensed a frisson of unease and when I called a third time without success I knew something was wrong. Karl was a bus ride away, so instead I rang the lovely couple next door, explained my concern and asked if they'd mind just checking that all was well. It wasn't. She called me back minutes later to say that she'd found Dad at the bottom of the stairs, he seemed to have taken a fall and whilst not completely unresponsive was clearly very unwell. They kindly called an ambulance and I alerted Karl, who left home immediately to get himself there. He rang me as soon as he could and explained that it was bad, Dad had been admitted to hospital with a suspected stroke and it would take a while to assess the extent of it. We made the decision to go up the following day but Karl called again in the early hours to say that he'd been summoned to the hospital and it wasn't looking good. We left immediately, another early morning journey up the M1 just six months after the last. We were too late, a kindly nurse who greeted us knowingly but said nothing, lead us to the relatives' room where Karl sat looking ashen and simply looked up and said, 'about twenty minutes ago'. Dad had not been alone, Karl was at his bedside and actually was unaware that he had died, it was so peaceful, it was only that a nurse had looked in at the same time that he knew. We were able to see him

194

however, and for that I was so thankful. He was still in his bed and had not been moved at all, lying on his side as he habitually had slept, and he did look at rest.

It was hard. Mum's death had been sudden and there was no way we could have anticipated it, with Dad we had not been present because we had chosen not to come the night before, it was cruel and I felt both guilty and cheated and it took a little time for me to have enough generosity of spirit to be thankful that Karl had been with him and he hadn't been alone. I was after all Dad's little girl, it should have been me. However, over the next few days I was to come to understand God's great mercy at work in this. Dad's relationship with Karl had been difficult and fractious for years, for many reasons and with responsibility on both sides. Karl, alone at his dying father's bedside, had the opportunity to make peace through the power of a gentle touch if not with words, and when the shock of it all abated, I was able to see that this would have been impossible had I been present. It was grace. My peace with Dad had already been made and although I was sad not to be with him at the end, once I'd forgiven myself for my tardiness, I had no other regrets.

There was grace too in the swiftness of his passing, he would have hated being infirm and dependent. One of his neighbours remarked that he simply didn't want to live without Mum, and although in the six months since she had departed he had taken good care of himself, I think there was truth in her comment. They were melded together and for him, there was no future without her. Too private to display any visible grief, the only telling thing he said to me after her death was, 'She was lovely wasn't she' It was a statement not a question and deeply touched me. When I was clearing the house a few weeks later, I found a poem he had written her during their courtship. It was neatly folded and stowed in the pages of a book. He was not an effusive man but that he kept it spoke volumes about his love for her.

So now we had to arrange another 'simple cremation', and following so soon on the heels of the first at least we knew what to do.

The funeral was to take place the following week and again Tom offered his services. It was a small gathering but no less honouring for that, and although this was for Dad, it was also a requiem for them both. I shared from my heart and then read a favourite poem of Dad's by Rupert Brooke and that nearly finished me, 'If I should die, think only this of me.......' He had introduced me to Brooke's poetry as a teenager and later had sent me a paperback copy of his collected works. He had been given the hardback version by a friend at college and his covering note said that it would come to me when he died. It seemed fitting and poignant to read from it. As with Mum, there was no fuss and although this without question would have been Dad's wish also, it was more for my own benefit that we kept it so simple. My concern for Dad's well being during the previous six months had kept any grief well tamped and I was very aware of my own vulnerability. Afterwards four of us went for a consolatory drink at a pub in the city that had been an old haunt for both Karl and I in years past. With my husband, my brother and my pastor, I raised a glass to my parents and we marked the end of an era.

There was much to be done, going through the house and sorting possessions, will reading and probate and eventually the sale of the house that had been home for both Karl and I at different stages. But there was no rush and we agreed to allow ourselves to breathe for a few days before embarking on it all. We headed home but I found it hard to settle, all the practicalities loomed too large, and I was soon back and engaged in what my parents had both agreed I was good at, 'getting things done'. It wasn't a gargantuan task, the house was small and they had never hoarded, but it was very final and desperately heart wrenching nonetheless. I left with several boxes of my own childhood stuff which they had lovingly kept, together with tins of old photos and a few of their personal bits and pieces as treasured mementoes. The samovar and the bust of Lenin, which were still on display, went to the tip but they are forever etched into my memory.

Since my own conversion in 1991 I had shared my faith freely with both Mum and Dad, and unsparingly I hope. But for all my sharing I had not been witness to either of them inviting Him to themselves and when they died, I was acutely aware that I had missed opportunities to actually lead them to Him. I berated myself time and again for my failure to do so and worried at what the dire consequences of that failure might be for them. However, God is only good and one day when I was crying out to Him in this regard, wallowing in self-pity and feelings of guilt, I sensed the closeness of Holy Spirit. He reminded me of a particular occasion with Dad, when he had shared a dream with me that had astonished him. It was so clearly a 'God' dream, a knocking on his skull and a voice asking, 'can I come in?' repeated three times. I went so far as to tell Dad that I knew exactly what that was, even that it was the voice of Jesus, but went no further. For someone who had spent her working life in sales, and had been relatively successful at it, this was pitiful in the extreme and I was staggered by my own reticence. We never got that moment back. But here in this one, I was comforted by the Comforter who tenderly showed me that my Dad's salvation was not dependent on my inability 'to close', but that what I had forfeited in that, was the blessing of being present at the closing. And from that point on the peace made sense, in respect of both of them. Mum had told me once, and much earlier, that she had come to a place of belief but wanted to keep it to herself, knowing that Dad at that time was still far off and in fear of causing a rift in her marriage. I was sure that she had chosen well. As for me, I was once again astounded by the grace of God and His goodness and kindness to me amid all my fear and failure. Whatever anxiety about my parents remained I released to Him, and there has never been cause since to consider it. His gentle discipline showed me what I had missed and His grace enabled me to take hold of my faith and believe for their salvation. Eternity is a very long time, I am so grateful.

Once the dust had settled and all the formalities completed we were able to look forward. The strain of the last six months in particular had begun to take its toll and we decided to take a 'proper' holiday. A few years before we married I had visited Southern Cyprus with Mum and Dad and loved the island, it seemed a fitting destination for recovery and it would be their money that was paying for it. We found a small company that specialised in Cyprus rentals and put a deposit on a modest maisonette in Coral Bay for a couple of weeks in early May. Spring in Cyprus is absolutely beautiful, a profusion of colour with wildflowers everywhere, and the temperature wonderfully warm but not the blistering heat of high summer. This was to be our first Mediterranean holiday together and after the cold of the Highlands in February and the damp of Somerset in the summer, we were both, but me especially, looking forward to two weeks of unbroken sunshine with absolutely nothing to do.

We flew on a Sunday evening and picked up a hire car which we had booked through the villa company. They also sent a representative to meet us whose job it was to settle us into our holiday home, so we followed his car out of the airport and along the main road. I was pleased at how well I remembered the place and was thrilled to be able to easily identify where I had stayed with Mum and Dad as we drove past. Coral Bay was a left turn at a crossroads a couple of miles further on, but when we got there our guide indicated right. We had no mobile phone back then, and no choice but to follow him, and as he drove up into the hills of Peiya we became more and more perplexed. He took us through a set of huge and imposing gates and down a long driveway and eventually came to a stop in front of a massive villa, standing alone facing out to sea. The Rep got out of his car and opened his arms in greeting and I started jabbering on about this not being right, we had booked a small maisonette in Coral Bay, for goodness sake, in the pictures one of the windows even had bars on it although the garden looked pretty, this wasn't right, he had made a mistake. He silenced me with a raise of his hand and said, 'lady, you have SERIOUS upgrade'. We were never to find out why, but we received it with thanks and later understood it as a blessing from heaven. He saw us in and showed us the basics and then left us to it. We were like a couple of gleeful kids as we explored, and the place was amazing. An underground garage and a basement with every conceivable laundry appliance. A sauna. Four huge bedrooms with bathrooms and spas. It was all marble floors and cherry wood furniture and leather sofas and chairs. Outside the sun terrace was bigger than our house in Chesham and ran the full length of the swimming pool and the view was breathtaking. Straight out to sea over orange and banana groves with Coral Bay nestling at the bottom of the hill. Idyllic.

It was the most wonderful fortnight. We explored in the mornings and lazed by the pool in the afternoons and so appreciated being away from the crowds. We hired a jeep and drove up high into the Troodos mountains and out into what was then, the wilds of the Akamas peninsula. We walked in the Valley of the Kings and lunched in Paphos where the pelicans come and eat from any proffered hand. There were some desperately poignant moments, visiting places I'd been before with Mum and Dad, and some tears were shed. But it was all of it very healing.

Before we left we went to look at the little maisonette that we had originally booked, it was exactly as we had expected and we would have enjoyed ourselves there I'm sure, but it was easy for us to recognise that we had been blessed above and beyond in the provision of Villa Danae and it had absolutely nothing to do with the Greek Goddess it was named after. We were to make Cyprus a holiday destination several more times in the coming years but the first was the best and a fitting memorial to Mum and Dad.

By the time we hit our fourth wedding anniversary we were thankful to find ourselves on a more even keel. We had visited the States a couple of times and seen the children in situ in their new home. It had been a challenging transition but they both rose well to the challenges they faced and we were so proud of them. I had accepted, at least as far as I was able, what was now the very strong possibility that we would not have children together. Acknowledging this actually brought some relief and although for a few years yet, there would be a smidgeon of hope that 'something would happen', it enabled me for the most part to put the thought out of my mind and get on with life.

As my strength was restored, I was able to do more and more and loved getting out and about visiting and getting involved with the pastoral life of the church. It was here that my own journey into prophetic ministry really began, encouraged by the prophetic words of others over me and some really good teaching. But now I was fitter I also began looking around for a regular part-time job that would get me out and into the world. It was harder than I thought and after a while despondency started to creep in. But God knows. One day, whilst eating his breakfast, Mike broke a tooth on a soft boiled egg. It was too ridiculous, but it was very definitely broken and at the front, and a dentist was required. An appointment was made and the tooth repaired and whilst he was waiting to pay his bill, Mike saw a notice propped on the reception desk. Dental Nurse required, full or part-time, please enquire. So he did, on my behalf and the lady on duty, who also happened to be the practice manager suggested that I give her a call to arrange to pop in for a chat. It had not crossed my mind to consider a job dental nursing, those days had been a lifetime ago, but something resonated in my spirit so I made the call and went in later that day. And when I left after an hour or so, having spent time with both the Practice Manager and its owner and Lead Dentist, I had a part-time job to go to. It was an odd feeling, in some ways it felt like a hugely retrograde step, but it also had such a 'rightness' about it and had presented itself in such a way that it seemed to have God's fingerprints all over it. On my first day, keen to make a good impression, I arrived way too early and as I sat in the car waiting for someone else to show up, I used the time to pray. Feeling a little nervous about fitting in, I 'presented my requests to God', finishing by asking for His peace for the day ahead, and as I felt it flood my soul I heard Him whisper four words that have since become my mainstay. 'Just be a blessing.' Over the next eighteen months, these words became the mantra that I repeated to myself often during any working day and that surgery became like the proving ground for everything that was to follow it going forward.

One joy was discovering that the dentist who had repaired Mike's broken tooth was a spirit-filled Christian and a member of a church that was known to us. It seemed confirmation to me that God's hand was in this placement, and however tested I might be at times, I was in His plan here. In fact, it was very much part of my healing and during the eighteen months or so I was there not only did I gain physical strength, I also learned a huge amount about forbearance and kindness and self-control. All lessons I was much in need of. Overall it was a hugely positive experience and I happily would have stayed indefinitely had there not been another curveball that was to have a defining and major impact on our lives. This time it involved Mike's mother, our one remaining parent, who for reasons that will become obvious, gets a chapter to herself.

Chapter 16

Mike's father had sadly died of cancer when Mike was just fifteen, and by the time I met her, his mother Jill had been widowed for twenty-eight years and living alone for many of them. She was a fiercely intelligent and fiercely independent woman who, though kindness itself at the core, did not suffer fools gladly. We warmed to each other immediately and getting to know her was a real pleasure. She was thrilled at the news of our wedding and the way God had brought us together. We saw a lot of one another during the three months of our engagement, and once we were married fell into a regular visiting routine, seeing her every couple of weeks for Sunday lunch. She was very present in our lives. It was a good thing; Mike's relationship with her over the years had been quite challenging for a number of reasons and this new start presented an opportunity for healing on both sides.

On the occasion of her seventieth birthday, about a year into our marriage, we took her out for a meal together with Mike's two younger brothers and their wives. We booked a table at a restaurant local to her home in Stanmore and she was greatly looking forward to the treat. It was a fun evening and we all enjoyed it although we noticed that despite all her smiles, Jill seemed a little distracted. It took her an age to decide what food she would like and then when the waiter came for the order, changed her mind several times before placing it. When the food arrived, she'd forgotten what she'd ordered and the whole evening she seemed, if not ill at ease, then just a bit unsettled. We dismissed it as an emotional response to a big birthday and for a while afterwards, her indecisiveness at the meal was a source of mirth for us when we all got together, with Jill laughing too, thankfully.

Sometime later during a Sunday visit to us, she made a very off-hand remark that she thought something was going wrong with her brain. It was a very strange thing to say and again we didn't attribute any degree of seriousness to it, but from then on we did begin to notice changes in her behaviour. The odd lapse of concentration, unusual levels of forgetfulness. On one occasion she arrived for lunch wearing a tea cosy on her head which she was adamant was a hat, and then she began to bring us gifts of things that she found lying around in her house, more often than not in the fridge, out of date jars of chutney and the like. Albeit quietly at first, alarm bells started to ring.

With her agreement a GP appointment was made, followed by an assessment at the National Hospital for Nervous Diseases in London and a referral to a Consultant Neurologist. Mike was with her throughout them all and returned home ashen from the last, having sat through the delivery of her diagnosis and the future prognosis. It was not good news. It was Alzheimer's disease and the pronounced outlook was bleak.

We were advised that in the short term, Jill would probably be able to manage quite well on her own with some support, but that it would be prudent, indeed necessary, to start making plans for the future, and we were keen that Jill herself be included as far as possible in that process. Whether she was really able to grasp what was happening or not, will always be debatable, but she was thankfully pretty sanguine about the inevitable changes that were to come and accepted with dignity that they were going to be necessary. For our part we informed ourselves as best as we were able, we read as much as we could find, we sought advice and we prayed. There were very soon only two options available to us, we either had to find Jill a place in a residential home equipped to care for dementia patients, or to take care of her ourselves. Despite the prognosis being so bleak and the time frame impossible to judge, we felt that it was important to consider her well being in 'real-time'. And in real-time she was a fairly young elderly lady, who although could easily become confused and forgetful also maintained periods of great lucidity. She was able to take care of her own personal needs and although she required a degree of supervision was able to manage well overall. The more we took everything into consideration, the less palatable the idea of placing her into a home became, and as a family we came to the decision that Mike and I would live with her and become her carers for as long as we were able.

Living in Stanmore was geographically untenable for us so there was upheaval all round at the start, as we amalgamated two houses and moved into a bungalow in the pretty village of Chalfont St Giles. Knowing that we had limited time, we had searched intensively to try and find the 'right' house, believing that we knew exactly what would suit us all best, but we just couldn't find what we were looking for. What became abundantly clear during this process, although we somehow managed to forget it time and time again, was that no matter what the problem, when we sought God before we sought a solution ourselves, He always provided the answer.

In this instance, it came in the shape of the first house that we'd viewed and had summarily dismissed because it didn't tick all of our boxes and was in a pretty poor state of repair. But at this viewing, unlike the first time, we could suddenly see its potential and began to imagine how we might adapt it to our needs. The timing of the sale of the Stanmore house and the purchase and renovation of this one dovetailed perfectly in the end, with a few faith-building opportunities built-in along the way. We resisted the very strong temptation to wobble and with the support of dear faith-filled friends, held fast to our trust in God for the way forward.

On a beautifully sunny spring day, full of good intentions and belief in what we were doing, we welcomed Jill into her new home. Ridiculously naive and in spite of all our research, I had imagined us living together harmoniously in this now beautiful house, sharing the space freely whilst respecting each other's privacy as far as possible. Resigning from my job to be at home with Jill full time, I had envisaged my role as her carer to be one of support, looking after her welfare and general well being, and that as family we would live companionably together. Within the first six weeks it became blindingly obvious that my imaginings were just that, and the reality of our situation was very different. Of course Jill didn't settle, she had undergone the biggest upheaval in her life for thirty years and we were the cause of it, and lucid enough still to recognise that, she was resentful and unhappy with us. During that short period, we were tried and tested and found wanting time and again as our reality completely failed to match our expectations. There were some sweet moments to be sure, but by the end of six weeks we were run ragged and beginning to doubt whether we had heard God well at all. Fortunately for us, His patience is limitless and just as we felt we were about to drown in a sea of good intent, He sent us a lifeboat in the shape of dear friends who lived around the corner.

Robbie and Colin, who were walking very closely with us on this journey and had already been a huge help and support, came round one Saturday morning when we were at our weakest, insistent that they talk to us. The previous night Robbie had a dream which she thought maybe a key for us, and knowing how we were struggling, was determined to share it. Thank God for true friends who are prepared to not take offence even when the opportunity is handed to them on a plate. I was not at my best, I was tired, sullen, angry, disappointed and confused and I absolutely did not want to spend time hearing about a dream, I was just done with it all. She pressed on regardless, and a stern look from Mike put me firmly in my place until she was finished. In her dream she had seen a removal lorry outside of our house, moving us out lock, stock and barrel and then driving away. 'Great, thanks', I thought, compounding my self-pity. Then, she went on to explain, in the dream she saw the lorry return and move us back in again but in a slightly different arrangement, Mike and I moving into number 9 and Jill to 9a. One of the earlier extensions to the house had been a granny annexe comprising bedroom, bathroom, hall, kitchen and sitting room. When we originally viewed it, this had been converted to three bedrooms and a bathroom, and in our own redesign,   had become a bedroom, bathroom, study and living room. But everything was still there and it even had its own front door. It was 9a.

The tiniest chink of light started to appear. I was reminded of accompanying Jill to an optical appointment at the London Eye Hospital just after she was diagnosed. It was pretty clear to the optometrist we saw that she was struggling to answer the questions asked of her and in the end the examination had to be abandoned, but it prompted the optometrist to share a little of her experience with her own mother, who was also suffering from dementia. In general her Mother was managing quite well, but ran into difficulties every time she had to make a decision, for example which room she wanted to be in, or which handbag to take if they were going out, her inability to choose causing her to become disproportionately distressed. Their solution had been to restrict the choice. They moved her into a small one-bedroom apartment and had confiscated all of her handbags bar one and had seen immediate change. She was calm and seemingly content and had never questioned once where she was or indeed, where all her handbags were.

As we pondered Robbie's dream and prayed, we realised that God had lead us from the outset, to a property that had been designed for the purpose we required of it, which at the time, so fixated on our own ideas, we had missed completely. Here He was, ever patient, offering to us through Robbie, the blueprint that He would have given us directly had we but asked.

We had created a beautiful house but it was a labyrinth, every visitor getting confused at some point about which door lead to where. We realised that much of Jill's restless wanderings probably resulted from her simply being unable to navigate the space, coupled with the fact that the space itself was too big. With humbled hearts we did a bit of re-arranging. Re-instating the kitchen in the annexe would have been too much of a hazard for Jill, whilst still in her own home there had been several incidences with appliances, from kettle to gas cooker, so instead the study became her dining room. We locked the interconnecting hall door from our side and moved Jill into 9a. It took me a while to come to terms with this, and I had to battle hard to overcome feeling like a gaoler, but Jill didn't bat an eyelid. As the optometrist had found with her own mother, the reduction in space was much more manageable and her acceptance of it easy. It truly was a Godsend and the lifeboat we needed to bring us into calmer waters and safely to shore.

As He had intended us to from the outset we all began to enjoy our new home. In His goodness He found a way to speak to us, even though, so caught up in our own self-reliance we had momentarily stopped listening for Him. What followed was another seven-year journey, full of challenges but hallmarked with huge favour and sustained by outrageous grace. During that time as Jill's condition gradually worsened, we watched her 'grow down' in every sense, and by journey's end our care was that required for a six-month-old baby inhabiting an eighty-year-old body; throughout it all, she was very present and although there were obvious changes, never once did we feel that we had lost her.

It was not an easy journey for any of us I suspect, and at times it was downright perilous but there were many sweet moments along the way and very many lessons learned by us. A major concern for me from the outset had been Jill's dignity, that we should fight to preserve it whatever the circumstances. This felt like a loving and valid concern, and I pursued it zealously, until one day I realised that actually it wasn't her dignity I was concerned about, it was my own. It began simply enough. Even at the beginning, there were days when her confusion was so great that simply getting herself dressed was a challenge, and it wasn't unheard of to find her fully dressed but with nothing in the right place. We laughed together on the day I found her with her underwear on the outside of her outfit but I was horribly embarrassed for her and she was laughing simply because I was, she didn't see the problem at all or have any desire to rearrange herself! Much later, when we found ourselves having to take care of her personal hygiene needs, I was desperate to afford her some modesty, and because that was practically impossible was always mortified afterwards, railing against how awful it all was. But the truth was the opposite. It wasn't awful for Jill, she had no concept whatsoever of being exposed or vulnerable, she simply submitted herself to a process that wasn't altogether unpleasant and after which she felt better, as we all do when bathed and clean and moisturised.

It quickly became apparent that for much of the time Jill lived in her own world and we weren't privy to the things she saw. This challenged our conversation as she would often remark on something that was completely ridiculous to us but as clear as day to her. She would sit in her living room looking at the lovely garden through the full-length windows and point at something we were blind to. She'd then tell us about the elephant or the giraffe or the plane flying across the sky being piloted by the pastor of her old church in Stanmore. Our immediate reaction was to try and explain that these things weren't real, through some misguided sense that it was important she understood, when the truth was it wasn't at all, and in fact the landscape she was seeing was much more interesting than ours. But it was hard to bear that this intelligent and erudite woman should be so denuded, and I let myself focus on how awful she would feel about herself if only she knew. But of course she didn't know and she was having great fun looking out at our suburban jungle, even if we couldn't see it.

One of our many helps in this journey was a day centre, run by the Red Cross which offered Jill a place every Thursday for a few hours, affording me a little break from what became relentless routine. My quest to preserve Jill's dignity was further stretched when she was brought home from her first visit with a carrier bag containing not only her clothes which had been soiled during the day but also a Pom-Pom, a ribbon and a somewhat ragged stuffed panda. I was embarrassed that I hadn't thought to send her with extra clothes to cover any accidents and thankful that the kind and attentive staff had kitted her out with spares, which they kept for the purpose of dealing with such things, but I was completely affronted by the toys. What were they thinking? I went to take them away and consign them to the bin when Jill grabbed the panda and started to cuddle it. Then she took the Pom-Pom and rolled it around and around in her hand, I was defeated. I settled her into her chair, left the piece of ribbon with her as well and retreated to the kitchen to try and make sense of it. When I took her tea fifteen minutes or so later, she was sitting chatting to the panda and stroking the ribbon, a picture of dignified contentment. Again, it was me who was offended on her behalf and my offence was of no good to her at all.

It took me way too long, but over time I began to understand that Jill's dignity was never in question. Her forbearance was amazing, she retained her ability to laugh at herself in adversity and in her lucid moments was always prepared to see the funny side. She may not always have been the most conventionally dressed but she wore well whatever she chose and with great poise and style. In the first couple of years she maintained her gift for conversation, even if the subject matter was visible only to her. She was in fact, one of the most dignified people I have ever met and that I got to serve her was nothing but privilege, whether it felt like it or not, and much of the time it didn't. The good thing was that as I began to understand that it was my problem, my preconceptions, prejudices even, that were causing most of our difficulties, I was able to bring them to God and allow Him to work in me to change them. And faithful as He always is, He did.

The toys in fact played a serious role in maintaining Jill's well being. She spent hours chatting with the panda and I imagine she imagined it talked back. She was interacting and communicating and whilst it had the air of the ridiculous about it, what did it matter if she was happy. Instead of continuously and hopelessly trying to keep her in our reality, we began to understand that the key was in embracing her unravelling, rather than fighting it. With God's help we were able to change our perspective and rejoice in what we had, realising that what was important was our communication, not the subject matter; that we could interact, not what we did. It had zero to do with dignity and everything to do with honour. And when the penny finally dropped, so did much of the tension we had been living in.

All of the help we received came to us at the right time and by the grace of God. He brought the right people from the right agencies alongside, just when we needed them and we continuously found favour and were blessed by their advocacy on our behalf. Time after time He inspired us with creative solutions to seemingly insurmountable problems, teaching us continuously that when we enquired of Him there was always a way, and generally when we didn't, there wasn't. There were many examples of this. Not long after we had moved Jill into the annexe, God gave me a picture of a rustic rope fence and a picket gate dividing the back garden. Mike ever practical, thought out the design and over a long weekend constructed it, delighting Jill with her own garden and a fence to stand and chat over with her 'neighbours', namely us. It also gave us outdoor space where we could sit privately and for which we were very thankful. Much further down the line when taking care of Jill's most personal needs had become necessary, He released to me, who had never ever designed or sewn anything more than the obligatory cushion cover in domestic science classes at school, a pattern for a sleep-suit, that was intensely practical but also stylish and comfortable and completely solved a very difficult and messy problem. The key always was enquiring of Him before we got into trouble.

It's easy to remember a key when you're struggling, less so when everything is running smoothly. At the stage where Jill was no longer mobile, we developed a routine for getting her out of bed and into the sitting room, where she spent much of the day. She was not a big woman, between us Mike and I were easily able to transfer her and it became a bit of a fun game getting from one room to the other. Of course, this was completely dependent on Mike being at home first thing and as far as possible he arranged his schedule to be so. There was a particular day when he was tied up on a job and completely unable to get back before lunchtime. Jill was happy, we went through the normal 'bed bath' routine, followed by breakfast in bed which she loved. Mealtimes were lengthy by then, very similar to feeding a toddler, and it was mid-morning before we knew it. Everything had gone well and I was feeling positive and capable and in good spirits, buoyed up by our progress. In that frame of mind it didn't seem right to me that she had to sit in bed until early afternoon, waiting for Mike to get home. After barely thinking it through and inspired by the self-righteous belief that I was doing a good thing, I decided to move her by myself. How hard could it be, I reasoned, we'd done it countless times together and I knew the manoeuvres. Swinging her legs out of the bed so that she was sitting on its edge, I positioned her arms around my neck. Then I bent my knees and braced my back, even in my confidence knowing that if she ended up on the floor I would not be able to lift her unaided. It actually was a very stupid thing to do and I think in that moment I knew it. Fortunately for me, God knew it too and at the moment of the lift that could have ended really badly, He sent angelic help. I didn't see anything but I certainly felt it, in my arms Jill was weightless, literally as light as a feather, and as I straightened my back my fear was that she'd shoot through the ceiling rather than end up on the floor! I literally carried her to the sitting room and settled her in her chair. She was laughing and I was crying and laughing and so very, very humbly thanking God for His goodness. Had I slowed myself down and enquired of Him before I made this reckless attempt, I am certain that He would have given me the wisdom to wait for Mike and infused me with peace about doing so. Jill was comfortable and happy and completely unaware of time, it was totally unnecessary to move her. But even in my bullish foolishness He was right there with me, an ever-present help indeed.

We knew things were probably drawing to an end about six months or so before they did. Although robbed of her mobility and speech and totally dependent on our care for her every need, Jill remained very much with us. As she regressed to what amounted to elderly babyhood, we learned how to communicate differently. At this stage I had overcome my antipathy towards the indignity of it all, recognising that what was important was our relationship, not what it looked like. Jill responded to touch and eyes and smiles and she often simply reflected back what she received. If I was grumpy, she would give me frowns and stares, if I was gentle and kind, affectionate and smiling then so was she. I tried to be this way all of the time, after all it made life much pleasanter for both of us, but I failed often. I can say that when this happened I always apologised to her and asked her to forgive me and in truth, this dear woman, so cruelly robbed of her faculties and in spite of it, always found a way to show me that she did. She could show forgiveness on her face, it was astonishingly humbling.

One day in early December we knew something was badly wrong. We had gone through our usual morning routine and Jill was sitting in her chair, now beside her bed, looking out at the garden which she loved. She had struggled to swallow her breakfast porridge but this had become a feature we were managing, and we weren't unduly concerned by it alone, but during the morning her breathing became laboured and although she didn't seem remotely distressed, we were, it was very loud. I rang our surgery and asked for a doctor to visit. They knew us well by now and were hugely supportive, a doctor was with us within minutes. Explaining the symptoms as I lead him to the annexe, I think he knew what he was coming to and deep down, so did I. He asked Mike to lift Jill from her chair and onto the bed so that he could examine her properly, and of course she really was as light as a feather by now so it was no problem. He took her in his arms like a baby and as he turned to lay her on the bed, she left. Straight from the arms of her son into the arms of Jesus. It was actually a beautiful moment. The doctor was wonderfully kind and patient, explaining to us what we had to do next and that there was absolutely no rush to do it. So when he'd left we sat with her for a good while before making the inevitable call to the undertaker.

We had said goodbye to our lovely spaniel Winnie about a year after our move, and there was a beautiful tender moment when her canine successor, Camber, a gorgeous whippet boy, jumped up onto the bed, lay down beside Jill and promptly went to sleep. He had joined us as a ten-week-old puppy and now six, had known her all of his life. He was content to lie beside her and it seemed fitting, she had really loved him. We named him in part after her father in law and Mike's Grandfather, Camile.

The funeral was arranged for the following week and having discussed how best to honour Jill, we felt it right to simply take it ourselves. There was no one closer and we desperately wanted it to be an uplifting occasion and a time of thanksgiving to God, as we knew she would also. Giving due honour in the twenty minutes allowed was a big ask but we did our best. No one was in any doubt by the end at our certainty of her eternal address. We exited to 'Happy Talk' from the musical South Pacific which was a favourite of hers, and so apt, knowing that she was now 'living the dream'. It was the hardest thing I had ever done and I only just held it together, but as I had rediscovered time and again in the previous seven years, it really is possible to do all things through Christ who strengthens us. A few days later I received a call from the undertakers inviting me to be included on their list of 'pet ministers', which I guess must say something. I declined, but Jill's wasn't to be the last funeral I was to conduct.

There was a lot of adjusting to do afterwards. Twenty four seven care is all-consuming and it took me some months to even be able to cope with the freedom that I thought I had craved. During our time together I had learned to live my own life in slots of twenty minutes and I found myself needlessly still rushing back home from anywhere I went. In fact the adjustment was so hard, that during it I began to rail against God. What had all that time, or at least the last couple of years when Jill was so completely dependant, actually been about? Why on earth had she been condemned to sitting in that chair, day after interminable day? What had been the point? She had given her life to Jesus years before, in fact one of our greatest privileges had been to see her baptised not long after we were married, she was saved. Why oh why Lord did you leave her to linger for so long? Of course the unspoken bit of the rant was, 'and take so much of my life looking after her?'.

One day a few weeks after the funeral, truly immersed in a trough of self-pity, I took Camber for a walk through the snowy fields not far from home. Even in this morass of misery, walking was where I met God best and I cried out to Him as I went, head down trudging through the snow. And as I bleated my heart out it was as though I saw jewels carpeting the ground where the light caught the ice crystals. Psalm 91 says that when we call, He answers and He did, and in my spirit I heard Him say in reply, 'Daughter, you still don't understand do you? Jill was already here, seated at my right hand. I left her with you for your benefit, that you might learn and come into deeper relationship with Me'. I stood rooted to the spot as my understanding cleared, and then I wept, really wept. Humble tears. Tears of joy. Tears of gratitude, that through it all He had been right there with us. And that while Jill sat seemingly purposeless and condemned to nothingness, she was in fact abiding in heavenly places and witnessing the jewel lined streets that she would eventually tread. No small wonder she had been so generous with her smiles.

This beautiful revelation brought me back to life and the plantings of what had been a very long winter season started to push through to spring. I settled my heart in the truth that whilst I served her, Jill my dear earthly mother in law, had served to bring me into deeper relationship than I ever imagined possible with my Heavenly Father and His Son and His Holy Spirit, I will be forever in her debt.

It was amazing and wonderful to receive revelation about Jill's journey's end and her future and I was immensely thankful and humbled by it, but even in the face of that certainty, it still took me a good six months to fully regain my equilibrium. It seemed that without her to care for my life had lost its purpose and I really did lose my way for a while. I can remember a day Mike and I took Camber for a walk in beautiful Chiltern woodlands and following a very slight and completely inconsequential disagreement over the map and a footpath, totally breaking down and turning into a gibbering wreck hugging a tree. Poor Mike was at a loss as to how to help me as I literally wailed my heart out. It took us both by surprise and left us wondering whether I should seek out some post bereavement help. But again, God in His goodness provided it before we even had a chance to look, and from an unlikely source at that. The following Sunday at church we listened to our assistant pastor bring a message which shifted everything for me. To my embarrassment, I don't even remember the content, but I vividly remember what happened in light of it. As I was listening with my ears to the voice preaching from the front, my spirit was caught by the still small voice inside, coaxing me out of the doldrums and back to life. That afternoon, and again walking Camber together, I followed Mike along a footpath we knew well, and without any consideration or forethought I heard myself saying to him, 'How would it work if I was to join you in the business?'. Following so quickly on the heels of my outburst a few days before, it stopped him in his tracks but as he turned to face me he could see from my expression that something had happened. We walked and talked for hours, Mike sharing that he had been hoping against hope that somehow this option might cross my mind at some point. Working together made huge sense, to maximise our potential and reduce the need to subcontract work away to other drivers.

Mike had actually been working as a subcontractor himself, until a couple of years before when he sensed a prompting from Holy Spirit to step out on his own. He had spent most of his working life employed by a major bank and had become disillusioned, grabbing voluntary redundancy when it was offered, but not before he had been totally imbued with an employee mentality. The idea of setting up a company himself was almost anathema to him, but Holy Spirit impelled, he grasped the nettle and did just that. He received his first booking before he finished delivering the flyers and after that, it had never stopped. He always had more work than he could handle and now Holy Spirit was impelling me to help him in it. As a concept it made perfect sense but practically it wasn't quite so easy to understand. The job in essence was driving, I'd been driving for years, how hard could it be? But this wasn't giving lifts to the airport for friends flying off on holiday, or picking up teenage kids from parties, this was providing five-star chauffeuring services to some top dollar folk, who were paying top dollar for the privilege. Although now a very long time ago, it had taken me five attempts to pass my driving test and even then I was helped by my doctor, who understanding how much I needed my licence to work, prescribed Valium to get me through it. I finally did, but hardly to a ringing endorsement from the Examiner, who at the end passed me with the words, 'I'm going to give you the benefit of the doubt'. Although I had learned to drive fairly well in the intervening years, I'd lost a lot of confidence during the time M.E. rendered me immobile and since my recovery had really only driven very locally and hardly ever with passengers. I also had and still have a problem reversing, I joke that it's an aversion to going backwards, but I do really have a difficulty in processing the direction of the steering wheel in relation to the actual wheels of the car if I'm physically looking over my shoulder, and only manage by relying on the rearview mirror. It works but is far from pretty and usually requires many corrections. Mike however foresaw no problems or at least, saw ways to overcome any that there might be and buoyed by his confidence in me, I agreed to give it my best shot. The licensing process and the local authority testing was a bit of a trial, the idea that I might fail a test to drive a private hire vehicle challenged my pride more than my local knowledge, but I passed without difficulty and within a month I was all set and ready to go.

It had been so long since I had worn any smart clothes that I remember feeling great donning the suit that I'd bought for the purpose, but as I got into the car to collect my first client I was reminded of a time many years before when I had kitted myself out with a designer sports kit to play Squash, only to discover that I had no aptitude for it whatsoever! I prayed this wouldn't be a repeat. However, when we follow God's leading we can be sure of His help, and the job went well and without incident and I arrived home elated, to be welcomed by Mike who had made sure he would be around to affirm me. We didn't look back. We were both occupied, our income increased and our business grew. It wasn't rocket science but we were masters of our own time which was hugely important to us both. My workload was much less than Mike's but it was enough to provide a significant contribution and it was hugely satisfying to be doing something together. Mike was wonderfully creative with the jobs he put my way and as far as possible only sent me to places he'd already been himself, so that he could brief me on any tricky manoeuvring that might be required. Always prepared, I was able to overcome any reversing challenges without the client in the car and save myself from embarrassment and them from fear! What I lacked in driving expertise, I made up for in PR. It was not difficult to judge whether a client wanted to talk or not and if they did, in my 'role' I found it easy to make conversation. Mike was continually amazed and would joke that I learned more about a client in twenty minutes than he had learned over years of driving them, and it was gratifying to discover that the years of sales training hadn't amounted to nothing after all. Once again God had given us a blueprint and blessed us richly as we followed it.

Chapter 17

Before we moved to Chalfont St Giles we had begun to feel unsettled in our church life and sensed that it was probably time to move on. We had visited a church in Hemel Hempstead on several Sunday evenings, having received notification about guest speakers who we were keen to hear and it seemed a very natural migration to plug ourselves in there, it was clear that we carried the same heart and values. It took a little while for us to fully settle, interrupted by our move which placed us a good forty minutes away, and made us wonder if we should look again closer to home. This we did but agreed that even with the distance, it felt 'right' and from that point on we dug into life as part of the Hemel Hempstead Community Church family.

It was a wonderful place to root. A real amalgam of folk from diverse backgrounds, all passionate for Jesus and committed to growing faith and family together. In it we found a place where we were both able to stretch our wings, Mike quickly becoming part of the worship team and over time me being released to pray, prophecy and preach.

Years earlier, back at St Andrew's and before we met, we were both deeply touched by the ministry of John Arnott and what became known as the Toronto Blessing, released through his church in Canada. He had visited to minister in Chorleywood several times and we had been to other meetings where he was speaking, each one marked by the presence and power of Holy Spirit, with testimonies of restoration, healing and salvations following. In the ensuing years

HHCC became a regular landing place for Catch the Fire Ministries and the European hub for Partners in Harvest, the associated network of churches that grew out of it. Twice a year leaders came in from all over the globe to spend four days together in the presence of God and each other, to join in worship, be encouraged and grow in faith and relationship. As the host church, we had the huge privilege of getting to serve at these conferences and we eagerly drank deep of all that was available. We have often reflected on how amazingly blessed we have been in our church life; to have experienced first hand the ministry of such giants of the faith in the places we have called home, is treasure indeed. And treasure that we continue to cherish.

Over the preceding years, many prophetic words had been spoken over me about moving in a prophetic gifting myself and early on in particular, specifically in the area of personal prophecy. I had always been intrigued by these and during the early years at HHCC began to take baby steps of faith, spurred on by the encouragement of leaders more concerned with allowing Holy Spirit to move than they were with the smooth running of a meeting. Faltering steps were dealt with gently and any falls with a helping hand back up. It was a really affirming place to grow and what had initially been intrigue on my part became a genuine hunger for more. I fed greedily on the teaching brought twice yearly at the PIH conferences and sought out other opportunities to hear prophetic ministers share their knowledge and experience. The bible tells us to eagerly desire the spiritual gifts, especially the gift of prophecy (1 Cor 14:1), and elsewhere to ask for the things we desire, so I did both, and unsurprisingly, because God is always faithful to His word and honours us when we are sincere, began increasingly to hear Him for other people. Whether it should have been or not, it was a wonderful surprise to me and continues to be so, even though I have now been ministering in prophetic encouragement for years. Witnessing the response of someone who has just received a word from God spoken through me, referencing things about them that I could not possibly have known, amazes me still. That I, who spent so many of my former years lying to achieve my goals should be entrusted to steward such a gift well, is nothing short of astounding and a constant reminder of my Heavenly Father's kindness and His redemptive work in my life.

I wish I could honestly say that it is a gift I have always handled with the utmost care, but sadly I can't. There have been occasions when I have released a word ahead of His permission for example, and then have had to accept that in so doing I have robbed the receiver of some or even all, of the blessing of it. Equally a directive word given 'out of time' can be positively dangerous and very costly, and I have to admit occasionally my growth has come at the expense of others in this respect. Thankfully whenever this has happened, Holy Spirit has been swift to rebuke and I have been able to make amends if only by confession and apology to the person or people concerned. It is a hugely sobering thought to recognise that your own mismanagement, whatever the reason for it, has cost someone their blessing and even worse, robbed God of the glory due to Him. These days I tread with the greatest care but remain so conscious of the fact that I am always only one step away from error. Prophecy is a marvellous gift, but it is a heady one and scripture contains many hazard warnings to be heeded for its safe use.

HHCC was a great nest to learn to fly from and it was our home for many years in the learning. Although a few of my fledgling attempts were less than glorious, the family there were always ready to encourage me back out to try again, and so was Mike, who released me generously from work commitments whenever appropriate ministry opportunities arose. It wasn't always an easy balance. I remember returning home late one night after being part of a ministry team at a German weekend conference, where I had been generously, if ridiculously, referred to by the main speaker as a world-level prophet, to discover that because he needed to and I was available, Mike had scheduled me to do an airport pick up the following morning. I was not best pleased. I showed my true colours the next day making my early exit from a church leaders' meeting to go to the job, departing with a flounce, an exaggerated sigh and the comment, 'I don't know, world-level prophet one day, taxi driver the next!' In fairness I said it with humour but deep down somewhere it betrayed my pride, and all these years later it still makes me blush to remember it. It is well that it does, pride and prophecy do not mix! I was to drive a 'taxi' for a good few years yet.

Holidaying in Cornwall became an annual event not long after we had moved to Chalfont St Giles. After a long slow learning curve, we finally recognised that we were better suited together in a coastal cottage with dog in tow, than on a beach in the Mediterranean, and for some reason I didn't understand, it was always Cornwall that beckoned. I had been there four times, twice on family holidays with my parents as a child and twice in my early twenties on jaunts with friends. None had been desperately successful, friction with my mother dominated the family trips, the other two occasions both marred by testy relationships of one sort or another, so it was not nostalgia that drew me back. Our first stay was at Port Isaac in a cottage situated right on the cove. It was February and winter storms were still raging, the waves literally broke against the downstairs windows on a high tide, as we sat snuggled under blankets with a fire raging. From there we explored North Cornwall and over the next few years worked our way down through the county basing ourselves in Pendeen, Mousehole, Porthleven and then round to Mylor and Restronguet on the South Coast. Every time and in every place at some point I would find myself saying, 'I could live here' and without doubt at each visit, I fell more and more in love with the place. And always we would meet someone who would tell us that they had come to Cornwall on holiday, stayed and made it their home, thereby watering a little seed that had been planted in me way back in the sixties somewhere near Mounts Bay. The drive home at the end of each holiday was always a huge wrench and I would spend much of the five-hour journey rationalising away what was becoming my dream. It was too far away, too remote, too seasonal, arguably too the very reasons for wanting to be there. The high summer would be

221

impossible, the traffic too slow, a laughable objection for someone living practically on the M25. But by the time we reached Reading, I'd normally managed to talk myself awake and was prepared to settle back into reality, which I always did.

Jill having left for her heavenly home and me adjusted to her going and settled in our business, it was time for us to think about our own options. The house in Chalfont St Giles needed significant work and in any case was not entirely in our ownership, we had consolidated everything to move there and it now formed part of Jill's estate, so we had decisions to make. It was tough, we enjoyed the village and had made good friends, but in the end, we had to accept that it was not going to be financially viable for us to remain there and we put the house on the market. During this time, which was actually hugely difficult for both of us, we strengthened and sustained our faith with the word of God from the second book of Samuel 7:10 which we printed out and stuck on the fridge and proclaimed every time we saw it, 'And I will provide a place for my people Israel and will plant them so that they can have a home of their own and no longer be disturbed'. We appropriated the promise and clung fast to it. It was a bumpy few months and we found ourselves challenged in many areas, not least of which for me was my entitlement. However much I tried to deny it, I eventually had to admit that I really did think that the years I had 'sacrificially' given to caring for Jill had earned me rights. Nonsense of course, all of it. There was no sacrifice, I had made a conscious and informed decision to serve Jill and in doing so had reaped blessings that hugely outweighed the harder moments, which in themselves had all been overcome by God's grace. The only right I had earned was to remain in thankfulness for all His goodness and to rejoice that we had all survived the experience relatively well. But I was too full of pride to see any of this and as pride will always do, it tied me in knots that took some time to unravel.

However, eventually, unravel they did and I was humbled to discover that even in all my sullen anger and disagreeableness, my husband continued to love me and our Heavenly Father to make a way for us. I repented, forgave and received forgiveness and we began to look in earnest for a new place to plant ourselves. Although from a business point of view it made little sense to us operationally, we decided to look closer to church in Hemel Hempstead. It was where we spent most of our time anyway and it did make sense that we were more available to participate in the day to day life of the fellowship. A new development under construction right on the edge of the town caught our eye. It appealed on several levels not least being that its position gave us easy access to the M25, so important for our business to function well. Our initial attempt to secure the show home property there, fell through with a crash when we were unable to sell the house in Giles within the very short time frame demanded by the developers. Our disappointment was tempered with relief at not having to commit ourselves to a substantial mortgage, and we continued to look at houses within our outright purchase range over the next few months, whilst we waited for a buyer to appear for No. 9. Whilst our searches yielded nothing suitable, a buyer in a good position to complete quickly did appear for our house and offered the asking price. We felt duty-bound to accept in order that the estate be settled, which for a short time left us with no idea of what we should do next, and then a marketing email popped up in our inbox for the final available house in the first phase of the development on the edge of Hemel, that we had looked at originally. We revisited. It was slightly bigger than the showhome and in a much better position, with a forward view over a communal green area that bordered the canal. I loved it and although I thought it a curious design for a family home with more bedrooms than living space, it would be perfect for the two of us and give us the ability to be able to comfortably host visitors at any time. We could both see it working but for one snag, it was way over our budget without significant borrowing. The agent was prepared to put a reserve on it for us for only a short time and we were both very quiet as we drove home, me trying to talk myself out of disappointment and into accepting that you can't always get what you want. Mike however had already made a decision, and motivated by his deep desire to provide me with the home that I wanted, and filled with a confidence that could only come from God, was preparing himself to call the bank. It was no small thing. Mike was fifty-seven, completely debt-free and self-employed. We needed a mortgage of £100k, the maths are not pretty. He was strong and very courageous and he blessed me beyond measure in his willingness to take this seemingly ridiculous step for my happiness, but we were both blessed in even greater measure by God who just a few years later made complete sense of it all for us.

It almost didn't happen, the timings in the end came right down to the wire and we literally had to dash to the developers to sign the contract with only minutes to spare. Thankfully we made it, and one Thursday in mid-June 2012 we uprooted from leafy Chalfont St Giles and re-potted ourselves in Hemel. Among our possessions was a blue ceramic planter containing a beautiful red rose called In Loving Memory, which we had bought two years before and planted in Jill's.

It was a roller coaster of a summer. We were booked to attend a Fatherheart Conference in the Netherlands, being held on a tall ship, sailing out of Harlingen and around the Waddensee for five days and commencing two days after our move. We'd both been looking forward to it for months and were determined to go, but I have to confess it was a stretch for me. The house was still in chaos with much of the unpacking left to do and it had become abundantly clear on moving day, that although we had already filled several skips in our downsizing efforts, there was still much left that needed sorting. It challenged me enormously to simply let it wait. Coupled with that, moving had left me emotionally drained which I understood, and physically really tired, which I didn't at first. It was only in the car on our way to the Channel Tunnel on Saturday morning, that it occurred to me that moving from a bungalow to a three-storey house might have something to do with it. I had climbed more stairs in the last two days than I had in the preceding ten years, no wonder I was aching!

Once we were on the train I relaxed a little but in honesty, I was not at my best and wrestled with my attitude throughout. Fortunately the host couple were absolutely amazing and treated me gently and with much grace. Towards the end of the conference, convicted that I should apologise for my own ungraciousness, I asked if I could have a word with them. Their response to my admission that I recognised I'd been a bit of a problem was an arm around my shoulder, a warm smile and the words, 'There are no problems, only solutions', spoken in that delightful Dutch accent that softens every 's' to 'sh'. It has since become a legendary phrase for us, whenever we face difficulties, especially with ourselves! Despite my behaviour, we made some good friends on that trip and although I couldn't see it at the time, I know that God was at work on my heart throughout.

Chapter 18

Arriving back in Hemel we hit the ground running, getting straight into work and arranging the house into at least a more organised sort of chaos. We'd been home about a week when we received a call from the couple who had bought the house in Giles, who in turn had received a call from the Queens Medical Centre in Nottingham, requesting us to contact them urgently about a patient they'd admitted a few weeks earlier, who they thought might be my brother. I rang immediately to discover that indeed their patient was Karl, and that he was very seriously, possibly gravely ill. It was a fraught dash up the M1 the following morning. At the last visit I made to that hospital, I was greeted by my brother who told me that my father had died twenty minutes earlier, and that association and the uncertainty of what would be waiting for me this time with Karl himself as the patient, were uncomfortable travelling companions.

Karl and I were very different people and although deeply and closely bonded emotionally had not been easy company for one another since my early twenties. Our paths had diverged as he immersed himself in perpetual studenthood and I pursued career and money, and although we had re-established our relationship on much firmer ground since Mike and I married, it wasn't always easy. Karl had been sceptical and then intrigued when I gave my life to Jesus. Finally convinced that I had not been swallowed up into some awful cult, he had begun to research the bible for himself but his approach never got past the purely intellectual and he quickly faltered. He watched the transformation in me and was amazed from a distance but he was completely unable to grasp the fact that it was available for him too. We had many long and frank discussions and I withheld nothing of my testimony from him, he even admitted his belief that I had experienced something of God and that he could see there was relationship, but without that experience first hand he was not willing to commit himself. Sadly he satisfied his need for 'experience' in other ways, pushing himself away even further from the truth. On my part, I doubt I was as understanding as I could have been and not yet at the point of recognising that I still had sibling issues that needed addressing, was often too harsh and judgemental. It had been over a year since we had seen each other, although we had spoken several times by phone. As I tramped through the labyrinth of hospital corridors to find the ward, I realised that our last conversation had been nearly six months earlier and felt a stab of guilt that I had been so caught up in our own situation, I was mindless of his. Eventually in the right location, I was shown to Karl's bed by a kindly nurse who would answer no questions herself but said she would arrange for the doctor to see me as soon as possible. The man in the bed, who only vaguely resembled my brother, was sleeping, and I was thankful for the few minutes this gave me to compose myself. He was shrunken, all skin and bone, yellow in pallor and clearly horribly ill. Even to my untrained eye, it was obvious that whatever was wrong must have been wrong for some time, and what had been a mere stab became a wave of guilt that threatened to overwhelm me as I sat there. Thankfully he opened his eyes before it could and although not exactly lucid, he obviously recognised me and gave a weak smile and a shrug that looked something like resignation. The Doctor showed up before too long and suggested that we go somewhere private to talk and I followed him feeling strangely like a frightened child, about to be scolded.

It was more of an interrogation than a scolding, completely understandable given the circumstances, borne out of concern and in no way unkind. It had taken nearly six weeks for Karl to admit to them he had a sister, and I was yet to contact him and give him our new address and number, so the details he had for me were out of date.

I can understand how it must have seemed a little suspect. Karl lived alone and had finally called an ambulance on the morning that he was unable to get himself out of bed. He had first consulted his GP about a really painful back a few months before and after preliminary tests had been referred to an oncologist for further investigation. From that point he had failed to keep his appointments. Tests carried out since his admission to hospital had shown advanced stage 4 cancer of the spine with metastases to lungs and liver.

My reaction to appalling news has always been to step outside of my emotional self and become intensely practical and pragmatic. No doubt I seemed a little cold to the young doctor when I simply stated the obvious, 'he's dying isn't he?' But he must have seen something of my heart in my face, because when he answered me he was so full of compassion that I broke down in front of him. He sat with me and let me cry, organised tea and then offered to answer any questions I might have, which I am sure he knew at this point would only amount to one, and that would be the one he couldn't answer definitively. He thought weeks rather than months and maybe not many of them. He referred me to the Macmillan team who he thought would be helpful and then explained that as the only treatment available was palliative, Karl would have to be discharged in the next few days and admitted into an end of life care facility that would be found for him locally. Reassuring me that he would be available until then should I have further questions, the Doctor took his leave and I returned to my brother, acutely aware that every conversation we would have from this point could influence his eternal address.

Karl was awake although a little confused and with more than a hint of paranoia in his conversation. He talked about conspiracy theories and being careful of what we said, as everything was recorded, but he also understood where he was and that he'd been there some time. The nursing staff assured me that the 'mind games' were a side effect of the strong medication and not abnormal, which eased my mind a little, and I tried to steer our conversation as gently as I could on to better things. I remember a really poignant moment when Karl leaned towards me and said, 'I don't think I'm going to get out of this one Liz', in all love I was able to answer him honestly and talk to him of Jesus and the open arms of the Father who was waiting to welcome him home, if only he would choose to go that way. He looked at me and sighed.

Several days later he was moved to a nursing home a few miles away and into his own room where he was much happier. He had never been much of a nester but at his request, I collected a few things from his flat which made the stark room more familiar, and I took in a CD player so that he could listen to the music that he had always so loved. It was a measure of the man, that even in such dire straits he could recognise the lack of sound quality and although he did listen to some audiobooks he avoided the music! My heart broke when I saw the state of his flat. To say it was squalid would be an understatement and I was mortified that he could have been brought so low to be existing in this way. The last time we had spoken he had seemed upbeat and untroubled but clearly that had not been the case. I was to discover later that he had been made redundant from his job around that time and could understand that it had probably hit him very hard. The idea of a 'normal working life' had been anathema to him until his mid-fifties when this job had come along. He surprised himself by enjoying both it, and the reality of a steady income, which enabled him to do more than he had ever done before. The loss would have been a blow. How long he had been feeling unwell I didn't know but it made sense that the events coincided and he simply stopped taking care of himself. All this stirred a tumult of emotions in me and left me feeling a complete failure as a sister, especially as a sister who understood salvation. It took much prayer and wise counsel to help me see that whilst undoubtedly I could always have done more, ultimately the responsibility was not mine to bear and worrying about it would only serve to diminish the time that we had left.

I travelled to Nottingham pretty much on alternate days from then on, to spend time with Karl and also to try and locate any friends he might have who would want to support him. Mike had suggested that it might be easier on me if I stayed in a hotel and cut out the travelling, and undoubtedly it would have been, but I just couldn't face being by myself at that time.

If our father had been an intensely private man, his son was even more so, but with his permission, I managed to contact a couple of his friends who were then able to speak to him by phone and to write, always Karl's preferred way of communication. He was grateful for the cards that he received and read and re-read the thoughtful messages they contained. Once in the nursing home, he didn't leave his bed other than to visit the bathroom and he was unable to manage that unaided for long. Our conversations were short and fairly stilted, due mainly to the heavy medication which alleviated his pain but often robbed him of his consciousness. I sat for hours just quietly reading from the Word and praying that he might encounter God in these times, and conscious or unconscious, each time I visited I read the Father's Love Letter over him, in faith that he would receive it.

The staff at the home were wonderful, it was a pretty grim place but their overall good humour and kindness brought it to life and I had no doubt that Karl was well cared for. We had prayed that he might be nursed particularly by someone who knew and loved the Lord and on a visit about a week after he was admitted, I met Anna. Karl was sleeping when she burst into the room, larger than life and singing a worship song I recognised in full voice. She quietened as soon as she saw me, but not before I had registered that here was a woman who clearly did know and love the Lord. She was a glorious answer to prayer and having not long before read Wm Paul Young's 'The Shack', it was not lost on me that God would bring alongside my brother a huge West Indian woman who saw sharing the love of God with her patients as the mainstay of her job. Of course, she was strictly forbidden to do this under institutionalised politically correct house rules, but she was fearless about her faith and was never deterred or somewhat amazingly, detected. Meeting her and knowing that Karl was in her care whenever she was working, was a huge relief to me. He may by then have not been eating much, but I knew that he was being fed with the word of God and I was full of faith that he would digest it.

A couple of weeks before we were due to leave for our annual Cornwall holiday and not at all sure whether we should go, the manager of the home called to let me know that Karl seemed to be deteriorating fast. Fortunately I was able to leave immediately and barrelling again up the M1, I prayed that I would not be too late. By the time I arrived he had rallied a little and she was apologetic about the urgency of her summons, but I was simply relieved to be there. I stayed at his bedside throughout the day and for most of the evening, quietly chatting to myself, reading, praying as Karl drifted in and out of consciousness. He knew I was there I'm sure, although he gave no response beyond a blink and a slight upturn of his lips. It was obvious even to me that things were coming to a close, but the doctor on duty explained gently that it was impossible to predict exactly when and that we could still be looking at days rather than hours. By the time the night shift arrived around 9:00pm I had made the decision to go home and return the next day, and I was so thankful when Anna came into his room as his overnight nurse. Completely non-judgemental when I told her my plans, she released me to leave, assuring me that she would be vigilant in her watching. I said goodbye to Karl, not believing that it would be for the last time but knowing that it might be.

Arriving back home around 1:00am and dog tired, I slept through the call from Anna at around 4:00. I woke naturally a couple of hours later and seeing she had left a voice mail immediately rang the home. Thankfully she was not quite at the end of her shift and was able to take my call personally. Karl had died at 3:33, she had been at his bedside and praying through Psalm 23. He had passed quietly and in complete peace. She went on to share that in her experience, it was not unusual for the patient to seem to wait for relatives to leave before departing themselves, and knowing his reluctance to cause fuss, this made some sense to me and eased my ache at having made the decision not to stay.

When our call was over and having arranged to visit one last time to collect Karl's few belongings, I was prompted to look up a scripture. John 3:16 is possibly the most well-known verse of all, but Father lead me to verse 33. In it, John the Baptist says of Jesus, 'The man who has received His testimony, has certified that God is true'. Karl had breathed his last at 3:33 that morning. It was enough. As had been the case with my mother and then also my father, I didn't hear my brother 'pray the prayer', but as with them, I knew only a deep deep peace at his leaving and was filled with hope for his eternal future. The kindness of God knows no bounds.

It was enough, but there was more to come. The next couple of weeks were taken up with the myriad practicalities that need attention following a death. Registration, funeral arrangements, clearing out and closing up the flat. None easy, but carried on a tide of grace it all came together without too many hitches. Whilst Karl had been at the nursing home I'd been able to make contact with a couple of friends from his Cambridge days, one of whom kindly took over contacting others, and having originally been concerned that his funeral would be a sorry affair, there was now a good group wanting to gather and pay their respects. Karl had been a gifted and enthusiastic musician since his teens, and music was a cord wrapped around practically all of his relationships, so it seemed natural having discovered all these folk, some of whom I vaguely remembered, to ask if any might like to bring a musical tribute in his memory.

The funeral itself was held at the Wilford Crematorium, a huge municipal site covering the South Nottingham district and where we had said our final goodbyes to my parents some years before, under the direction of our dear friend and pastor Tom. This time it seemed only right that I should lead the service myself and I was sure that it was what Karl would have wanted. I had had a dream a few nights before he died in which I saw him packing a rucksack and walking away, to the accompaniment of Peter, Paul and Mary singing

'Leaving on a Jet Plane'. Clearing out the flat, I found the rucksack and was reminded that he had rarely gone anywhere without it, so it seemed fitting to sit it atop the coffin, together with the beloved fiddle that had brought him and others so much pleasure. We entered the chapel to the strains of Sandy Denny's 'Who Knows Where the Time Goes' and left to Fairport Convention's 'Meet on the Ledge'. I spoke honestly in my short address, of the depth of our relationship despite our differences, of Karl's soft and gentle heart, sometimes disguised so well, of his response to my finding salvation and finally of my hope for his. One of his old university friends said a few words, and then another musical friend from Nottingham gave a rendition of Hooligans Jig, an old favourite for both of us from way back. Through smiles and tears everyone clapped as she finished, and someone said 'play it again', so she did. I doubt there are many encores played at funerals! I'm not sure that the chapel staff knew quite what to make of us but I was certain that Karl had a smile on his face. We retrieved the fiddle before the curtains closed on the coffin, but let the rucksack remain. It seemed appropriate, it had gone with him everywhere else. To my knowledge, Karl had never been on a jet plane, but reminded of the dream, I was thankful for the assurance it gave me that he was fully prepared for his journey.

We had arranged a small send-off at a pub in Ruddington, a village near our old family home, and everyone joined us there to spend a little time catching up and reminiscing. Mike and I had only really come to know them through this time, but we mixed well and we were so glad that we didn't simply disperse after the ceremony. The landlady had given permission for us to make music, so the fiddle came out again. It was delightful and I know that Karl would have been astonished that it was all in his honour. One of the Cambridge crowd had even composed a tune for the occasion which he called 'A Waltz for Karl', it was beautiful and there wasn't a dry eye in the place as he played it. Later on, we decided that we should give him the fiddle in Karl's memory, knowing that he would want it to be played and cherished. I am sure it has been both.

In fact that same friend was compelled to contact us a couple of weeks after the funeral, to tell us about a dream he'd had that he felt was significant. In it he had heard a ringing phone and on answering it, heard Karl's voice saying 'hello'. In the dream his response had been to ask who it was, and hearing Karl's voice again saying, 'it's me, Karl', had replied, 'but it can't be you, you're dead!'. 'Oh don't worry about that' Karl laughingly replied, 'that sort of thing is always happening around here'. It seemed like yet another gift of assurance to me and I received it thankfully, explaining it as best I could. It gave great pause for thought to the dreamer, another hugely clever scientist, who I hope by now has been able to find the truth in it for himself.

It had been a mark of Karl's life that anything he undertook should be with the least possible amount of fuss. He had made his departure three weeks before we were due to leave for Cornwall enabling us to take the holiday which by now, we really both needed. We were grateful. It had been a hard summer but we had seen much goodness in it and welcomed the opportunity to take some time to relax and process. I was desperately sad that things had become so hard for my brother and at the same time hugely thankful that he was now out of pain, free and in joyful wonder at his new surroundings.

Chapter 19

As it always had done, the break in Cornwall did us good and although there were still a few loose ends to tie when we returned home, we felt sufficiently restored to step into the new life in Hemel that we hadn't yet really been able to establish since we moved. We sorted the house out and met with friends, hosted a few visitors and fell into what would become a normal pattern for a while. It was fun discovering our new surroundings, and we were pleasantly surprised at quite how much countryside was still on our doorstep, despite our now distinctly urban address. Whilst I had been so consumed with events in Nottingham, Mike had been hard at work marketing our business and was seriously blessed to discover that not only were we very capable of maintaining our existing client base, which we had thought might become a geographical challenge, there were countless opportunities to expand it locally. He simply used the blueprint God had released to him at the outset and applied it again, and it began to bear fruit just as quickly as it had the first time. Actually, the development where we lived became home to many business people who then became our clients. Although always aware that we had a sizeable mortgage and needed to work hard, we were able to easily let go of the burden of it, trusting God as our provider. Life was good and although we weren't certain of how things would unfold long term, we determined to live it well where we were.

Years before, whilst we were still caring for Jill, I had received a prophetic word from a highly respected minister at a weekend conference in Wrexham. The whole thing had been a treat, Mike releasing me to attend and arranging for carers for his mother, but it was way more than that. The word itself was one of those 'to the moon' words, that seemed so completely impossible to be laughable, but as I listened to the recording afterwards and again and again in my hotel room, it seemed like I had been handed a precious gift that however outlandish it might seem in that moment, I must absolutely not despise. So I prayed, thanking God and giving Him my 'yes', not simply to the bits I could identify with but to all of it, in its entirety. Returning home, I shared the word with Mike, with whom it also resonated and with our Pastors for their discernment and my accountability. After about a week and the first flush of excitement, embroiled back into 'normal' day to day life, not seeing any way at all that any of this word could be fulfilled any time soon, I put the tape into a drawer with a sigh. Back then my expectation was still skewed towards disappointment and although a little flicker of hope in my 'yes' remained, it took some time for me to fan it back into flame.

At the Partners in Harvest Spring conference held at HHCC, more than a year after we had said goodbye to Jill, God reminded me of this word. I'd hurried home at lunchtime on the second day to take Camber for a walk, thinking how inconvenient it was that I had to, when I heard that still small voice whisper very loudly in my ear, 'When you go back this afternoon, I want you to introduce yourself to someone from Germany'. My first response was way less than enthusiastic and then He reminded me that part of the word given to me in Wrexham, had been about ministry in Germany. Remembering this, my second response was simply abject fear. I had no grid for this and no idea how to make an approach to an unknown German, that would make any sense to them and not seem outrageously arrogant. Fortunately for me, I am more moved by my awe of the Lord than my fear of man and after a little wrangling, I again gave Him my yes. However, back at the conference, the afternoon was torture. There was no opportunity at the beginning of the meeting, nor in the tea break and sitting through the final session, that wet blanket feeling of disappointment began to settle itself on me. Here we go again I thought, not meeting the mark, never quite getting there. As the meeting closed I hovered around for a while but I just couldn't see a way forward and I walked dejectedly towards the door wearing my failure and self-pity like a coat. Thank God for those He puts around us at the right time. Bryan, a truly lovely man and our Operations Manager was standing by the door and touched me lightly on the arm, 'Are you ok Liz, you're looking a bit dejected?' I explained why, he took me by the shoulders, looked me in the eyes and said, 'oh that's no problem, I know Rainer, he's lovely, come on I'll introduce you' and with that he practically frog marched me to the front all smiles and laughter, and made the introduction. From then it was easy, Mike who was also around manning the sound desk, joined us, and very soon we had agreed that I would go as a delegate to a PIH conference in Germany to be held a few weeks later.

I have always loved travelling, but if God had enquired of me where I would like to go, Germany would not have been my answer. I have no connection there whatsoever, my memories of travelling there on business a lifetime ago, weren't wonderful and were mainly dominated by the discomfort of being stuck for a night at Frankfurt airport due to fog; so when I arrived at the conference, I was more than a little confused about why I was there. God is so faithful. During the next three days, He began to birth in me a love for that nation and its people that whilst I didn't understand it, astounded me. As did the opportunity to share a little of my testimony and to bring some prophetic encouragement to those gathered. It was a good few days and although I was certainly way out of my comfort zone, I felt embraced and affirmed. Connections were made and the seeds of friendship sown and on returning home I imagined it would springboard me into the fulfilment of Gods word from Wrexham, and braced myself for the invitations that surely would come flooding in. Except they didn't. However, encouraged by one of my spiritual fathers who was at the conference himself, I returned the following year, this time more as part of the team and on a firmer footing, and also more than a little abashed by my previous arrogance. There was still no flood, but there seemed to be an acceptance and as relationships were forged, ministry opportunities in different churches began. Each time I visited, my love for that nation and its people deepened and it has become a favourite place for me. One pastor, who has become a friend and whose church I have visited multiple times, remarked once that I 'carried something that enabled me to speak to the German people in a way they can receive without offence'. I was completely unaware of this but am seriously blessed and humbled to be able to do so. The connections in Germany also opened the doors to others in Europe, particularly in Belgium and The Netherlands. Reflecting on it as it unrolled before me, I came to more of an understanding of God's goodness to me in this, and why these places are of particular importance in my story. So many years before, back in my twenties, the Low Countries and Germany had been my territory as a computer hardware broker and I had spent two weeks out of every month over there for a time. Whilst always operating within the law, it was a business of sharp practice and often less than honourable, selling and taking payment for equipment not yet sourced and often not fulfilled within agreed time limits, sometimes causing huge pressures for the client. And here I was, re-born and being used by God to bring prophetic encouragement to people in those very nations! He is a redeemer indeed and it is not lost on me that yet again He should take something so broken in my life and mend it completely.

There is always more. One of the Dutch connections opened a door for me to spend some time in Kosovo, formerly part of Yugoslavia, and governed until 1992 by the Yugoslavian League of Communists. I had holidayed there alone back in the eighties, to the joy of my parents who imagined it might help me reset my political thinking, it didn't, but I remembered it fondly as a beautiful country and I was pleased to accept the invitation. Still reeling from the horrors of the Yugoslav war in the 1990s, Kosovo is now an independent state, building well for the future but still suffering from crushing poverty and deprivation and in desperate need of Jesus. What an honour to be used in that place to touch people with His love, bringing His truth through the ministry of the prophetic. One man gate crashed a ladies meeting and was told he could stay if he kept quiet and stood at the back. He gave his life to the Lord in that meeting. Another young man of eighteen, from a devout Muslim family, came to one meeting and the same night had an encounter with the person of Jesus in his bedroom. He returned the next day and gave testimony publicly, praying the prayer of confession with tears of joy. There were many testimonies of lives touched and restored and healed, and despite the language difficulties God always spoke in such a way that they were able to understand. I have visited since and it is always a huge blessing to me. Again, it seems redemptive, ministering at a church in a country considered by many to formerly have been part of the Eastern Bloc. Its significance is not lost on me.

As doors began to open for me to minister in Europe, other doors about which I had no idea at all began to appear on the horizon at home. We often hosted visiting speakers at HHCC and were blessed to have connections with many different ministries. Our Associate Pastor was chaplain to the Police Force in the town and one Sunday, towards the end of his tenure with them, an Officer who was chairman of the local Christian Police Association and a friend, was invited to come and minister to us. My past experience at the hands of the Police had been far from edifying and although I had received huge healing and deliverance from the trauma surrounding the incident back in my early teens, a residue of disaffection with them remained. This manifested itself in caustic remarks, in response for example to a news report, or following a patrol car on a blue light and suggesting with a sneer that they were late for their lunch perhaps. Not really serious in itself but not for nothing does the bible say that out of the overflow of the heart the mouth speaks (Luke 6:45). In this vein, I was not enthusiastic about hearing this man at all, but I was part of the leadership team and knew that I had a responsibility to be there, and taking that responsibility seriously I went with the best grace I could muster, and I am so thankful that I did. Keith preached a testimony based message centred around a well-known police axiom, 'every contact leaves a trace', and as he told story after story of how Jesus had used him to impact the lives of those he encountered during the course of his work as a traffic sergeant, something began to stir very deeply in my spirit. At the end of his talk and the powerful time of Holy Spirit ministry following it, I knew that I had a word from God to release over him and I found myself standing in front of this huge man, who represented an organisation that had been anathema to me for practically my whole life. Part of this word had to do with open doors and was wonderful, as unbeknown to me that very thing was actually happening in his life and the word carried huge confirmation for him. It also was to open a very unexpected door for me. As the service closed I realised I had been so impacted by his message that I wanted to be able to do something more, and as we were leaving I shared this with our Associate Pastor. In the few moments I had to consider it, I imagined that my 'more' would look something like offering prayer support from a distance, but immediately he had other ideas. About to retire himself from the role and tasked with looking for a possible successor, his response to me was, 'Liz, you'd make an excellent Police Chaplain, why don't I get you the application form?' My response was less decisive, praying for them from a distance was one thing and I thought I might be able to overcome my remaining prejudices to do that, but volunteering as a chaplain was taking it to a whole other level and I seriously questioned my capability to do that, without even asking myself the question of did I want to. Agreeing to give it some thought and get back to him, I went home almost wishing that I'd not said anything at all!

In my experience, when God wants to nudge us into action, He keeps nudging until we act, and after a few days of wrangling with the proposition in prayer, I knew that this was a door I was to push. I asked for the application forms and submitted them to Police HQ and before long I received a phone call inviting me for interview. I had not been inside a police station since 1973, apart from once as a youth leader taking a youth team on a treasure hunt around Chorleywood and making an enquiry at the local information desk, so it was with huge trepidation that I pulled into the car park in Welwyn Garden City. I had no idea what to expect or how I would respond to any sort of questioning in that environment. I was met at reception by the secretary of the Chief Inspector I was due to see and although she was lovely, followed her literally quaking in my boots, to his office. She knocked on the door and opened it at his 'enter', and there sitting behind a huge desk was a huge man in full uniform, and another sitting with him to the side. Oh my word, for a second all I wanted to do was turn tail and run away, but as he rose and proffered his hand in greeting, every vestige of my nervousness left and I found myself completely at ease. We chatted and exchanged information and opinions in the lightest of atmospheres for over an hour, and he concluded the meeting by assuring me that he thought I would be an asset to the service and would be in touch in a few days; there were posts in several locations to fill and it was simply a matter of agreeing which one would be the best fit. Sitting in the car and taking a moment to reflect before leaving, I realised that what had just taken place really was huge and dwarfed the size of any desk or man. I drove out of that car park whooping with delight, knowing that God had, in the last hour, completed yet another level of healing in me. I had been cleansed of that residue of disaffection and any fear associated with it, and was finally free. Forty-three years after my first police interview, I had completed my second and what had back then been a disaster, God had turned to good; every contact leaves a trace indeed!

As promised, a few days later I received a letter offering me a chaplaincy posting at HQ rather than in Hemel. This left me in a bit of a quandary, as I'd hoped to be representing our church in our town, and I asked for a little breathing space to consider it. We were about to leave for our annual Cornish holiday and I said I would confirm once we were back. In truth, my reaction was mixed, equal parts disappointment and relief. I reasoned that maybe the whole exercise had been a 'Jehovah Sneaky' to enable me to finally get free of the past, and I was so very thankful for that, it far outweighed the disappointment. I had decided not to pursue it further before we left for Cornwall, but held off making the call anyway as we'd agreed that's when I would respond.

On a summers evening sitting in a pub garden by the canal enjoying an early drink, Mike rocked my world. We had been in Hemel three years and whilst we weren't unhappy, neither had we ever really felt that we were 'home'. This feeling was compounded each year when we visited Cornwall, so much so that the vague dream we had once had of relocating ourselves there, had become a ten-year plan that we felt we might realistically be able to fulfil. We were only three years into that plan and a long way from accruing the finance we needed to achieve it. In all of our time together I had never once heard Mike express anything like a grumble about the day to day grind, in fact completely the opposite, he was effusive about how blessed we were, but that evening something changed. He said he felt that he would be unable to sustain our business for much longer, he sensed a shift, as though the grace had lifted. My initial reaction had been total shock, and then fear. We had saddled ourselves with this huge mortgage, which we were nowhere near to paying off, what on earth would we do? what would he do? I could understand his dissatisfaction but couldn't see how we could do anything other than simply keep going and staying thankful. Knowing this would be my response he was quick to suggest I calm down and just listen. Always a whizz with figures and a careful and responsible steward of our finances, he went on to explain that we were actually already in a better position than we had thought we would be, and that we ought to be able to significantly reduce our original timeframe of ten years. As my world gently settled itself back on its axis, I started to get excited at his next suggestion, which was to extend our upcoming two week holiday to three weeks and spend the first of those checking out the property landscape around Falmouth, which we thought was where we wanted to be. We agreed that this would simply be a reconnaissance exercise that would help us to re-assess our forward planning and that we would be disciplined in restricting it to that first week, not encroaching on the holiday, which we were both in need of. Having worked seriously hard during that year, we had pushed the boat out and booked a beautiful cottage on the waterfront at Restronguet and knew that we would not be able to extend our time there, but we were able to find a less extravagant alternative in a nearby village for that first week and in any case, it seemed right to keep the business end of our stay separate to help us focus.

We logged ourselves onto several estate agents websites and were encouraged by what we saw; we looked at the details of properties that seemed affordable and allowed ourselves to engage in some dreaming about those that weren't. Many years earlier we had begun to understand the power of specific prayer, and in this vein we made a list of the features we would like in our 'forever' home, which was also helpful as it concentrated our minds and our searching. We arranged to view several houses during that first week but purely as a scouting exercise and in spite of our head in the clouds dreaming, when we arrived in Cornwall our feet were still very firmly on the ground.

Each of the places we looked at had merit but none was quite right and even though we absolutely didn't want to progress immediately, after five days of viewing we were a little deflated. However, as we enjoyed a yummy Cornish tea by the waterside and reviewed our week, we realised that actually we had made good progress. Our house in Hemel was a new build and although it was beautiful and probably also because a lot of construction was still going on around us, I longed for a house with 'character'. On the first day, we had viewed two properties one an impressive stand-alone new build, and the other a beautiful Georgian village house. I was surprised to discover that on balance and for many reasons, I preferred the new build, much to the relief of my husband who had foreseen a retirement consumed by maintenance, which did not fill his heart with joy. It was enormously helpful to recognise this, as it would seriously refine our search parameters going forward. We had also made good headway in identifying the areas we didn't want to be, again very helpful in this respect. So, when we moved to Beach Cottage to begin our holiday proper, we were happy that we'd made progress and determined that we would return the following spring to continue our searching. However, God it seemed, had other ideas. Three nights later in the early hours, I was woken by Holy Spirit giving me a very specific instruction. Having settled our thinking about the way forward and being nudged awake from a very deep sleep, I was slow to respond and when I did, it was in protest. He told me to pick up my iPad and look again at the Right Move Property website, 'but why?' I whined, 'we have done nothing but that for weeks, we have seen everything there is to see, it's pointless'. In His infinite goodness, He persisted, gently admonishing me in the process; He also suggested that I changed our geographical search parameters slightly. With less than good grace, I did this, with 'I told you so' thoughts going through my head as I trolled through property after property we had already seen, and then up popped something we hadn't. An architects impression of the style of house we had been looking for but hadn't found. I scanned the details, it sounded perfect, and amazingly even the 'in the region of' price indicator was not prohibitive. I woke up and read carefully and then sighed in resignation when I saw the location. Impossibly, it was in a village we had never heard of, seriously, we had looked everywhere, and was situated on the north coast, the other side of the county altogether. I was on the verge of grumpiness but I kept reading and saw that it was in fact, only eight miles from a place we knew well, in the area we wanted. My spirit stirred, I marked the page and counted the hours until I could reasonably wake Mike and share all this with him. Over breakfast we checked the map and even though it meant breaking our own rules, we decided to drive out that way and take a look, rationalising that we could visit nearby Porthtowan afterwards in holiday mode. So we loaded the car with our beach things and Camber the Wonder Whippet and headed across the county.

It took just over twenty minutes, and the village when we found it, was delightful and completely new to us. We parked the car and had a wander around, quite taken by its higgledy-piggledy qualities which we found really appealing. As we walked along the main street an imposing house under construction at a crossroads impressed us both, but neither mentioned it to the other, thinking that it would be way beyond our financial reach. Crossing the road we found the place we had been looking for and although the house itself did look good, we knew straight away that it wasn't for us. The drawing had shown one property on a reasonable plot, but it was obvious that a second was to be built immediately alongside reducing the outside space to practically nothing. Hey ho, we thought, well we've discovered a new village and had our eyes opened to other geographical possibilities so it hasn't been time wasted. As we were about to leave the builder came out, asking if he could help, and hearing our explanation suggested that if we wanted more space we should look at the house on the crossroads, he was building that as well, commissioned by the owners, who he thought would probably be on site. We looked at one another and although we both thought it was an impossibility, curiosity got the better of us, so we agreed and followed him.

We have a God of the impossible. Although still ostensibly a shell, it was obvious that the place would be lovely. Despite its imposing appearance it actually wasn't a huge place, just three bedrooms but the floor to ceiling windows and a gallery arrangement upstairs created a real sense of spaciousness. Our eyes opened wider as we looked around and realised that box after box on our wish list was being ticked. In fact, the stairs were not yet in place but Mike climbed a ladder to look at the upper floor, and came back down grinning, 'you can see the sea', my heart leapt. The first house we had looked at had been a new build and it was beautiful and for a moment we had been tempted but it had no view whatsoever and in fact was next to an industrial estate. But it did help me to recognise the value to us of a new build, and here we were standing in one with a sea glimpse, if not a full view. In our conversation with the couple who were selling, we learned that they were planning to put the house on the market within the next few weeks and although reluctant to divulge too much information assured us that the asking price would be in line with other comparable properties. We also learned that they had moved from Hertfordshire when they retired which seemed too ridiculous for coincidence to us. We left them having agreed to return the following week when the stairs were installed and we drove away knowing we had some serious thinking to do.

A couple of years earlier the Lord had released a word to me about the 'suddenlies' of God, our understanding of and preparation for them, and I had shared this word extensively in the places I had been invited to minister since. We wondered whether we might be about to experience one for ourselves and determined that whilst we would not allow ourselves to be carried away on a wave of excitement, neither did we want to miss anything that God might have for us. We returned to the house the following week, the stairs now duly in place, and after saying hello I raced up to the first floor, Camber at my heels. It was a glorious day and the sun was streaming in through the huge window. I stood and looked out over the rooftops and sure enough, there was the expanse of the sea shimmering in the distance. Could this really be ours? We were still way ahead of our plans, it had never been our intention to go further than to scope out the market. I could hear Mike downstairs in discussion with the sellers and turned to go down to join him; glancing back for a final look I saw Camber lying stretched out in the sun at the window. And in that moment I think I knew it would be. After a little negotiating they agreed to proceed with the sale privately for the benefit of both parties and we shook hands on our deal, arranging to meet up again a few days later to sort out an escrow account to secure the purchase. Everything about it was astounding, not least that we had appeared just prior to the interior being fitted out and so were able to largely input our own specifications. Once the escrow was in place and them assured that we weren't simply having a holiday 'romance' with the idea of living in Cornwall, they bent over backwards to accommodate our preferences where they could. As for us, we simply had peace that this indeed was a 'suddenly' of God. How very like Him to do for us what He had released to me as a word for others.

We were also by now more than a little excited, and for the first time ever I was eager to get back, crossing the county line out of Cornwall with anticipation rather than deflation. Buoyed up by the ease of our purchase we returned home believing that selling our house in Hemel, on which the move was contingent, would be equally simple. So confident were we in a quick sale that we actually held off putting it on the market for a month or so, concerned that we would find ourselves out of the house before the Cornwall build was complete, which was expected to be early spring. It was a surprise to us then, when finally having listed it with an agent we received almost no response. Finally a family booked to view and because they had a very distinctive name, we did an internet check out of curiosity and discovered that they were active in a vibrant church known to us locally. Thinking that this made sense of the delay, I thought this must be it, we had prayed for the right family to move into the neighbourhood and we only needed one buyer, so we reasoned it would be them. Another suddenly. They were quiet at the viewing and very polite and complimentary about the house, but they gave us no further clues and offered no information about themselves, leaving no opportunity for us to open up any meaningful conversation. Despite that, we were still surprised when the agent called to say that they felt the layout wrong for them and wouldn't be making an offer. The next viewing wasn't for weeks, tempting us to despondency but then when the agent told us it was a lady Rabbi and her family, again

I thought, this absolutely must be it, surely. Again a lovely family and again very complementary but again not interested. It was now mid-November, traditionally the worst time to sell, Mike was steadfast which was amazing, as money was being drawn down from the escrow account to cover the cost of materials required in excess of the original specifications, which we would lose if we failed to complete on the house purchase by the end of March. We had agreed that if this did become the case it would go on to the open market and we would have to bid again at that point. As is so for most, we needed to sell in order to buy, and we had exposed ourselves to a heavy financial hit if things didn't go to plan. We revisited God's promises to us and the sequence of events that had got us to this place and still we could see nothing other than His hand, so we continued on, me greatly helped by Mike's quiet confidence which went some way towards making up for the deficit in my own.

The bible warns us against giving ground to the little foxes that come to destroy the vine (SS 2:15). It embarrasses me to confess that not only did I give them ground I stood at the gate and positively welcomed them in. I began to question myself and my ability to hear from God at all. What right did I have to expect that we would be so outlandishly blessed so far ahead of time? Once the wobbling started it was hard to stop it and although at some level I remained in faith, it was the sort that came through hanging on by the fingernails and hoping against hope, rather than taking hold and believing. By the time the interim between Christmas and New Year came around with no buyer in sight, I needed help. Having invited fear in, it had taken hold and robbed me of any excitement for the future and all of my joy, and I am so thankful that Father God did not give up on me as easily as I gave up on our dream. Holy Spirit woke me one night with instructions so clear that it was impossible to miss them, directing me to request some specific ministry and where to go and get it. I may have been in fear but I was not confused about why and so the following morning I made a call and an appointment. Determined that I had a thorough understanding of the reason for being there, I was confused by the issues that arose, none seeming connected with the fear that was gripping me. But with the guidance of Holy Spirit, the counsellor lead me through a series of situations concerning my relationship with Karl, which in turn had resulted in impeding my relationship with Jesus as my brother and friend. The hour or so that followed was deeply healing on so many different levels and although I hadn't identified it as any sort of contributory factor to my current fearful state, fear had left all the same. I drove home from Birmingham with Jesus as my companion, who reassured me throughout the journey that all would be well. And for my part, I determined to put myself constantly 'on watch' lest fear try to assail me again.

From that point on, although we still received no interest in the house I was able to stand my ground in faith, together with my seriously amazing husband who never faltered, even when we got so close to the wire time-wise it really did seem impossible. One of the biggest lessons in my faith journey has been to let go of trying to second guess just how God will act in a given situation. When we put the house on the market, I went through just such an exercise and imagined that I knew exactly who our house would appeal to. In my head, our buyer would either be a well-heeled executive or couple, or a single who would look to subletting a room or two to pay the mortgage. The configuration of the place didn't lend itself easily to family life, having more bedrooms and bathrooms than living space, and this had been borne out by the reaction of the Christian family who originally viewed it. During this time, they actually bought another house on the development with a different floor plan and moved in whilst we were still there. We welcomed them with flowers and a kind word, but I had to dig deep from the well of my generosity to do it. With only a few short weeks to go before the house in Cornwall would be wrested from us and put on the open market, we received a call from the estate agent, a family would like to come and view. We said yes of course, but any hope I had for a sale evaporated when I opened the door to a young couple with three, very small children and a pushchair. We took Camber for a walk whilst they were there, leaving the agent to show them round and we trudged across the park, consoling ourselves with the thought that at least it was a viewing, and perhaps was a sign of more appropriate interest on the way.

The phone rang almost immediately we returned, and as we had thought it would be, it was the estate agent who had always been faithful in reporting back. Not interested in hearing yet another consolatory word, I busied myself with something in the kitchen but became aware that the call seemed to be taking longer than usual. As I listened at the door I heard Mike say, 'tell them thanks for the offer, but they'll have to do better than that if they're serious'. Amazingly this family, so unsuited to the house in my ridiculously dismissive mind, wanted to buy it, true they had made an equally ridiculous offer but the agent seemed certain they would come back. Sure enough, a few minutes later she did with the offer significantly increased and much nearer our asking price, although not quite near enough. She said she'd get back to us. Mike has a remarkable ability to remain dispassionate and level headed in negotiations, qualities that I lack completely when the emotional stakes are so high; so agreeing that my input would probably be more of a hindrance than a help, I took myself off. We had to choose stair carpet for Cornwall, so I walked along the canal to the carpet store in the shopping park nearby. The next twenty minutes were hilarious, I was chatting with the salesman who was showing me different carpet options when Mike called to say that they'd increased their offer which was now even closer to our asking price, they clearly were serious and he was confident they'd go further, we just had to hold our nerve. I wasn't sure I could, but he promised me that we would accept if they didn't and he was sure they wouldn't withdraw, he just wanted to let me know. Of course, the carpet salesman knew as well because I blurted it all out to him and as there were no other customers at the time, the two other staff members also heard. The next call from Mike was another in the same vein and the tension mounted, and then he rang again, their final offer was within spitting distance of the sale price and even though that had been reduced in the interminable wait, it was still on the high side of market value. We said yes, I yelped in delight and the store staff all clapped. But seriously, the best was yet to come.

The agent, congratulating Mike on the sale went on to explain that the offer was a bit unusual. The buyer was actually not the couple themselves but the Father of the wife, a businessman who now lived in Dubai and wanted to gift it to his daughter. They had completed financial checks and all was in order, we had ourselves a cash buyer who wanted to complete quickly. In fact, it transpired that they had seen our house advertised from the outset but had not been in a position to go ahead until now and had been concerned all along that they would be too late. Only God. Every time I do it, I cry in the re-telling of this story, it is such a beautiful picture of His grace and goodness to us. A loving earthly father giving a lavish gift to his daughter mirrored by our Heavenly Father giving such a gift to us, realising our dream. All the time He knew and He bore with me in love and patience as I tried to second guess Him, even healing my heart of pain and re-introducing me to Jesus, as I gave in to needless fear. He is forever looking for opportunities to help us come to maturity in faith and I certainly grew in mine during this time.

The price differential between outer London and Cornwall enabled us to buy outright and left us with a tidy sum to live on until Mike's pension kicked in a few years later. And in the end we arrived in Cornwall ahead of schedule, taking vacant possession in early March. God's timing is always perfect and He knew all along just how this would work. I gave thanks that neither the first Christian couple, now resident in their house across the way, nor the lady rabbi, nor any of the few others that had come to view had been interested; preventing us from accepting any offer that might have come with added complications and stalled us. And I humbly repented for my lack of faith.

The house in Cornwall which had been built on the site of another, retained its name, which was Homestead. We decided to change it. One purported origin of the name Hemel Hempstead, our physical home for three and a half years and our church home for over thirteen, is Heavenly Homestead and that seemed to us a better representation. It was a big day when we received the necessary approval enabling us to fix the Cornish slate nameplate to the wall, the fulfilment of an appropriated promise. We thank God for this 'home of our own,' and its new name which generates comment from all who see it, some asking and is it? To us, it is indeed.

It did very quickly become 'home' and despite acutely missing our church family we were in no doubt that this was where we were meant to be. During our first few months I was keenly aware of a sense of 'rooting', something wholly new to me and a joy to discover, not least because it helped allay the only real concern I had about our move. On one holiday, years before, when we were very much still in the dreaming stage of our plan, I stood at the kitchen window of our holiday home very early one morning and watched the sunrise over St Michaels Mount, such a stunningly beautiful sight that it took my breath away. In that moment I was arrested by the thought of how simply awful it would be, if that view were to become so familiar living here, I might fail to see it. If I might stare vacantly out of a window one day and no longer see the beauty of the place before me. Where would that leave me and my dreams? Well, six years on, and every day I look out of our upstairs window at the view estate agents would describe as a 'sea glimpse' and I am still astounded by it, even on the days when the mist is low and it's not really visible, there is joy simply in the knowing.

A year or so after we arrived, I was reflecting one day on the journey that brought us here, and how everything in it had dovetailed together so perfectly in His hands. There really were no obvious loose ends but a thought kept coming back to me that I couldn't resolve. When we returned to Hemel from that last Cornish holiday, I had made the promised call to the Inspector at Hertfordshire Police and explained what had transpired. It was easily clear to both of us that pursuing the Chaplaincy role there was no longer viable, as the time I had left was way too short to establish any meaningful relationships. He was very gracious and wished me well and I was slightly relieved that I didn't have to decline his offer without any apparent valid reason. Although I was immensely thankful to have gone through the process which enabled me to understand that my healing in respect of the Police was complete, I couldn't shake the thought that there was more to come. It is God, there is always more. Sure enough, almost another year on, at a prayer meeting one evening whilst I was engaged in ministering to someone, my ears caught the leader of the meeting calling folk to pray for a young woman, a police officer, who had been given permission to establish a prayer room in her station. There was no time to speak with her at the meeting but after several very obvious Holy Spirit nudges, I went to see her and enjoyed a couple of hours with her and her husband, also a serving officer, sharing glory stories. A week or so later she contacted me to say that she had been speaking with the Force Lead Chaplain and there was a vacancy at a nearby station if I was interested. To be honest I didn't really know whether I was, but again Holy Spirit kept on nudging so a meeting was arranged. I have been volunteering as a Police Chaplain ever since. Not only had Father God lead me through this healing journey and into freedom; by making this path straight He also completely redeemed that one awful incident, that had derailed much of my life. It is one of my greatest joys to be able to serve the men and women of the organisation I had so completely reviled. Only God. He really does never leave loose ends.

But I have to. I began this account taking a very bad photo on the New Brighton Ferry, at a time when developing prints was a costly business. It was actually developed by my Dad in the under-stairs cupboard of our first house and is included at the front of this book. Today I can take limitless shots on my iPhone heedless of expense and store them on a cloud somewhere in cyberspace, to view as I choose. It seems a fitting analogy for how far I've come in the intervening years, how far God has brought me, saving, refining, moulding and shaping along the way. He is not finished yet but I live easy and secure in the knowledge that He who began a good work in me, will bring it to completion.

Every contact leaves a trace indeed.

Author's Note

The pages you have read contain no fiction, but in some instances I have chosen to alter names for reasons which I hope will be understood.